P9-DLZ-132

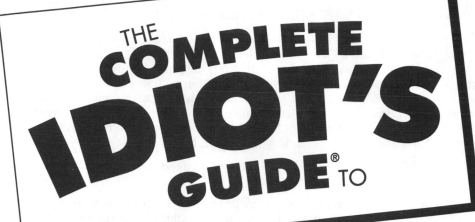

THE COMPLETE IDIOT'S GUIDE® TO

Saltwater Aquariums

by Mike Wickham

alpha books

A Division of Macmillan General Reference
A Pearson Education Macmillan Company
1633 Broadway, New York, NY 10019

To Sharon, the most exquisite fish in the sea. I love you.

Copyright © 1999 by Mike Wickham

Macmillan General Reference books may be purchased for business or sales promotional use. For information please write: Special Markets Department, Macmillan Publishing USA, 1633 Broadway, New York, NY 10019-6785.

International Standard Book Number: 1-58245-029-3
Library of Congress Catalog Card Number: LOC 99-10861

01 00 99   8 7 6 5 4 3 2 1

Interpretation of the printing code: The rightmost number of the first series of numbers is the year of the book's printing; the rightmost number of the second series of numbers is the number of the book's printing. For example, a printing code of 99-1 shows that the first printing occurred in 1999.

Printed in the United States of America

Contents at a Glance

Contents

12 Popular Fish for Beginners 145

Foreword

The marine aquarium hobby in North America saw a rapid upsurge in interest in the late 1980s, as the advent of miniature reef aquariums became popular. Fortunately, the rest of the marine hobby also benefited from these improved filtration and aquarium designs, and a new paradigm for marine aquariums came into being. Sterile aquariums with bleached corals and equally sterile looking fish have fortunately become a thing of the past, as the benefits of more natural systems become widely recognized.

However, in the last few years a new lethargy has set in among marine aquarists, due, I believe, to the needless increase in complexity and the confusion this can bring. There are now so many options for how to set up a marine tank and most new hobbyists are faced with such a bewildering array of equipment and philosophies that they often give up in disgust.

We live in a world of increasing complexity. It is just this increased complexity that has spurred a return to more simplistic ways of doing things. This can be seen in any number of areas, such as holistic medicines, the advent of more "natural" herbal remedies for depression and the common cold, and the increasing numbers of people who are turning to a more simplistic, less materialistic lifestyle. A more holistic approach is also evolving in the marine aquarium hobby, as more and more people come to realize that the organisms control their own environment. The numerous webs and chains of life that can exist in more natural aquarium systems interact in a way that modifies and maintains their environment. As we gain a better understanding of their actions and roles in the closed ecosystems we have established, we begin to better appreciate the intricacies of the natural world. Although I do not believe that we will totally abandon the need for technology in our home aquaria, I can see already that many of what were once considered "must have" pieces of equipment are no longer in use by most hobbyists.

Barriers to travel and communication have all but disappeared. I live on an island 3,000 miles away from the nearest landmass; a place that only 200 some years ago was unknown to Western civilization. Yet today I can write this Foreword and e-mail it within a few minutes to the author at his home in Arkansas. With the advent of electronic communications, one of the last barriers to the spread of information is rapidly disappearing. Yet for all these marvels, what you are holding in your hand is still the most popular method to disseminate information. What is sad is that so few of us use it, when doing so would make many of our endeavors oh so much easier.

Which brings me to this book by Mike Wickham. In these pages, he demonstrates that marine aquarium keeping need not be complex. That it is within the grasp of anyone who has the necessary temperament and who is willing to exercise patience and be observant.

By bringing a slice of nature into our homes, we take on a responsibility for the welfare of the inhabitants of this little world. In exchange for your diligence, you will be rewarded with a glimpse into a world that few have experienced and fewer still have learned to appreciate. In this increasingly complex world, the opportunity to sit back and watch a small slice of nature unfold in your home is a reward beyond measure. These miniature worlds help us to maintain a link to the natural world from which we arose.

J. Charles Delbeek
Honolulu, USA
January 1999

J. Charles Delbeek is co-author of The Reef Aquarium, *and is a noted writer and lecturer. He works with the Waikiki Aquarium.*

Introduction

I got my first aquarium in 1964. I was just a kid, and it took me several months to save up enough money for a little 5-gallon starter kit. My parents didn't want me to buy it, because they thought that I would quickly lose interest. I suppose they also feared that they would get stuck taking care of it!

Still, it was my money, so they let me make the purchase. As it turns out, my little 5-gallon aquarium sparked my parents' interest in fishkeeping, too. When a local dime store ran a special on 10-gallon starter kits, my mom surprised me by offering to buy a second tank for me. She really shocked me, though, when we got to the store and she said, "What the heck, let's get two more!" Before you knew it, we had over 40 aquariums in the house and a little fish-breeding business. And so fishkeeping has turned out to be not only a lifelong hobby for me, but also a profession. Yes, I kept my interest in those dazzling denizens of the deep.

The aquarium hobby offers something for everyone. Most hobbyists start with a small, peaceful, freshwater community tank. Some prefer to keep large, aggressive varieties, while others find fun in watching fish spawn and rearing the babies. Many hobbyists graduate to the saltwater hobby, with its spectacularly colored fish and amazing invertebrates. Who knows? You may end up doing all of the above, and more!

How to Use This Book

As you read *The Complete Idiot's Guide to Saltwater Aquariums*, you will soon recognize that it is very much like your aquarium—in the sense that it shares something with ecosystems. In an ecosystem, if you change a parameter (by adding or removing a species, for example), it will affect something else. For every action there is an equal and opposite reaction.

The information in this book is very similar to that. Just about every fact in every chapter relates in some way to the information in other chapters. Skip something and you may change the whole picture in your tank. Change something and you may find unexpected consequences. It's a ripple effect.

Anyway, as you read this book, you will find a few topics interwoven through many chapters. So many things interrelate that it is impossible to separate them entirely. Still, I came up with a logical plan. The book is divided into five parts. The topics are laid out in the order you will most likely need to learn them.

➤ **Part 1: An Introduction to Fishkeeping.** I start by telling you some things you need to know before you buy your first aquarium.

➤ **Part 2: What Stuff Do You Need First?** I'll follow with detailed instructions on buying equipment and assembling it into a functional aquarium. This is sometimes the most confusing part of fishkeeping.

➤ **Part 3: Your Denizens of the Deep.** The ocean is full of interesting life. In Part 3, the real fun begins as I introduce you to them.

➤ **Part 4: The Tank Is Running; Now What?** Water is the lifeblood of your aquarium. So in Part 4 I will tell you everything you ever wanted to know, but were afraid to ask, about water. Heck, 10 bucks says that I'll tell you a few things about water you never would have thought of asking! I'll also talk about the scheduled maintenance of your aquarium, including how to feed your fishy friends. And finally, you'll find an introduction to reefkeeping.

➤ **Part 5: Oceans of Trouble.** Part 5 is the troubleshooting section. I'll discuss some common problems that hobbyists encounter, how you can prevent them, and how to deal with them if you didn't.

How much would you pay for a book like this? You might expect to pay a jillion dollars, but not with this special offer! But, wait. . . don't get out your checkbook yet, because there's more. That's right! If you act today, I'll also throw in a Table of Contents, an Index, and several informative. . .

Appendices! I end the book by pointing you toward other sources of information, giving you some sample shopping lists and telling you how to find a local aquarium society, if you'd like to join a club. I'll even tell you about some cool, fish-related places you can visit on vacation.

Now how much would you pay?

But Wait! There's More!

As you read this book, be sure to check out the little boxes on the sides. Throughout the book, you will find boxes that give you extra pointers by highlighting various important and interesting bits of information. Watch for these boxes:

Fish School

Look here for definitions of unfamiliar words. There is also a Glossary at the back of the book, in Appendix A.

Fish and Tips

Check here for helpful hints that save you time and money, and make fishkeeping easier.

Something's Fishy

When something is not quite right, we say that it's fishy. These boxes contain warnings and safety tips.

Fish Tales

Look in the Fish Tales boxes for fun and interesting fishy facts.

You can also expect a few boxes thrown in just for giggles, like this one:

The top reasons it's fun to be an aquarium fish are . . .

. . . you get free seafood at every meal.

. . . you have your own personal human slave to make your meals and clean your house.

. . . nobody thinks you look stupid when you swim into the wall.

. . . every time a new family moves into your neighborhood, you get to beat up the parents and eat their kids.

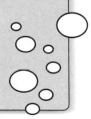

Time to Say Thank You

Special thanks to Dennis Hare and Richard Graham of the Aquarium Center in Randallstown, Maryland. Thanks also to Phil Concepcion, Jeff Edgerton, and Mark Ozolins of Exotic Aquatics in BelAir, Maryland. Big thanks to Charles Delbeek, for writing the Foreword to this book. Extra thanks to the gang at CompuServe's Fishnet Forum. Finally, a big ol' hug and eternal thanks to my editor, Beth Adelman, for not murdering me in cold blood when I missed my deadline—at least, not yet!

Trademarks

Part 1
An Introduction to Fishkeeping

Soon you will have your very own aquarium, filled with dazzling saltwater fish. You probably can't wait to start spending all your money on your aquarium and supplies, setting it up, and then stocking the tank with your favorite species.

Before you do that, though, let's talk about why people get into the hobby and what benefits you can expect from it. There are many ways to enjoy aquariums and fish. You want to be happy with your choices, so I'll point out some things you need to consider before you pick a size and style of aquarium. I'll help you figure out the best choices in equipment. You'll also learn how to choose a good dealer—one who will end up being your friend in the business.

Chapter 1

Why Keep a Saltwater Aquarium?

In This Chapter

➤ Attractions of the aquarium hobby

➤ Why fish are fun

➤ Why invertebrates are interesting

➤ Why an aquarium may not be right for you

Imagine yourself snorkeling in the Indo-Pacific. The sun warms your back as you glide through the crystal waters, patrolling the edge of a reef. Like an Impressionist painting of maroon, yellow, and blue, encrusting sponges and algae create the backdrop. Colorful colonies of soft corals sway in the surge. A pair of clownfish, brightly striped in orange and white, undulate fearlessly amidst the stinging tentacles of a bubble-tipped anemone. Colonies of acropora coral extend countless stony fingers toward the water's surface, searching for light and current. As you approach, a school of black and white damselfish dart into the acropora forest for safety, and a crab scuttles into a hole in the rock. A school of blue tangs passes by, their bright yellow tails waving hello as they pass. A blenny, with its feathery eyebrows, nibbles algae from the reef.

The reef is like an underwater garden, but the "flowers" are animals—corals extending their feeding polyps. Iridescent fish flit about like insects. In the substrate, worms, crabs, starfish, and hordes of other animals make their homes. There is an incredible diversity of life on the reef. Everywhere you look, you will see something different swim or crawl by.

Next time you're in the South Pacific, make sure you go for a swim. But in the meantime, you can enjoy the spectacular beauty of the tropical ocean in your very own home. Scenes similar to these occur every minute of every day in a properly installed aquarium. There is always something going on. Every time you look, you will see something you hadn't noticed before. Exotic fish and invertebrates provide an endless array of shapes and colors. And they tantalize you with a spectacular exhibit of interesting behaviors.

Aquarium keeping is a hobby you can really get into! Rob maintains this 600-gallon aquarium, owned by Horan & Associates.

Be an A"fish"ionado

What is it that attracts so many of us to aquarium-keeping? What is so special about these slimy, cold-blooded creatures that makes us want to fork out our hard-earned dollars for them? What is it that makes us want to fawn over them like they are our own children? OK, well, maybe we don't fawn over them like they are our children. I know I don't—that is, not since I finished therapy.

Living Furniture

There are lots of reasons that people are drawn to aquariums. But when asked, the most common reason given for taking up fishkeeping is that the person thinks the aquarium will look good in their home. A properly lit and attractively decorated aquarium can add natural beauty to any room. And these days you can buy stands and canopies that are furniture-quality and will fit right into any decor. The aquarium becomes a piece of living furniture.

Your aquarium is live art! It is like a picture frame that holds an ever-changing portrait of Mother Nature. It adds a window to the outside world that is unaffected by weather or season or geography. Properly maintained, your tank will always provide you with a breathtaking scenic view.

An aquarium can be a small tank on a countertop, or it can dominate an entire wall. Some people even build aquariums into the wall or use them as room dividers. You get to be artistic and decide what contribution your aquarium will make to the room.

Mellow Out

One great benefit of this hobby is a subliminal one. Fishwatching is relaxing. It is known that petting a dog or cat will make your blood pressure drop to calmer levels. The same thing happens when you watch fish. Except, of course, when you see your $2 fish trying to kill the $50 one!

Fish Tales

A recent study at the University of Pennsylvania, conducted by doctors Aaron Katcher and Alan Beck, showed that watching an aquarium for 20 minutes did a better job of relaxing dentists' patients than hypnosis!

Learn About Nature and Science

Your aquarium is educational. It is a miniature ecosystem. It will give you an opportunity to learn how fish, invertebrates, and algae interrelate and how they are affected by light, current, water quality, and the environment. You will have the opportunity to delve or dabble in ichthyology, microbiology, chemistry, horticulture, aquaculture, taxonomy, and many other fields.

But don't let those big words scare you off. You don't have to be a genius or a scientist to be successful with your aquarium. Even a complete idiot can do it, with a little preparation. I'm living proof!

Fish School

Invertebrates are animals that lack a backbone or spinal column. They can be soft like a jellyfish, or hard like a crab.

Fish and Tips

Be sure to check out the appendices I've included at the end of this book. In them, you will find a list of places to go for more information. I even put together a recommended reading list.

Prepare to learn a lot! In this book, I teach you all the basics of setting up a saltwater aquarium. I also cover some topics that are a bit more advanced. As you will see, there are several styles of saltwater aquariums you can choose from. Some are relatively simple. Some are on the cutting edge of aquatic science. The style you choose will depend largely on how much you want to learn—and how much you want to spend. Just remember that no single book will tell you everything you need or want to know. After you read this book, don't hesitate to investigate others.

By the way, not only will this hobby teach you some things about science and nature, but you may end up learning some new things to teach others, as well. Only a few years ago, corals were thought to be impossible to keep alive in captivity. Now, thanks to dedicated hobbyists and scientists, we have gained enough knowledge to get them to grow and reproduce in captivity—and we have only just begun. There is so much more to learn. Perhaps you will uncover some new facts and secrets!

Learn Respect for Living Things

Before you buy a car, it helps to take driver's education. Before you buy your aquarium, do a little reading. The more you know, the better your chance of success. You want your fish to live. Your fish want you to want them to live. They depend on you. You can't write them off as dependents on your tax return, though. Sorry.

Don't forget that fish are perishables. This does not mean you should think of them as expendables! Often, customers have wanted to buy fish against my recommendation. They know there is a good chance that the chosen specimen will not survive with their other fish, but they buy it anyway. "Aw, heck," they say. "If it dies, I'll just get something else." I get annoyed when this happens. The fish they kill aren't too happy about it, either!

If you don't show respect for the fact that fish are living beings—if you consider them to be expendables—you really should forget fishkeeping and take up stamp collecting or some other hobby.

Lights! Aquarium! Action!

OK, I have listed many reasons why people enjoy the science and art of keeping aquariums. But for me, the biggest appeal is that a properly decorated aquarium with the right mix of inhabitants is just plain beautiful. It has living color. It has fluid motion.

A good aquarium will have all the elements of a never-ending movie. In your tank, you will find comedy, drama, and suspense. You'll laugh. You'll cry. You'll never eat another shrimp cocktail again. Just kidding. You won't laugh or cry.

Sometimes you'll watch your aquarium for fun and sometimes you'll watch it to wind down. Try this some evening: Turn out the room lights, switch off the television, erase the 1-900 numbers from your speed dialer, and just sit there for a bit watching the fish. Feel the tension slipping away? Try it when you are having trouble falling asleep. It can work wonders.

If It's Not Easy, You're Doing It All Wrong

Fishkeeping is easy, but fish plus water does not necessarily equal success. You need to learn a few things to succeed. This is even truer with a saltwater aquarium than it is with a freshwater tank.

It surprises me how many people walk into a fish store, ready to buy fish, knowing only that fish live in water. They have no idea what it takes to keep a fish alive. They don't even have the tank purchased or set up yet. It doesn't dawn on them that some fish won't get along, that many fish and invertebrates consider each other to be lunch, that some critters can give painful stings to humans, or that water can't be used straight out of the tap.

These aspiring aquarists don't know what temperature is required or that rapid temperature changes can kill a fish. In fact, unless a fish is floating upside down—dead, bloated, and stinky—they wouldn't be able to tell if it is healthy or not! By the way, if you're reading this thinking to yourself, "Uh-oh. . . that's me he's describing," don't worry. It is not a problem, because you are taking steps to learn. For some people, learning would be too much trouble. Their tanks are destined to end up collecting dust in the attic or garage. Yours is not.

Fish and Tips

If you have to spend more than 10 minutes per week maintaining your saltwater tank, you are probably doing something wrong. Seriously. How many hobbies do you know with that kind of work–enjoyment ratio?

Still, you don't have to take a college course to learn how to keep an aquarium. There are a few basic rules to follow, and if you stick to them, things will go well and you will spend lots more time enjoying your tank than maintaining it.

Those Amazing Aquatic Animals

Did you know that the male seahorse is the one that gives birth to babies? Or that clownfish start out their lives as males but change into females when the need arises? Did you know that some species of fish show parental care and guard their young, while others disperse thousands of eggs into the water current? Did you know that there are fish that keep their eggs and babies in their mouths for safety? There are fish that share their burrows with guardian shrimp, too.

Fish and Tips

Another easy thing about fishkeeping is dealing with them when you go on vacation. They can be left for two or three days with no food, and no harm will be done. If you plan to be gone longer, have a friend feed them, or buy an electronic fish feeder to dispense food automatically while you are away.

Did you know that the corals you see in curio shops are the dead skeletons of colonies of animals? Or that decorator crabs cover themselves with bits of sponge, seaweed, and debris for camouflage? We all know that lobsters and crabs live on the bottom, but did you know that they start life as free-swimming microscopic larvae—part of the ocean's vast population of zooplankton?

Interesting behaviors provide many good reasons for a person to want to keep fish and invertebrates. You will find that many of these animals have personality, too! They will come to recognize you and to look forward to your presence—well, either your presence or the presence of the can of fish food in your hand. It's hard to tell.

Marine animals can display intelligence, too. The octopus can learn how to unscrew the lid from a jar to get at a delicious crab inside. Octopuses have even been known to climb into the aquarium next door for a meal and then slither innocently back to their own tank. Fish will even do things that make you laugh. I once had a fish jump out the tank and hit me in the head as I walked by. I'm not sure why it did that, but I probably deserved it.

The real reasons I keep saltwater aquariums are . . .

. . . blennies make great cat treats.

. . . I like my sushi fresh.

. . . heavy aquariums keep tornadoes from blowing away my mobile home.

. . . fish geeks attract all the hot babes.

. . . the *National Enquirer* says fishkeeping is recommended by three out of four Elvis impersonators.

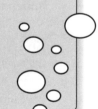

Reasons Not to Have an Aquarium

Frankly, I can't think of a single reason why a person would not want to keep an aquarium, but I can think of several reasons why a person would not deserve to keep one. This is particularly true of saltwater aquariums, as they tend to fall at the advanced end of the hobby. Compared with freshwater aquariums, there is less margin for error and more things that can go wrong.

Fish are living things, and although they require a very small commitment on your part, they do require a commitment. If you are not a responsible person, if you are not willing to do the tiny little bit of work required to keep the fish fed and the water changed—and if you would look at your tank so rarely that you wouldn't spot disease until it was way too late—then you really should forget about getting an aquarium. It is not fair to make the animals suffer.

The fact that you are reading this book puts you 20,000 leagues above 95 percent of the people who keep fish. It also puts you in the group that will have the highest success rate. Way to go! Smart move!

Anyway, now that I've listed reasons why you may or may not want to keep tropical marine fish, let me end this chapter by saying welcome to an interesting hobby. Whether you keep a single small tank for the kids or a larger one to decorate the living room, or become so involved with fish that your basement fills up with aquariums or you open an aquarium shop of your own, there is something in the hobby of fishkeeping for everyone. Enjoy!

Fish and Tips

If you don't feel up to doing the maintenance yourself, consider hiring one of the companies that provides aquarium maintenance services. Many dealers offer this service, and you also may find individuals or aquarium service companies listed in the Yellow Pages.

The Least You Need to Know

➤ An aquarium is living art.

➤ The hobby teaches about nature and science.

➤ Watching fish will relax you.

➤ Fish and invertebrates display amazing behaviors.

➤ The inhabitants of your aquarium depend on you. Be responsible!

Chapter 2

What Kind of Tank Is Right for You?

> ## In This Chapter
>
> ➤ Charting a course
>
> ➤ Freshwater vs. saltwater
>
> ➤ Big bruisers vs. peaceful pygmies
>
> ➤ Fish vs. invertebrates

Probably you have seen aquariums before and already have an idea of how you think your tank should look. Perhaps you saw a nicely decorated aquarium in a restaurant, in a doctor's office, or at a friend's house. Maybe Captain Picard's lionfish in *Star Trek: The Next Generation* caught your eye or Andy Sipowitz's fish in *NYPD Blue*.

Then again, maybe you have never seen or noticed any aquariums before. Perhaps this tank is not for you, but for a son or daughter who has an interest. Either way, before you buy any equipment or critters, some planning is required. It will be easier to make your aquarium turn out the way you expect if you have some expectations to begin with.

So take time to notice your friends' aquariums. Note what you like about them, what you tolerate, and what turns you off. Visit some public aquariums—and by public aquariums I mean fish zoos, such as the National Aquarium in Baltimore or the John G. Shedd Aquarium in Chicago. Public aquariums are popping up all over the country these days, so there is probably one within driving distance of you.

Keep in mind, however, that many public aquariums concentrate on local species or species that are way too large to be appropriate for your aquarium. So what you see in a public aquarium is not necessarily what you can do at home. Still, the public aquarium is a great place to get ideas.

Most aquarium and pet stores have at least one display-only aquarium set up in the shop. These tanks are fully decorated to give you an idea of just how good an aquarium can look. Although the particular fish in a display tank won't be for sale, the same species are usually available for sale elsewhere in the store. A dealer's display-only tanks can be very good sources of decorating ideas, since many dealers were devoted hobbyists long before they became dealers.

The National Aquarium in Baltimore. (© National Aquarium in Baltimore, Ron Haisfield)

Some dealers decorate their stock tanks, too, but most decorate them only sparsely or not at all. You see, it can be more difficult to net fish out of a tank that is heavily decorated—especially in saltwater aquariums. Corals snag nets easily and provide many places for fish to hide. Saltwater fish are not afraid to dive under the sand or hide deep in the fingers of coral skeletons to escape capture. For example, a triggerfish can lodge itself into a hole and lock the spines on its fins so that there is no way to remove it. You just have to wait for the fish to come out on its own.

Freshwater vs. Saltwater

Before buying your first tank, you have some decisions to make. The most important is to decide whether you want to keep freshwater fish or saltwater fish. This is a book about saltwater tanks. Before you proceed, you should consider if a saltwater aquarium is right for you—or if a freshwater aquarium would be a better place to start.

Let's start by defining some terms. *Freshwater* is the type of water that we drink. It is relatively salt- and mineral-free. Freshwater starts out as rain and eventually wends its way to the ocean. On its way there, it travels through rivers, streams, and lakes, picking up trace amounts of salts and minerals as it goes.

Saltwater, or seawater, is what we find in the oceans. The ocean is like a big dead-end lake—the water flows in, but only leaves via evaporation. So all the dissolved salts and trace minerals deposit there and have built up to high levels over millions of years. Saltwater is undrinkable for humans and most animals.

Fish School

Saltwater tank, seawater aquarium, and **marine aquaria** are all synonyms.

All water has some salts and minerals in it, but there is a big difference in how much you will find in freshwater compared to seawater. You could almost think of saltwater as highly concentrated freshwater or of freshwater as greatly diluted seawater.

All of this is a roundabout way of saying that freshwater fish and saltwater fish require very different water chemistry. You normally cannot plop a freshwater fish into a saltwater aquarium, or vice versa, and expect it to live. Besides the water chemistry difference, there are other differences as well. Let's talk about the differences that will help you make the right choice.

Your First Aquarium Should Probably Be Freshwater

Except in this chapter, you probably won't find me discussing freshwater aquariums anywhere else in this book. This book is designed to tell you how to properly—and easily—set up and maintain a marine aquarium. But your first aquarium probably should be a freshwater aquarium. Why? For several reasons.

First, a saltwater tank has less margin for error. The water quality parameters are more exacting. The ocean is the most stable environment in the world, so the organisms living in it are not used to big changes in their environment. If you are not careful, you can create conditions that stray from acceptable levels. For example, if a lazy freshwater aquarist lets 25 percent of the water evaporate from his tank, the fish may not notice much. In a marine tank, though, a 25 percent evaporation loss would increase salinity (how much salt is dissolved in the water) by 33 percent! Remember, only the water evaporates—not the dissolved salts. They just become more concentrated.

If you are a beginner, the extra margin for error provided by a freshwater tank could make the difference between initial success and failure. The water chemistry in a freshwater tank can fluctuate a bit more before it causes problems. Freshwater holds more oxygen than saltwater, too. Also, the toxicity of ammonia, which is excreted by the fish, increases with the pH of the water in the tank. Since saltwater has a normally high pH, the risk is always greater.

Next, saltwater aquariums are a bit more difficult to maintain than freshwater. You have to premix seawater in a separate container whenever you do water changes. *Salt creep* will cause you to have a bit more cleaning to do—how much depends on how many bubbles you have bursting. You see, when bubbles burst, they splash. When those splashes dry, unsightly salt deposits are left behind. (Don't worry, I'll talk about ways to limit this problem later in the book.)

Fish School

Salt creep is (1) unsightly mineral deposits that build up where water splashes and dries, (2) affectionate slang for a saltwater hobbyist.

You also may want to consider that saltwater fish are considerably more expensive. Although there is a whole range of prices, the most popular freshwater fish will cost you between $1 and $2 each. Marine fish, on the other hand, will average closer to $20 each. So it is probably a good idea to learn the ropes of fishkeeping with something a bit cheaper. Also, your initial investment in equipment for a saltwater tank will be somewhat greater.

Don't forget to consider availability. Dealers usually stock many more varieties of freshwater fish. In fact, unless you live in a larger metropolitan area, your dealer may not stock marine fish at all. It takes a larger investment in equipment and knowledge to keep saltwater fish, and your dealer may not be able to justify that investment to serve what is typically a minor percentage of his clientele. After all, he has to turn a profit or he will disappear.

Fish Tales

According to a survey by the American Pet Product Manufacturers Association, about 11 percent of American households keep freshwater fish, while only 0.6 percent keep saltwater fish.

Finally, diet is a factor. Most freshwater aquarium fish will readily accept flake food and survive quite well—even if that is all they are offered. With saltwater fish, though, only the hardiest would survive long on that diet. Be prepared to offer more of the frozen seafoods that your dealer carries.

So far, I have listed many reasons why a saltwater tank may not be your best choice for a first aquarium. But that doesn't mean your first tank can't be saltwater. If you choose the saltwater route, this book will show you how to do it right. If you decide to go the freshwater route, pick up a copy of *The Complete Idiot's Guide to Freshwater Aquariums*, by yours truly.

Positively Beautiful

OK, so much for negatives. What are the positives of saltwater aquariums? Foremost is the color of the fish. Saltwater fish would easily win any competition for most brightly colored. There are many spectacularly beautiful species. Bright colors—often iridescent—and bold patterns are common. The attractive coloration of saltwater fish is definitely what draws most people to keep them.

But wait—there's more! I haven't even mentioned the invertebrates. For the freshwater aquarium, you would be very lucky to find a store that carries even a half-dozen varieties of snails, clams, crabs, or shrimp for your tank. But it is a different story for the saltwater aquarium. There is a huge selection of invertebrates, including corals, anemones, urchins, starfish, crabs, shrimps, snails, clams, and much, much more. In fact, there is even a style of aquarium—the reef tank—that emphasizes invertebrates. I will talk about reef tanks later in this chapter.

Size Matters

Consider what size tank you want to set up. While the space you have available and your budget will be factors, a major consideration is the types of animals you plan to keep. If you want to keep large fish, plan on buying a large tank. You cannot crowd your fish or they will die. Also, big fish require more gallons of water per inch of fish length than small fish. More about that in Chapter 11 on picking fish.

Besides making sure that your tank isn't too small for its inhabitants, you must make sure that the inhabitants aren't too small for one another. Big critters eat little critters. With rare exceptions, you cannot mix large species with small ones. That is, not unless you want the small ones to be bait for the lunkers.

Fish and Tips

Most experts recommend that your first saltwater aquarium be no smaller than 29 or 30 gallons. Tanks that are this large and larger provide a more stable environment and help ensure success.

Charting a Course

Every aquarium is unique. Probably no two look exactly alike. However, saltwater tanks tend to fall into four general categories: fish-only tanks, reef tanks, lagoon aquariums, and semi-reefs. The requirements of these four types of aquaria are different in various ways, including appearance, required equipment, and (most important) the types of animals that can be safely kept within.

Once you set a course, it can be difficult to change midstream. For example, if you set up a tank with groupers or lionfish, you won't be able to add peppermint shrimp to that tank later. They would quickly become tasty peppermint snacks for those large fish! Choose a course and stick to it. It will help you pick compatible species.

The Fish-Only Aquarium

The fish-only marine aquarium—that is, an aquarium that excludes invertebrates—is the most common type of saltwater setup. It is the simplest form of marine aquarium, and is set up using the same basic equipment as most freshwater tanks. The same undergravel filters and outside power filters are commonly used. Fish-only marine aquariums tend to be less expensive and less demanding than the other styles of saltwater aquariums.

The fish-only marine aquarium uses artificial corals, coral skeletons, rocks, and plastic plants for decoration. Probably the most common example of this is the antiseptic-looking display filled with bleached white coral skeletons set against a dark background. Colorful fish flit between the dead corals. This appears quite unnatural, but it is a holdover from the days when live rock was not available and no one knew how to keep corals alive in captivity. Using coral skeletons to decorate a tank was as close as anyone could come to having a natural display.

Live invertebrates are generally not kept in this aquarium, for a couple of reasons. First, they add certain requirements to the upkeep of the tank, and second, the medications that are used to treat many saltwater parasites are lethal to invertebrates. Medicating the fish in a marine aquarium can be difficult or impossible when invertebrates are present. If you mix fish and invertebrates, be sure to follow the guidelines on quarantining new arrivals religiously! See Chapter 22 on stress and disease.

Fish School

An aquarium containing a mixture of small peaceful fish is called a **community tank.**

The Reef Tank

Most experts consider the reef tank to be the most advanced type of aquarium—either freshwater or saltwater. Most would consider the reef aquarium to be the most beautiful style of saltwater aquarium, as well. It certainly is the most natural style. In a reef tank, sometimes called a mini-reef or micro-reef, the emphasis is on the invertebrates (particularly live corals), and fish play a lesser role.

Despite the fact that most saltwater fish come from reefs in the wild, most of these fish cannot be safely kept in a reef aquarium. Why not? Because they feed on corals and other invertebrates! In the wild, Mother Nature has mechanisms to keep everything in balance. But an aquarium is not a complete ecosystem. As hard as we try, and no matter how much we spend, our aquariums will never be large enough to achieve the same natural balance. We will always have to intercede to keep the water quality acceptable, and if something dies or is eaten, it will be the dollars in our wallets that replace it, not the mechanisms of Mother Nature.

Reef tanks are set up very differently from most marine fish tanks, and I devote Chapter 20 to them. For now, I'll just touch on the basics of what constitutes a reef

A fish-only marine setup uses artificial decorations that enable you to keep the widest variety of species. (courtesy All-Glass Aquarium)

aquarium. The first is the use of *live-rock*. Live-rocks are natural, porous, calcareous rocks that are harvested from the ocean. While the rocks themselves can't be alive, we call them "live" because of the range of organisms that come along for the ride. Sponges, algae, corals, and more coat the external surfaces, while the nooks and crannies inside the rock are inhabited by worms, crabs, shrimp, copepods, and count-less forms of larvae and microplankton. Helpful nitrifying and denitrifying bacteria also come with the rock.

Live-rock is used extensively to form the basis of the reef in your aquarium. More exotic species of corals, other invertebrates, and fish are added to round out the display. In a sense, live-rocks and their encrusting sponges, algae, and corals become the garden of your reef, while the fish and other invertebrates become the buzzing, flitting creatures in that garden.

Another difference between a reef aquarium and a fish-only marine aquarium is the intense lighting. Most corals, anemones, and a few other inverte-brates harbor symbiotic organisms within their tissues. Without enough light to photosynthesize properly, these organisms, and their symbiont hosts, will die. And no, a typical aquarium full-hood with light is not nearly enough light! Check out Chapters 7 and 20 on lighting and on reef aquaria.

Fish School

Live-rock is porous rocks that have been harvested from the ocean, along with a healthy growth of attached marine flora and fauna.

Reef aquariums emphasize keeping live corals. This magnificent custom aquarium belongs to Chip and Jean Lubke.

Powerful protein skimmers (also called foam fractionators—try saying that three times fast!) are also required in reef tanks. Unlike other filtering methods—which merely trap waste until you clean the filter or break it down into byproducts that are removed when you change water—protein skimmers actually remove waste from the system. Waste bubbles out into a separate cup and no longer has contact with the aquarium water. I will talk about these useful devices more in Chapter 5 on filtration. By the way, I highly recommend protein skimmers for any saltwater aquarium, not just reef tanks.

Finally, most reef aquarists use some type of undertank sump for their setup—usually a trickle filter, but sometimes a separate smaller aquarium. The sump provides a place outside the tank for housing filtration, heaters, and protein skimmers, and for adding replacement water and additives.

I know that I used a few confusing terms in this section, but I explain them in more detail a bit later. Also, be sure to check out the recommended reading list in Appendix C for sources of more information on reef tanks. There is no way to fully cover this advanced topic in just part of a book.

Fish School

Symbiosis is a close association between two or more species, especially one that offers mutual benefit. For example, the anemone provides shelter to the clownfish. In return, the clownfish brings food to the anemone and helps drive off predators.

The Lagoon Tank

The lagoon tank is a specialty tank that falls somewhere between a fish-only marine tank and a full-blown reef tank. In a way, a proper lagoon tank looks more like a planted freshwater tank than a saltwater tank. It is dominated by fancy macroalgae and a few rocks.

Since most hobbyists picture coral decorations for their saltwater tank, not many who are looking to start a marine aquarium would envision their saltwater tank looking so green. But the lagoon tank lets you do a couple of things that don't usually work in the fish-only marine setup. First, you can culture fancy macroalgae, which come in various forms and colors. (Of course, you must avoid fish species that would eat the algae—which includes many of the most desirable species. Save them for the fish-only aquarium.) Second, you will be able to add a few hardy invertebrates. While you won't be able to keep live corals or many other species that would prosper in a reef tank, the lagoon tank will support various shrimp, crabs, featherduster worms, and more.

The lagoon tank is especially great for certain species. Most marine fish sold in stores come from tropical reefs. However, there are a few species that come from an entirely different habitat. The endearing seahorse is probably the best and most popular example. This fish is not found in the high-current areas of the reef. It is too slow to compete for food there and too poor a swimmer to avoid the stinging tentacles of corals and anemones. You won't be keeping live coral in this corral!

You can keep a variety of very interesting animals in a lagoon tank.

Rather, the seahorse is found in the grassy inland lagoons. Here, the current is weaker and plants, not corals, dominate the landscape. The prehensile tail of the seahorse

Something's Fishy

Be careful to pick species that won't decimate the macroalgae and the invertebrates in your lagoon tank, and avoid adding fish that are too competitive for the slow-moving seahorse.

grabs handily onto the grasses to anchor the animal in place to wait for passing prey. The seahorse is much better suited for the lagoon tank. One nice thing about a seahorse tank is that it can be a bit smaller—perhaps only 10 or 20 gallons.

Another reason the lagoon tank is ideal for seahorses is that it is an ideal habitat for tiny mysid shrimp and the nearly microscopic crustaceans called copepods (pronounced *KO-pee-pods*). These tiny critters hitch a ride on the live rock and macroalgae that you introduce to your tank. Then they settle in and multiply like crazy. They function as harmless scavengers, but their main advantage is that once they are established, they become a delicious snack that is continuously available for your seahorses. The more nooks and crannies, plants, and rocks in your lagoon tank, the more copepods you will have and the happier your seahorses will be.

The Semi-Reef Aquarium

The semi-reef aquarium is a hybrid between a fish-only or lagoon tank and a reef aquarium. The semi-reef adapts many of the principles that make the reef aquarium a healthy place to live. It relies on live rock to provide a natural, nonartificial appearance, and it incorporates live-rock and protein skimming as part of the filtration. It may even include more intense lighting than a typical fish-only marine aquarium. Various compatible invertebrates and fishes find residence in the semi-reef, but most corals (particularly stony corals) do not.

Although the semi-reef aquarium is not for keeping live corals, the use of live-rock allows some invertebrates and fish to be kept together.

The Coldwater Marine Aquarium

Most of the animals we keep in saltwater aquariums come from tropical climates, but a few hobbyists have found delight in keeping critters from temperate parts of the world. There are some beautiful and hardy species of sea anemones—huge pink and green ones, for example—as well as fish and other invertebrates that come from colder waters.

Special chillers (refrigeration units) are necessary to keep coldwater aquariums at sufficiently low temperatures—usually around 60° to 65°F (17° to 18°C). These animals do not fare well at typical room temperatures, so do not attempt to keep them unless you are willing to spend several hundred dollars for a proper chilling unit.

I mention this type of aquarium only briefly, because you are unlikely to find these coldwater animals in stores. The demand is small and the equipment is expensive. However, if you live near the beach, you may be able to collect your own coldwater specimens. Be sure that your local regulations allow it, of course. While I won't be specifically discussing coldwater aquariums elsewhere in this book, most topics will also apply. Rules regarding water chemistry, diet, and so forth should be the same.

Something's Fishy

Not any old refrigerator will do. Aquatic chillers are specially designed to withstand corrosive saltwater.

Brackish Aquaria

Many species of fish live in coastal areas and have evolved to tolerate large ranges of salinity. They can survive in freshwater, saltwater, and anything in between. The "in between" is brackish water. Most species sold as brackish are actually juvenile saltwater fish. They belong to species that spawn in the coastal waters. The youngsters live in the tidal estuaries and mangrove lagoons until they are large enough to move out to sea.

Pure freshwater has no salt. Seawater has a lot—roughly 24 teaspoons per gallon. A brackish tank is kept somewhere between those two extremes. Some hobbyists keep as little as two teaspoons of salt per gallon of water in their brackish tanks, but anywhere up to 12 teaspoons per gallon is suitable, and most brackish species tolerate full seawater. Indeed, most fare better in pure seawater.

Obviously, you cannot throw any species into a brackish tank. You must pick suitable species of fish and plants. Most aquatic plants will not tolerate excessive salt. Since the brackish tank is not truly a marine aquarium, I'm going to skip it in this book. For a list of popular brackish fish, check out *The Complete Idiot's Guide to Freshwater Aquariums*.

Biotopes for Purists

A *biotope* is a sample of a particular geographic environment. The reef tank and the lagoon tank are examples, but to be a purist about it, you would need to take things a step further. Most aquariums are set up with a mix of species from the various oceans. Many of these species would not encounter one another in the wild. While they frequent the same type of habitat, they would not be found in the same biotope.

To set up a true marine biotope, you would not only provide proper habitat for the animals and plants within, but also would choose species that would only be found together in the wild. For example, the Caribbean royal gramma would never see a coral beauty angel from the Indo-Pacific.

You may want to attempt this purism. While it will limit the number of species that you might keep in any particular aquarium, the up side is that it would be an even more natural environment, so you will be likely to see more natural behavior. Heck, you may become the first person to get a certain species to breed in the aquarium!

The Least You Need to Know

➤ If this is your first aquarium, you may be better off starting out with a freshwater tank. There is more margin for error.

➤ Big fish eat little fish. Even big peaceful fish eat little fish!

➤ Big fish need big aquariums.

➤ The three most common styles of marine aquarium are the fish-only aquarium, the reef tank, and the lagoon aquarium. Pick one, and choose your equipment and inhabitants accordingly.

Fishie Freddy's
Tropical Fish Store

Chapter 3

Finding a Dealer You Can Deal With

In This Chapter

➤ Which is more important: quality, selection, or price?

➤ How to determine if your dealer is a doofus

➤ I tell you where to go . . . shopping

If you are to be successful with your saltwater aquarium, the first thing you need to do is find a qualified dealer. Life will be much easier for you if you can find a good place to shop. Besides offering the appropriate merchandise, your dealer should be helpful and knowledgeable. You need someone you can turn to for advice.

Before you can decide which dealer is best for you, you first have to find a dealer who carries saltwater fish and supplies. The aquarium hobby is large, and there is hardly a pet store around that doesn't carry fish and aquariums of some kind, but the majority of those stores only stock freshwater fish. You see, the saltwater aquarium hobby is just not as widespread—mostly because it takes more technical expertise to be successful, and also because it is a more expensive hobby.

So some of you will be unlucky. You may find yourselves living in an area where there are few, if any, pet shops or aquarium stores, and the ones that you do find may not carry saltwater fish. You may have to travel some distance to find a store to serve your needs, and even then, the selection might be quite limited.

Some of you will be much luckier—particularly those who live in a major metropolitan area. Big cities are likely to be populated with many pet stores, including several specialty aquarium shops. Your chances of finding saltwater fish and supplies will be much greater. You will find better selection and more competitive prices. Lucky you!

But whether you live in the city or a rural area, you need to find a good dealer. You need to find someone who sells the equipment you need, who stocks the fish you covet, and who can offer advice when you need it. You need to find a dealer you can think of as a friend in the business. OK, so let's talk about the things you need to look for to find the right dealer.

Dead Fish Stink

Dead fish are a warning sign! A dealer whose tanks are littered with dead fish is a dealer who doesn't know how to care for them properly. If he can't keep his own fish alive, how is he going to be able to offer advice that you can trust to keep your own fish alive? Further, do you want to risk buying from tanks that are full of dead and diseased fish?

Avoid stores where there are lots of dead fish. They are bad news, pure and simple. Now, having said that, let me qualify this statement a little. Fish are livestock. Livestock is perishable. That means that fish can die. Eventually, even healthy fish will die—of old age or accident, or maybe some other healthy fish will decide to have them for lunch or bite them to death. So it is unreasonable to expect that you will never see a dead fish in your dealer's tanks, even if he is the best dealer in the whole wide fishy world. You just shouldn't see too many or see them too often.

Fresh Fish

When buying fish to eat, you want them as fresh as possible. When buying fish for your aquarium, you want them to age a little bit. In other words, buying new arrivals is a bad idea, because they are suffering from shipping stress.

Something's Fishy

There is nothing more tempting than showing up on your dealer's delivery day to pick out the coolest specimens before they even go into the tanks. Avoid this temptation! Getting first pick is not worth the risk of buying a highly stressed and possibly sick fish.

Imagine being crammed into a small plastic bag and then thrown into a dark box with a bunch of other fish. In transit, the box gets tossed around, and it may sit on a dock where it is roasted or chilled. Imagine being locked up that way, without food and swimming in your own waste, for up to 48 hours. That is what many fish go through to get from the exporters in Asia to the tank in your home. Worse, they have been through similar travels as they went from collector to jobber to exporter, and they may have had further stressful stops on the way as they passed through the hands of transshippers and wholesalers here in the United States.

Shipping is stressful, and stressed fish are more likely to get sick. As someone who has years of experience medicating fish in a store, I can certify that it is mostly the new arrivals that get sick or die. So avoid buying new specimens until they have been in the store for at least a few days, and don't hold it against your dealer if he has a few tanks under medication. Some dealers quarantine new arrivals in the back room before putting them in the sales displays.

How can you tell if a fish is a new arrival or not? Believe it or not, I have quite a few customers who are in the store often enough that they know what is new and what is not! Unless you are one of them, though, you won't be able to tell by looking at the fish. So the only way to know how long a fish has been in your dealer's stock is to ask. Some dealers put an arrival date on the price tags to guide you. The longer your dealer has had a fish in stock, the safer it will be to buy it.

Fish and Tips

Even fish get jet lag. Saltwater fish are mostly caught wild on the far side of the globe. When they arrive at your local shop, they have been through many transfer points and sealed in a bag in a dark box for perhaps a couple of days. Upon arrival, many will lie on the bottom of the tank. Don't worry. They just need time to recover from the stress of the trip.

Take Your Medicine

If the water in an aquarium is an unusual color, it probably means that the tank is under medication. Your dealer may treat tanks because the fish in them are obviously sick, or he may medicate new arrivals solely as a preventive measure. Do not buy from medicated tanks!

However, there is an exception to this rule. Most dealers keep their saltwater fish stock tanks under continuous copper medication. With so many fish coming in and out, this prevents outbreaks of protozoal parasites in the store. You would be hard-pressed to find a dealer who does not use this medication, and in fact, you should probably hope that your dealer does. This does not mean that you should do the same in your home aquarium, though!

Look for the Good Stuff

While dead fish are a bad sign, lack of them is not necessarily a good sign. Your dealer may be lousy at keeping fish alive but may be very good at regularly searching out and discarding dead bodies. So it is also important to look for healthy stock. Look for fish with bright eyes, clear skin, and erect fins. Look for fish with energy.

Look for fish with an interest in life. Are the fish active, or is everyone lying around or hiding? (Note that lying around and hiding is normal for some species, though.) If you are interested in purchasing a fish, ask to see it eat. Don't worry—your dealer won't look at you like you are nuts. This is a common request with wild-caught saltwater fish. A fish that eats is probably in good shape.

Feel free to stick your hand near the front glass to see if the fish come running for food or at least show habituation to humans. However, please do not touch the glass or tap on it. Sound travels through water much more easily than it travels through air, so tapping on the glass is like pounding a drum in a fish's ear. It can frighten a fish very badly and can cause injury. Besides, touching the glass leaves finger marks that make it harder to see the fish.

Something's Fishy

Don't buy a fish that isn't eating. It may be sick, or it may require a highly specialized diet that cannot be provided in captivity.

A Predilection for Large Selection

There are hundreds, maybe thousands of species of fish and invertebrates available in the aquarium hobby. Your dealer won't be able to carry them all, but the more tanks he has, the better his selection will be and the more fun it will be to shop there. I hope you live somewhere where your neighborhood aquarium stores are large operations with a large selection.

There are very few farm-raised saltwater fish or invertebrates. Almost all are wild-caught, and some are seasonal. Because of this, the supply of inhabitants for your marine tank can be quite variable. For example, small clown triggers can only be found during a certain time of year, and when there is a typhoon in the Philippines, divers won't be collecting fish at all!

While large aquarium stores are more likely to have a larger selection, don't overlook the smaller stores. The most important consideration is the health of the livestock. Sometimes the largest store around has the most disease-ridden fish because the staff is just too busy or lacking in expertise to give the fish proper care.

Look for a large selection of supplies and equipment, too. Does the dealer carry more than one brand of various items? Choice is good, although a person can be scared away by too many choices. Don't be afraid to ask for your dealer's advice if the choices are confusing. Still, my feeling is that a dealer who carries only one brand of most items is a dealer who doesn't understand that everyone's needs are not the same. Your dealer's recommendations are going to be very valuable, but there still should be some flexibility.

Ask the Experts

Your dealer can't help you if he doesn't know what he is doing. As a novice, you are at a disadvantage because you don't know what you are doing, either! So how can you tell if your dealer is an expert or a doofus?

Obviously, it would be foolish to assume that everyone who works in an aquarium or pet store is an expert. There are no academic degrees required to own or work in a fish store, and there aren't even any official tests to pass. Even the best stores with the most

You know your dealer is a doofus when . . .

. . . you tell him you want to buy a blue damsel and he fishes out a red fish.

. . . you ask if he has crabs and he just looks insulted and says, "Of course not!"

. . . you say you'll take the starfish and she asks if you mean the one that looks like Demi Moore.

. . . you ask her to show you her fishnets, and she hikes up her skirt and points at her stockings.

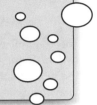

knowledgeable staff have to fill empty positions once in a while. That means that even the most highly recommended establishments may have a few trainees running around. So in addition to evaluating a store, be sure to evaluate the individual salespeople who will be helping you. A salesperson who knows his or her stuff can help you learn your stuff.

It is not always easy to evaluate a salesperson. A person can spout incorrect information with such confidence that they seem believable. You've got to be careful that your salesperson doesn't serve you some baloney with your fish!

Now, this may not be easy, especially since you are new to the hobby. The only way you will know if someone else knows what they are talking about is if you arm yourself with a little knowledge beforehand. The more you know before you walk into a store, the better you will be able to tell what kind of advice you are getting. If you at least know the basics, you will be able to tell if the information given to you by a salesperson agrees with what you've already learned.

Fish and Tips

Dedicated pet and aquarium stores are usually much better sources for quality stock and supplies than stores that simply wedge a pet department in between the shoes and the sporting goods.

Fortunately, most employees will at least know the basics. So even if you get a rookie to wait on you, they probably will be able to help you with most common questions. Still, if you feel that a salesperson is not yet ready to answer the questions you ask, don't be afraid to ask if there is someone with a little more experience available to help you—even if you have to come back later.

To evaluate the salespeople at your local shop, listen to how they answer questions—not just your questions, but those of other customers, too. Does the salesperson have an answer for everything? This may indicate a salesperson who likes to bluff their way through a conversation. You need someone who is willing to say so when they don't know something. Does the salesperson hesitate before each answer and then give

Fish and Tips

There are many ways to skin a catfish. Getting different answers to the same question does not necessarily mean any of the answers are wrong. Rather, differences may reflect personal preference. For example, one dealer may recommend fluorescent lighting, while another recommends metal halide lights. Both methods will work.

vague responses? This could be a sign that they don't really know their material or are making it up.

It can be helpful to look for a consensus. If you ask the same question of a couple of salespeople or even in a couple of stores and get similar answers, you are probably getting good advice. Don't overdo this, though. Only use this technique when you are initially evaluating the quality of a dealer, or if you have particular reason to believe that the salesperson gave a wrong answer. Your dealer can't turn a profit if he has to have employees help you twice for each sale. And if he can't turn a profit, he can't afford to hire and keep good help. Further, most salespeople feel insulted when they overhear a customer asking someone else the exact same question. It makes them feel like that customer wasted their time, and may make them feel less inclined to spend time with you on your next visit.

Courtesy Should Be Common

Let's say you walk into a store. A little bell on the door jingles as you enter. The cashier is leaning against the counter, her back to you, and doesn't even turn around to catch your eyes, give you a nod, or say hi. You walk around for a bit, browsing the merchandise on the shelves. So far, there has not been a salesperson in sight, but maybe you hear a couple of people giggling and goofing off in the back room.

You spot a new product and want to ask questions about it. There is no one to ask, so you roam around a bit more and notice an employee speaking to a customer on the phone. You wait nearby, hoping to get help when he gets off the line. Bad move. It turns out that it he is not talking to a customer, but to his girlfriend. After a few minutes, you realize that it will be a while.

You wander from the equipment section to the fish department. Maybe someone there can help you. Aha! There's a person wiping algae from the glass in the tanks. Finally, someone who works here! You approach, hoping for help. As you get near, the person doesn't even look up to acknowledge your existence. So you stand there a moment, hoping to be noticed.

Finally, you say, "Excuse me. I have a question on this product. Can you help me?" The employee sighs and makes a face. It is pretty obvious that he would rather be wiping algae.

"Is this a good choice?" you ask.

Without elaborating, the employee replies, "Yeah, it's good stuff," and then turns to start wiping algae again.

"I don't understand how it works. Can you tell me about it?"

The employee takes the bottle and starts reading the directions to see how it works. He's reading the same label that you read when you first picked up the product. Obviously, this employee isn't all that familiar with the product.

OK, so what is the moral of this story? The moral is that all of the employees in that shop should be retrained, replaced, or rented out as doorstops!

One thing is obvious: Someone else deserves your business. Go someplace where you get a little courtesy and service. Go someplace where they smile and say hi when you come in the door, and where they at least make eye contact and give you a nod as you pass them in the aisle. Go someplace where the salespeople actually come up and ask what they can do to help, rather than waiting for you to put them in a hammerlock to get their attention. Find a store where they are happy to see you.

There is no substitute for friendly, helpful, courteous employees. Find a dealer who shows interest, not just in the products, but also in you. Your dealer should look out for your interests as well as his own. You don't want a salesperson who is only looking to make a sale for the sale's sake. You don't want to be sold products that you don't need or that don't work.

Luckily, most employees in aquarium stores are people who signed on because they share your interest and joy in the hobby. In fact, an aquarium store is one of the few places you can shop where it is common for employees to talk you out of buying something!

A good salesperson can help you by suggesting additional products that you need or may find useful—items that you may not have considered—but he won't try to offer you a product for every little problem. Sometimes there are simpler, cheaper, or even free ways to solve your problems, and your dealer should be willing to volunteer that information.

Special Services

Many dealers have more to offer than the usual merchandise and advice. A good dealer will offer some extra professional services. Some are even free. Here are some examples:

➤ **Water testing.** You bring in a sample from your tanks, and they do a quick analysis for you. Usually this service is free, but some dealers charge small fees. I still recommend that you have your own water test kits on hand, though. If you run your own tests, you can still feel free to call your dealer for advice on what to do when the readings say that something is wrong.

➤ **Equipment repair.** Most pumps, filters, heaters, and lights are repairable. A few dealers offer repair services, usually charging only for parts. Be aware that you may have to leave the item for repair at their convenience, and you may have to wait for parts to be ordered. Unfortunately, most dealers don't carry much in the way of replacement parts.

Some dealers offer water testing services. Here, Alexandra runs a pH test.

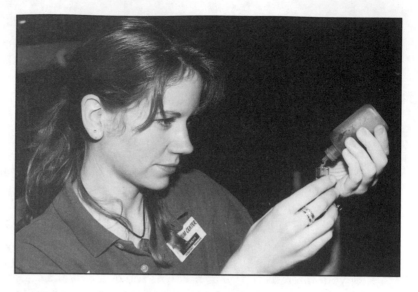

➤ **Instructional seminars.** These are usually free, so take advantage of them. Usually they will be on topics suited for beginners, but advanced topics may be covered as well. Sometimes guest speakers who are big names in the trade may be brought in. It is a great way to learn, have fun and maybe even make some new friends.

➤ **Aquarium drilling.** Yes, most glass can be drilled with the proper tools. More and more people are having holes drilled in their tanks to allow for undertank plumbing.

➤ **Aquarium maintenance.** This is where you pay your dealer to come to your home or business to install or perform routine maintenance on your aquarium. Usually the service is performed on your own equipment, but some dealers even have arrangements that allow you to lease the aquarium setup. Services are usually tailored to each customer. It can even be set it up so that the service occasionally swaps fish and decorations in your tank, giving you something new to look at. Most aquarium service companies will have you sign a contract that explains your obligations and theirs.

➤ **Disease diagnosis.** All tropical fish stores offer free advice on treating fish diseases. Granted, some are much better at it than others. You may even get lucky and find a store that is willing to look at your sick fish under a microscope. This is not very common, though, and the stores that perform this service are likely to charge a small fee. Still, if it helps you choose the right medication the first time, it is worth it.

➤ **Custom-built aquariums and cabinets.** Of course, custom units cost more than off-the-shelf models, but it is possible to get custom sizes and finishes to match your existing furniture.

➤ **Convenient business hours.** Offering great service and services is very important, but it is especially nice if they are offered when you can take advantage of them. Ideally, your favorite dealer will be open seven days a week and until 9 p.m. on six of those days. My condolences to those of you living in areas where the shops close at 5 or where the owners set a different schedule each day to suit their convenience. That happens too often when hobbyists open a business. They don't always realize that it is not just a hobby anymore.

Fish and Tips

Better dealers offer live foods for sale. It is highly entertaining to watch fish eat the way they do in nature. Goldfish, guppies, brine shrimp, and blackworms are the most common live foods you are likely to find offered, but there are others, and an exceptional dealer will have them available for sale, too.

How Much Is That Fishy in the Window?

It is a Saturday afternoon and you are shopping for aquarium supplies at Super Duper Tropicals, your favorite aquarium store. Today you happen to be thinking about setting up another aquarium, so you are looking at the various filters that are available. Let's say you find two similar filters of two different brands. Both are rated at the same number of gallons per hour and are designed for the same size aquariums, but they use different types of filter media. One filter costs $5 more than the other. Interestingly, you can buy the cheaper filter for $1 less at D&D Tropicals down the street. (By the way, in this example D&D stands for "Dead and Dying.")

Of the two brands of filters, which is better? Which one will you buy? Since it appears that the dingy store down the street may sell at a lower price than your favorite store, will you go there to buy it?

Every dealer has a different method of pricing his merchandise. So as you shop around, you may find a large range of prices for the same items. Prices will vary from store to store and by geographical region. Welcome to life. Yes, everyone loves to get a good deal. None of us wants to pay more for an item in one place than we would if we bought it somewhere else. I hope that you find a good bargain every time you go shopping. But keep this in mind: Price is not everything!

Fish and Tips

Don't be ruled solely by low price. Quality and service are more important!

Your money should be buying more than just merchandise. When comparing prices, consider what else you are getting for your money. If your dealer is helpful, be willing to pay a little more for that. Does he offer free water tests, pump repairs, or other services? Is there a guarantee on the livestock he sells? Does he carry hard-to-find items? If so, taking advantage of such "free" services should be worth something to you.

A good dealer can actually save you money, even if his prices are a little higher than average. He can do this by steering you away from products that you don't need or that are inferior. A good dealer provides advice that will keep you from killing your expensive fish. And a good dealer will help you out with free advice, even when you are not making a purchase (but it would be wrong to expect him to do so if you are planning to make the purchase somewhere else).

When you are lucky enough to find a good dealer, help keep him in business by shopping there. Don't reward the shady guy down the street with your dollars. Low price is desirable, but I put it at the very bottom of my list of factors for deciding what is and isn't a good store to patronize. Let price be the deciding factor only when all else is equal.

Now I'll Tell You Where to Go

There are many places to shop for fish and supplies, and I don't just mean aquarium and pet stores. Let's talk about some of these choices and the advantages and disadvantages of each. I will admit up front that I'm about to stereotype some of these options for you, but my descriptions will be based on what you would commonly find. However, let me emphasize that every seller should be judged individually. There are good ones and bad ones of every type.

Pet Stores

The most common source of fish and supplies is the local pet store. Most pet stores sell fish, birds, hamsters, reptiles, and an array of other pets and supplies. Most pet stores are neighborhood mom-and-pop operations—that is, single locally owned stores, as opposed to parts of a larger chain.

Many pet stores have a specialty based upon the interest of the owner. But whether the owner's favorite is the bird department or the fish department, sales of fish and supplies typically account for close to half of a pet store's business. So even if a pet store isn't a specialized aquarium store, there is a very good chance you will be able to find someone knowledgeable enough to help you. Pet stores are good places to shop.

Tropical Fish Specialty Stores

The ideal place to buy your aquariums, fish, and supplies is a dedicated aquarium store. Unfortunately, there are not many of them out there, except in the larger cities.

Dedicated aquarium stores are great. Aquariums are usually a passion for the owners and most of the employees. So the chances of finding salespeople who know their stuff, who will steer you right, and who don't mind a little friendly fish-related chat are excellent. When people like something, they learn about it. So you are most likely to get good advice, find the best equipment, and the healthiest fish in the dedicated tropical fish store. Count your blessings if you've got one nearby.

You may recall my earlier note that many pet stores only carry freshwater fish. Tropical fish specialty stores, on the other hand, usually stock saltwater fish as well. In fact, you may be lucky enough to find a store that carries only saltwater fish and supplies.

Pet Supply Superstores

The pet business is changing. A few years ago, it was dominated by small, neighborhood pet shops. In recent years, chains of giant retail pet superstores have sprung up. These stores tend to specialize in the sales of supplies. That is, to keep overhead low, they carry little or no livestock. Some of these stores are truly pet shops with no pets.

One thing I must give the superstores credit for is that they have brought a degree of professionalism to the pet business. The stores are large, nicely laid out and merchandised, and the selection is good. Since they specialize in pet-related merchandise—as opposed to being a pet department in some other type of operation, such as a garden center—there is a semi-decent chance that you could find the equipment you need and someone to advise you.

Unfortunately, the odds of that are not as good as they could be, because most of these stores put their emphasis on selling self-serve goods, particularly dog and cat foods. So you may have an easier time finding someone to answer questions about your cat than your catfish.

There is such a thing as a tropical fish superstore, but it is a fairly rare thing. You can find a few around the country, mostly on the East Coast. Still, the ones I've seen have been all worth the trip. It's a lot of fun to walk into a huge store and find upwards of 600 aquariums full of dazzling fish and invertebrates, supplies galore, and wall-to-wall fish geeks!

Mass Merchandisers

Most of the mass merchandisers (that is, the various XYZ-Marts) have pet supply departments, and some even carry a few pets and fish. If you know your stuff, you may find some good deals there.

On the other hand, if you are new to the hobby, I recommend that you avoid these places. Check them out later, when you have a better idea of what you are doing. For now, you need to get good advice to get started right. Unfortunately, the pet departments in these stores are almost always staffed by employees who have insufficient training. Often, it is the clerk from the shoe department or auto parts section who will end up dipping your fish. As I like to say, "They don't know the difference between cichlids [pronounced *SICK-lids*] and sick fish!" If you don't know the difference either, that only further emphasizes my point that you need to find a store that has an experienced and knowledgeable staff available.

One thing the mass merchandisers may have going for them is low prices. However, their selection is likely to be small, and occasionally the merchandise is inferior. Mass merchandisers tend to carry little in the way of livestock. Worse, it is doubtful that they will carry any saltwater livestock at all. (Though if you ask me, that is probably best, because they are usually ill-equipped to keep the fish alive.)

Mail Order

There are a few large mail-order pet supply operations around the country. They sell a wide variety of merchandise at very good prices. In fact, I've sometimes seen stuff for sale at prices less than what your dealer pays through his distributor. You can find some very good bargains via mail order, and these companies offer quick shipping.

Fish and Tips

If you buy from a mail-order company, it is major uncool to go first to your local dealer and have him spend time educating you on what stuff to buy and how to hook it up, only to have you turn around and buy it somewhere else. When you find a good dealer, keep him in business by shopping there.

But beware the downside. First off, you need to be familiar enough with the products to order them sight unseen. Ordering a product over the phone is no substitute for being able to look over the item in person at your local shop. You can't read the package and instruction booklet ahead of time, and you don't have an easy way to compare quality and competing brands.

Another disadvantage of mail order is that you have to wait for delivery. If the item is something that you need in a rush, it is not feasible to wait a few days for it to arrive, and paying extra charges for overnight shipping is likely to eat up any savings that came from buying via mail order. Plus, what happens if the item is defective when it arrives? You've got the time and expense of packing it up to ship back and the delay of waiting for a replacement, refund, or credit.

Fish and Tips

Certain items, such as aquariums and gravel, are too breakable or heavy to ship, and are rarely available by mail.

Another disadvantage is that the telephone order taker doesn't always know what items are in stock. Heck, they may not even be in the same building! So you may be placing an order for an item that they don't even have, and the law gives them 30 days before they have to let you know about it.

Most merchandise available via mail-order will be aquarium supplies. There is little available in the way of mail-order livestock, and frankly, by the time you pay expensive air freight to ship it, it could cost you more than buying locally. However, if you are looking for a large quantity of live-rock, you may find some pretty good deals.

Because most mail-order livestock is shipped via air freight, be prepared to take time (usually on a moment's notice) to make a trip to the nearest metropolitan airport to pick up your shipment. By the way, when I say "metropolitan airport," I mean one that is large enough for the jumbo jets to fly into. Your local county airport is just not going to do.

Despite all this, mail-order can be a good way to shop if you are an experienced hobbyist and know what you are getting. If you live in a rural area, you may not have an aquarium shop anywhere nearby. You may have no other choice than to order supplies through the mail.

Garage Sales

I probably should have titled this section "Risky Business." You can find aquariums for sale in the classified ad section of your local newspaper. You will find them in the occasional garage sale, too. Depending on how much you know, you could get a really good deal or waste a lot of money.

When people sell used equipment, it is usually because they failed to keep their fish alive with it. Granted, this may be because they didn't know how or didn't keep up with the general maintenance. However, it also may be because they bought inferior equipment. So if you buy used equipment, make sure it is the same stuff you would have bought new, had you gone to a dealer.

Anyway, until you know your way around the hobby more, I recommend that you avoid purchasing used equipment.

> **Something's Fishy**
>
> There is no warranty on used equipment. It is common for people to buy boxes of used equipment only to find that some of it doesn't work, that it is missing pieces, etc. Plus, you don't know if grandma unwittingly washed everything with a toxic soap to clean it up for the sale.

The Least You Need to Know

➤ Avoid dealers with sick and dying stock.

➤ Find a dealer who is knowledgeable.

➤ Seek dealers who are courteous and willing to spend time with you.

➤ Quality is most important, followed by selection and price.

➤ It's usually best to shop in a dedicated aquarium store, but a good pet store will suffice. Evaluate each dealer individually.

Part 2
What Stuff Do You Need First?

Nobody gets into the aquarium hobby because they think pumps and filters are cool. Spectacular fish and invertebrates are the attraction! Still, you can't have the animals if you don't have the proper life support. So prepare yourself to learn about equipment and how to select the right components for the job at hand. There are many choices, though, so the results will be up to you. Check out the shopping lists in Appendix B for added help.

Knowing what to buy is one thing. Knowing how to put it together is another. The last chapter in this part, "Some Assembly Required," will give you detailed, step-by-step instructions. I even drew some illustrations to guide you.

Chapter 4

Choosing a Tank and Stand

In This Chapter

➤ Deciding between glass and acrylic

➤ Tips for choosing the best size and shape of aquarium

➤ The difference between starter kits and complete outfits

➤ Choosing a proper aquarium stand

Aquariums come in many shapes and sizes. The rectangular box is the most familiar, but there are some other shapes available, too. You will find hexagonal and octagonal aquariums, as well as pentagons and tanks that fit perfectly into a corner of the room. There are even spheres and other tanks with curved front panels. Standard aquariums range from 2.5 gallons up to 300 gallons, but custom sizes may go even larger. But before I talk about how to choose specific aquariums, there are some things to consider.

Make Sure It Will Fit

Decide where you will put your aquarium before you buy it. Take time to measure the space, and you will be sure to buy a tank that fits in the spot you picked out. Write down all the measurements and take them with you when you go shopping.

When you are deciding where to put the tank, appearance is not the only thing to consider. Here are a few more things to think about:

➤ Be sure to locate the tank where it is not going to block access to a door, window, electrical circuit panel, or the like.

Fish and Tips

If you put your tank near a door, particularly an exterior door, note the direction the door swings. Be sure to allow safe clearance or install a doorstop device in the floor. I once had a windstorm blow my front door open, and it swung around so far that the doorknob went through the front of my aquarium!

➤ Don't put the aquarium too near a heating duct, cooling duct, or radiator. These may cause temperature extremes in your tank.

➤ Allow enough height for both the tank and the stand, and don't forget to leave enough room to open the lid so you can maintain the tank.

➤ Be careful to keep the aquarium from sticking out into an aisle where it will block traffic. Remember that you may need to leave a bit of space behind for any hang-on-the-back filters, overflow boxes, or protein skimmers. At the very least, you must allow enough room for electrical cords, air lines, or filter hoses to run behind the tank.

While you are measuring, it is also a good idea to consider the strength of your floor. The construction in some older homes may not be strong enough to hold a large aquarium. If your floor bounces a lot when you walk on it, then it probably is best not to put a really large tank there. Bouncing is not very good for aquariums anyway, as it can twist and crack your tank.

But don't let me scare you too much. Most sizes of tanks will be safe in almost every house. It is only when you get into the larger tanks—say, 75 gallons or larger—that a weak floor could be a factor, and even then, I would say that it is probably only a problem in construction older than 30 or 40 years. If the floor joists are of the modern typical 2 × 8, 2 × 10, or 2 × 12 construction, I doubt that there is any need to worry.

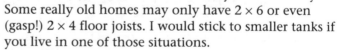

Some really old homes may only have 2 × 6 or even (gasp!) 2 × 4 floor joists. I would stick to smaller tanks if you live in one of those situations.

Acrylic May Be Idyllic

Modern aquariums may be made from either glass or acrylic. Both types have advantages and disadvantages, and you will need to decide which features appeal to you most. The chances are high that your dealer will stock only one type, so you may need to shop around to find the style you want.

Fish and Tips

Water weighs around 8.4 pounds per gallon. Figuring that a filled aquarium weighs roughly 10 pounds per gallon should help you estimate its total weight. So a 10-gallon tank would weigh around 100 pounds, a 75-gallon tank would weigh around 750 pounds, and a 300-gallon tank would weigh a ton and a half!

Most people who choose acrylic aquariums do so because of their distinctive appearance. Both tank and stand tend to be made of this space-age plastic. They have a clean, modern look, and acrylic can be formed into more shapes than glass. An aquarium with fish is a work of art, and acrylic has more of a modern art look to it.

If you want, you can buy your acrylic tank with a solid-color back panel (usually blue or black) built in. There will be no need to buy an additional background, but you won't be able to change it, either, if you ever get tired of the color.

Acrylic tanks are usually manufactured using single-piece construction of the sides. That is, a single sheet of acrylic is heated and bent to form the front and sides of the aquarium. So the corners are seamless, rounded, and completely transparent. Acrylic is more transparent than glass, too, so you don't get the very slight greenish tinge that you get when looking through thick panels of glass.

Acrylic tanks have a clean, modern appearance, and can be formed into more shapes. (courtesy Cole Enterprises)

Acrylic is lighter than glass. Less weight makes the tank easier to move around when empty. (Never move a full tank! You may twist and crack it.) Two people can easily carry a large empty acrylic aquarium, while it may take four or more to move a large glass tank.

Acrylic is also stronger than glass. Yes, it can be cracked or shattered, but it takes more force to do it. Acrylic tanks are usually assembled using liquid solvents to weld the seams together at the molecular level. So an acrylic tank is effectively a one-piece deal with seams that are difficult to split. That is, the best ones are. It depends on the manufacturing technique. There are some brands out there that use thick acrylic glues to bond the panels, instead of the thin liquid solvent. Those tanks aren't as strong.

Acrylic tanks are more flexible than glass tanks. This means they can take more twisting and bouncing about before they break. That has made them more popular on the West Coast of the United States. Why? Well, partly, it's just a California sense of style, but mainly it is because acrylic tanks withstand earthquakes better than glass.

While flexibility may help an acrylic aquarium survive an earthquake, it does have its disadvantages. Once the tank is filled with water, the weight of the water presses out on all

Fish and Tips

You can drill acrylic with typical household tools. So if you want to install plumbing for through-the-wall or through-the-bottom filtration, you can do it yourself.

the sides. This causes a slight bowing of the panes. (This happens with glass, too, but not as much.) This is not a strength problem and shouldn't even cause any distortions in your view of the fish, but it does have a downside. Depending on the lighting in your room and your angle of view, the curved surfaces may pick up excessive reflections of room lights in an annoying manner.

Because the sides bow more easily, acrylic tanks have their clear tops welded on, to strengthen the sides of the tank. Cutouts allow access for filters, heaters, feeding, and maintenance. There is no need to buy a separate glass cover for an acrylic tank. The integral top also prevents much of the mineral buildup that you could get at the edge of a glass cover.

Compared to glass, acrylic has most of the advantages, but it has one disadvantage—and it's a fairly big one. Acrylic is softer than glass, so it scratches easier. Much easier! If you or your fish are prone to knocking large rocks against the sides, you may soon find your tank scratched.

There are special kits available for buffing out scratches, but they aren't fun to use, and prevention is better. There are liquid polishes for tiny scratches, and kits that use abrasive screens of variously sized mesh to rub out defects.

Is Glass First Class?

Personally, I prefer glass tanks. Glass is not as strong as acrylic, but it is plenty strong enough—unless you live on the San Andreas fault!

Something's Fishy

You need to be more careful when scrubbing algae on your acrylic tank. It is not safe to use razor blades on acrylic, and even some algae pads are too rough and can cause damage. Be especially careful not to get bits of gravel between the acrylic and the scrubber pad.

Glass tanks are made by gluing panes together with silicone rubber sealant. Of course, the corners are not transparent because of this, and are not smooth and rounded like acrylic. Rather, glass tanks have sharp angles on the corners—polished, so that you don't get cut on them. Since the corners aren't rounded, you don't get the funhouse mirror distortion that you get on the corners of acrylic tanks.

Plastic frames are glued onto the top and bottom of glass aquariums. Mostly, they are decorative, but they do provide some added strength. Solid black and dark or light woodgrain finishes (referred to as walnut or oak) are most common. There are some other colors you may find, including granite and whitewashed oak. Choose the color that best matches your stand or the decor of your home.

Like acrylic tanks, some brands have solid-colored backgrounds built in. You may even find models with integral mirror backs. These tanks reflect the decorations inside the tank to make it appear twice as deep. Pretty cool, huh? Of course, the downside of a mirror background is that you may see the reflection of a familiar fool looking back at you!

Plate Glass or Tempered?

Aquariums may be made of plate glass or tempered glass. Most small tanks are made of plate glass. There are two types of plate glass. The cheaper *rolled glass* is more commonly used in windows than in aquariums. The liquid glass passes between rollers to make the sheets of glass. It is a bit more wavy than float glass. *Float glass*, the type usually used in aquariums, is manufactured by pouring liquid glass onto a bed of liquid mercury. The glass floats on top and cools to form the smoothest, most perfect type of glass.

Something's Fishy

Tanks with built-in mirror backgrounds are probably not a good choice for saltwater aquariums. For starters, any saltwater splashed on the back of the mirror may corrode it, ruining the appearance. Also, many saltwater fish are highly territorial with others of their own species and see their own reflections as a constant threat.

Some larger tanks are manufactured entirely or partly of tempered glass. Tempered glass is manufactured in a process that makes it stronger than an equal thickness of plate glass. This means that thinner sheets of glass can be used to keep the cost down, resulting in a cheaper and lighter aquarium. An advantage of tempered glass is that it is harder to break than plate glass. Do not try to drill tempered glass, however. It will shatter!

Usually, you won't have a choice between plate glass and tempered glass. Most sizes will only be available in one style. So which should you choose? Well, if you want to drill the aquarium, tempered glass is out of the question. Otherwise, it probably doesn't make much difference. You shouldn't be hitting your aquarium hard enough to break it. But if Junior likes playing baseball indoors and you think your tank may take a hard enough whack to break tempered glass, get plate glass. There is less chance of losing the entire contents of your tank on the floor. Personally, I prefer plate glass tanks.

Reef Ready

Most glass aquariums can be drilled for through-the-glass plumbing of filters. As I just mentioned, tempered glass is the exception. Both glass and acrylic tanks are often available predrilled, with plumbing installed, ready to connect to the proper filter. These tanks are commonly referred to as *reef-ready*, because reef tank hobbyists tend to prefer to put their filters in the cabinet underneath the tank. Freshwater hobbyists use reef-ready tanks, too, though.

Nice Shape! Big Footprint!

Aquariums come in all shapes and sizes. Before I continue, remember that the size of your space, and the size and behavior of the critters you intend to keep, will play a role in determining the shape and size of your tank.

What shape aquarium is best? For starters, you need maximum surface area to promote the exchange of oxygen and carbon dioxide in your tank. That means the top should be the same size as the middle and the bottom. This includes most shapes of tanks. It probably only rules out spheres and those tanks with slanted fronts that have recently hit the market. Rectangles, hexagons, pentagons, and the new bow-front or Euro tanks are fine.

How much space an aquarium takes up on the stand—in other words, the dimensions of the bottom—is called the *footprint*. Go for the big footprint. Wide, low aquariums are better than tall, narrow ones, because they maximize the surface area per gallon.

> ### Something's Fishy
>
> The downside of tempered glass is that if it does break, it will shatter into a million pieces. You will lose every drop of water in the tank, every time. Plate glass, on the other hand, cracks when it breaks. Depending on where the crack(s) occur, you may not lose all water from the tank. If the tank bottom cracks you will lose it all, but if only a top corner cracks only a little water will leak out.

As an example, let's look at two aquariums. One is 20 inches long by 10 inches wide by 10 inches high. The other is 10 inches long by 10 inches wide by 20 inches high. You can see that both tanks have the same volume of 2,000 cubic inches (calculate volume by multiplying length by height by width). However, the first tank will have a bigger footprint, providing it with a water surface of 200 square inches (calculated by multiplying length by width). The second tank will have a water surface of 100 square inches—only half as much.

> ### Fish and Tips
>
> Avoid tall tanks. It will be hard to reach the bottom in a tank that is more than 18 inches deep. In tanks 30 inches deep, how do you reach the bottom to root a plant or clean the back glass?

Both tanks hold the same amount of water, but one has a footprint and surface area twice the size of the other. The larger surface area allows for better exchange of oxygen and carbon dioxide at the surface. The larger footprint provides more room for fish to swim—fish prefer swimming back and forth to swimming up and down—and it also provides more bottom territory for fish to stake out. In other words, your fish will be more comfortable in the wide, low aquarium than in the tall, narrow one.

Bigger Is Better

Always buy the biggest tank that you can afford and that will fit in your designated space. A bigger tank provides

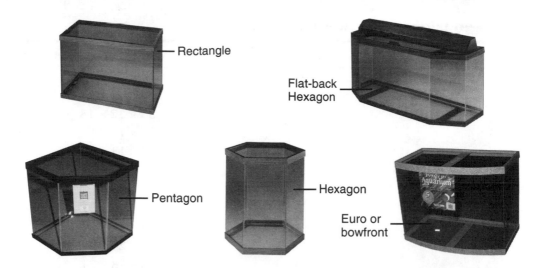

Some typical aquarium shapes. (courtesy of All-Glass Aquarium, except pentagon and Euro, courtesy of Perfecto Manufacturing)

a more stable environment and is safer for your fish. If a fight breaks out, a larger tank also makes it easier for a fish to dodge bullies. The loser can't get away if there is nowhere to run! Besides, it takes almost the same amount of time to maintain a small tank as it does a large one.

The best reason to buy the biggest tank you can afford is that you will quickly wish you had more room to keep more species of fish! As a dealer, I hear this lament all the time. You will be surprised by how fast you can fill an aquarium, given all the choices of interesting species that are available.

The following table contains typical sizes of aquariums. The sizes highlighted in bold tend to be better values on a dollar-per-gallon basis and make especially good starter kits. Choose the largest that will fit your budget or space. Remember that saltwater tanks should be no smaller than 29 gallons—to allow for territoriality and to provide a stable environment.

Fish and Tips

Aquariums are sold in standard sizes and dimensions, but the stated size of the tank, in gallons, is based roughly on external dimensions. To calculate the *true* volume of your aquarium, measure the *inside* length, width, and height (all in inches), multiply these figures, and divide by 231 to get gallons. So if a tank had inside dimensions of $30 \times 10 \times 10$, you would multiply those numbers to get 3,000 and then divide by 231. You end up with 12.98 gallons. True gallon capacity is almost always less than the capacity stated on the label.

Starter Kits vs. Complete Outfits

Your dealer may offer some saltwater starter kits. This is often the easiest way to get going and may even come at a special price. But let me define my terms before I

Aquarium Sizes and Dimensions

Shape	Gallon Size	Length × Width × Height (in Inches)
Rectangle	20	24 × 12 × 16
	20	30 × 12 × 12
	29	**30 × 12 × 18**
	30	36 × 13 × 16
	40	48 × 13 × 16
	45	36 × 13 × 24
	55	**48 × 13 × 20**
	58	36 × 18 × 21
	75	**48 × 18 × 21**
	89	36 × 24 × 24
	90	48 × 18 × 24
	100	72 × 18 × 18
	110	60 × 18 × 24
	120	48 × 24 × 24
	125	**72 × 18 × 22**
	135	72 × 18 × 24
	150	72 × 18 × 28
	180	96 × 18 × 24
	180	72 × 24 × 24
	200	84 × 24 × 25
	220	84 × 24 × 25
	265	84 × 24 × 30
Hexagon	20	18 × 16 × 20
	27	18 × 18 × 24
	35	23 × 20 × 24
	45	22 × 22 × 24
	60	27 × 24 × 28
Flatback Hexagon	23	24 × 12 × 20
	26	36 × 12 × 16
	33	36 × 13 × 20
	52	48 × 13 × 20
Pentagon	44	22 × 22 × 24
Euro (bowfront)	28	24 × 15 × 19
	46	36 × 16 × 20

proceed. When I say *complete aquarium kit*, I mean one that includes *everything* that you need to set up the tank properly—except your choices of decorations and livestock. Anything less than that I call a *starter kit*. Whatever is missing from your starter kit, you will need to purchase separately, according to your taste.

I can tell you right now that you are not going to find complete kits for $19.99! A complete 29-gallon saltwater setup will probably run 10 times that, without the stand. Do not scrimp on equipment. It keeps your fish alive. Don't risk killing off a hundred dollars' worth of fish to save a couple of bucks on equipment. Sheesh!

The following is a shopping list of items that I believe make up a complete fish-only saltwater aquarium kit (see Chapter 20 on reef tanks for a separate list):

➤ Aquarium

➤ Full-hood with light

➤ Filter system (typically, an undergravel filter and outside power filter)

➤ Heater

➤ Thermometer

➤ Gravel (crushed coral)

➤ Gravel vacuum

➤ Food

➤ Net

➤ Tapwater conditioner

➤ pH, ammonia, and nitrite test kits

➤ Hydrometer

➤ Sea salt

➤ Beginner's book (this one!)

➤ Protein skimmer

➤ Aquarium stand

Something's Fishy

Avoid mini tanks! Don't even think of using a fishbowl or one of those small gumball machine or Garfield the Cat tanks for saltwater fish. You will fail. I don't care how many fish are pictured on the box.

If your budget is tight, you could get the gravel vacuum later. You won't need it for a few weeks anyway. Some people consider a protein skimmer to be optional in the fish-only marine aquarium, but I highly recommend adding one. And finally, if you have a counter or shelf strong enough to hold your aquarium, you may not need the aquarium stand at all. For those of you who need a stand, read on.

Taking a Stand

Make sure that your aquarium stand is strong, flat, and level. Remembering that a full aquarium will weigh around 10 pounds per gallon, you can see that it may not be safe to put your tank on a shelf, table, or countertop that wasn't designed for it. If the stand wobbles or twists, your tank may break! Your best bet is usually to buy a commercial aquarium stand. These stands are designed to hold the weight, and they will match the decorative frame on your tank.

Angle-Iron Stands

The least expensive variety of aquarium stand is a simple angle-iron stand. These stands usually come in a black finish, but are sometimes available with a copper finish. (The copper matches up pretty well with both oak and walnut finishes, its color falling somewhere between.) These stands are fully welded and preassembled. Many are double stands. That is, they have a shelf on the bottom where you may place a second aquarium.

Most aquarium stands are 24 to 30 inches high. Angle-iron stands can also be purchased in lower models. Only a foot or so tall, these stands may be useful when a tank needs to be closer to the floor.

Wrought-Iron Stands

Also called deluxe-metal stands, wrought-iron stands are fancier versions of angle-iron stands. They have decorative scrollwork instead of straight legs and cost just slightly more. Other than that, the features are similar to those of angle-iron stands.

Knock-Down Stands

There used to be wrought-iron versions of knock-down stands, but I haven't seen them for years.

I believe they are no longer being made. Knock-down stands are similar to angle-iron stands in utility, but they have the look of wood. Today's knock-down stands typically consist of two wooden shelves and two wooden side panels. The stands come with bolt sets, and you assemble them at home in just a few minutes. Usually made of particleboard, they have an applied woodgrain laminate finish. Knock-down stands are doubles, so you can also put a second tank on the bottom shelf.

You may also stumble across commercial knock-down stands made of stained 2 × 4 lumber. Though not fancy, these stick-built stands can be sturdy and quite inexpensive.

Cabinet Stands

Cabinet stands will cost a bit more than other styles, but they are the best choice. Doors on the front allow easy access to the inside, where there is room to store food, nets, and other supplies. Plus, the cabinet hides any electrical cords, air lines, or filter hoses that run down the back of the tank. The open design of other stands does not provide these benefits.

Cabinet stands will hold a single tank on top. They come in a variety of finishes to match the various styles of aquariums and room decor. I've seen black, white, oak, walnut, granite, black oak, whitewashed oak, and other styles. Your dealer may even be able to special-order custom finishes for you.

Something's Fishy

One disadvantage of knock-down stands and some cabinet stands is that, being made of particleboard, they can be damaged by water. If your tank ever leaks, or if a filter hose pops loose and soaks the stand, there is a very good chance it will warp and be ruined.

Cabinet stands made of wooden panels and planks are a better choice than those made of particleboard with a vinyl finish. Particleboard can be ruined by water.

Aquarium Enclosures

Less commonly seen, aquarium enclosures are the fanciest and most impressive of aquarium stands. Enclosed stands consist of a cabinet stand and a matching canopy. Often, they will be designed as one piece with side supports. The tank slides in from behind. All you see is the aquarium's glass and the cabinetry. The aquarium frame is completely hidden.

I have even seen versions that had matching cabinets above and below. With those, you pop open the top doors to access the tank for maintenance. Enclosed stands are the best-crafted stands you can buy, but they are not as easily found in stores, and they are not cheap.

Homemade Stands

If you are handy with tools, there is nothing to stop you from building your own aquarium stand. Heck, you may end up building yourself a whole fish room at some point! You can build fancy cabinets to match the rest of the decor in your room or do something simple with 2 × 4s. I've seen stands made of concrete blocks alone, or concrete

Fish and Tips

Modern aquariums rest on their bottom plastic frames, so they don't touch the stand in the center, but only around the perimeter. Because of this, it may surprise you to find stands that are open on top, with no central support. That is perfectly fine and comes in handy if you ever want to plumb through the bottom of the tank or see what is hiding under your undergravel filter.

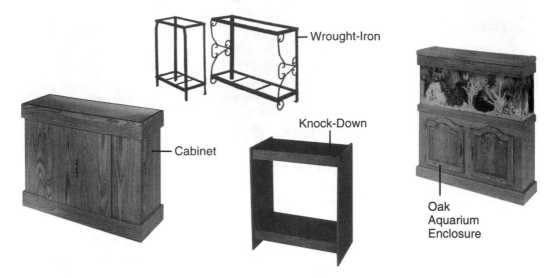

Different types of stands. (courtesy All-Glass Aquarium)

blocks with 2 × 4s threaded through them. If you build your own stand, just be sure that you know what you are doing and make it sturdy, flat, and level enough to support your aquarium properly.

Decorative Canopies

The term *canopy* is used in two ways in the aquarium trade. The most common use is *glass canopy*, which is the hinged glass cover that sits on top of an aquarium. *Decorative canopies*, sometimes called *caps*, are something different. The decorative canopy is an added furniturelike piece that sits on top of the aquarium, hiding the top frame and your lighting system. It gives a nicer architectural look to your aquarium setup and matches the finish of your aquarium stand. Canopies open on top to give you access to the tank.

The Least You Need to Know

➤ Measure your space before selecting an aquarium size.

➤ Buy the biggest tank you can afford.

➤ Long, wide aquariums are better than tall, narrow ones.

➤ Know the difference between starter kits and complete setups.

➤ Your aquarium stand must be flat, level, and strong.

Chapter 5

Filtering Through the Filter Choices

In This Chapter

➤ Learn the basics of filtration

➤ Become familiar with some common styles of filters

➤ Decide which style of filter is right for you

➤ Explore air pumps and connectors

➤ Examine optional powerheads

Without a filter system, your aquarium would quickly turn into a cesspool. A filter system is the life support of your aquarium. Like your heart and lungs, it circulates and oxygenates the water, and like your liver, kidneys, and intestines, it collects and processes waste. Without filtration, you would have to greatly reduce the number of fish you keep in your aquarium. You would also have to increase the frequency of water changes.

Filters keep the water clear and the fish happy. Don't forget, though, that filters are equipment. They need regular maintenance or they will fail to function. Your filter helps clean the tank, but *you* have to clean the filter. Chapter 19 on routine maintenance will cover that topic in depth.

Your filter is not a miracle worker, though. Don't even begin to think that your filter can remove all types of waste. It can't! Even if you maintain your filter regularly, there are still dissolved wastes that can only be removed by making regular partial water changes. Further, those water changes help replenish lost trace elements. Filters *do not* eliminate the need for water changes.

The Basics of Filtration

When you go filter shopping, you may be presented with a huge array of brands and styles. If you ask which type is best, you may get many different answers. There are a lot of ways to filter a tank, and there's no such thing as the "best" way. Both art and science are involved in picking a filter. It may take more than one type of filter to do the job properly.

Later in this chapter, I'll discuss the common styles of filters that you are likely to encounter. But first, I'll talk about the three basic types of filtration that your filter system must provide:

➤ Mechanical filtration

➤ Biological filtration

➤ Chemical filtration

Fish and Tips

In addition to removing dissolved waste, chemical filtration helps keep the water clear. Without the use of activated carbon, your water may be quite transparent but may develop a yellow cast from the buildup of dissolved organic materials.

Mechanical Filtration

When most people think of filtration, they are thinking only about mechanical filtration. Mechanical filtration means physically sifting out particles of solid waste by passing the water through some type of filter medium. Filters almost always provide mechanical filtration of some form. For example, an undergravel filter collects sediment in the gravel bed, while outside power filters trap detritus in various types of disposable or reusable media.

Biological Filtration

Biological filtration is probably the most important type of filtration. It works by using helpful bacteria to break down fish waste, particularly the ammonia that the fish excrete. Be sure to read Chapter 15 on cycling your new tank for full details on the ammonia cycle.

All filters provide some biological filtration, but some are better at it than others. Filters that provide more surface area for helpful bacteria to colonize are more efficient. Also, filters that have reusable media can be better choices. When you throw away disposable media, you also throw away a good portion of your helpful bacteria colonies. So the new medium must be recolonized with helpful bacteria before it works at maximum efficiency.

Chemical Filtration

Chemical filtration uses certain chemical compounds to remove dissolved wastes. Granular activated carbon (similar to charcoal, but much better) is the most common chemical filter medium used, but there are other products, including various resinous beads for softening water and removing copper, phosphates, organics, and other metabolized products. Zeolite (sometimes sold as ammo chips) is sometimes used to remove ammonia, nitrates, and phosphates.

Chemical filter media are almost always disposable. That is, after some use the media will no longer be able to adsorb the impurities that you want to remove. In fact, if they become fully loaded with waste and your pH changes, the chemical filter media could potentially release some nasties back into the aquarium! So always change your chemical filter media on schedule. I recommend that you replace activated carbon monthly. Zeolite and resinous beads (some are rechargeable) should usually be recharged or replaced monthly. Follow the manufacturer's instructions.

There are some chemical filtration products on the market that claim to be good for up to six months. While these are excellent products, you should never try to stretch their useful lives to that point, unless you have an unusually low bioload. (The bioload of your aquarium is determined by the size and number of waste-producing animals introduced into it.) Rather, replace these products every month or so, just as you would replace activated carbon.

Something's Fishy

Activated carbon is not rechargeable! You may hear people say that you can recharge it by baking it in an oven. However, that is not true—not unless you have a special superhot, low-oxygen oven. You don't! After a month, throw away the old carbon and buy new.

Filtering Through the Choices

Don't be surprised to find a perplexing array of filters in many brands, shapes, and sizes at your local shop, and don't be afraid to ask your dealer for advice in picking the right filter or filters for your tank. Later in this chapter, I'll talk about some common filtration combinations used for marine aquariums. But first, let's look at the various styles of filters out there.

Undergravel Filters

Undergravel filters are one of the oldest styles available and are still a good choice in many instances. There is no filter medium to replace—the gravel is the filter medium—so they are very cheap to operate. Undergravel filters trap sediment in the gravel bed. You use your gravel vacuum to clean the gravel when removing water for your regular partial water changes. This makes them very easy to operate, since the cleaning takes place during your partial water changes.

Undergravel filters work on a simple principle. The filter consists of a perforated platform, which rests under the gravel in your tank. Rising from the filter are one or more lift tubes (usually one inch in diameter). An air line with a small air diffuser hangs inside each lift tube. An air pump sits outside the tank and drives the filter.

Fish and Tips

Powerheads make a better choice than air pumps for powering an undergravel filter in a marine tank. The extra bubbles generated by an air pump cause more salt spray and will result in more salt deposits collecting on the underside of your tank's cover.

Air is pumped down the center of the filter lift tube(s), and as the bubbles rise from the bottom, they push water ahead of them. The effect is that water gets pulled down through the gravel, pushed through the slots in the filter plate, and then pulled up the lift tube and back into the tank, where the cycle begins again.

As the water travels down through the gravel, debris gets trapped between the stones (mechanical filtration). Additionally, helpful bacteria living on every particle of gravel will break down the ammonia that is excreted by the fish (bio-filtration). Some models of undergravel filters have small activated carbon cartridges atop the lift tubes. These cartridges provide minimal chemical filtration. I usually recommend removing them, though. I believe they restrict water flow a bit too much, and there are better ways to provide chemical filtration.

Pick gravel that has the correct particle size. Particles one-eighth to one-quarter inch in diameter are good. If the gravel particles are too large, the spaces between them will be too large to easily trap small debris—it will wash right through. Worse, large spaces between the gravel allow food to become trapped where it can't be reached by the fish. This results in pollution. Do not use sand with an undergravel filter; it will sift down through the filter plate and clog the filter.

Undergravel filters used to be considered a necessity for the marine aquarium, and many still consider them to be so, because they are excellent biofilters. These days we have other choices, too, including fluidized-bed filters and trickle filters. Properly applied, any of them can be good choices.

Fish and Tips

For the undergravel filter to function properly, you need the right amount of gravel. Gravel is the filter medium in this system. Use a layer $1^1/_2$ to 2 inches deep. If the gravel isn't deep enough, it will have a very hard time trapping debris.

There are some instances where undergravel filters are a bad choice, though. For example, undergravel filters are great for fish-only marine tanks but are poor choices for reef tanks. Why? Because in a reef tank there will be so many live-rocks and corals in the way that you won't be able to vacuum most of the gravel. The undergravel filter would become a waste trap that cannot be easily cleaned.

Another instance where an undergravel filter would not be the best choice is in a tank where the fish dig a lot. Engineer gobies, jawfish, and other species constantly rearrange the gravel and would constantly stir the sediment. If their digging exposes the filter plate, water will tend to take that open pathway, rather than filter down through the gravel where the filtration takes place.

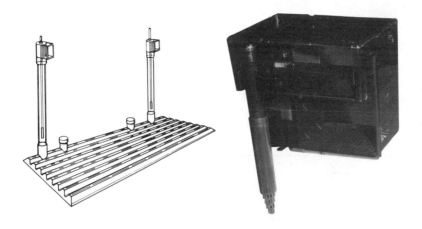

A typical undergravel filter (left) and outside power filter.

Outside Power Filters

Outside power filters hang on the back of your aquarium and contain disposable media. The motor is built in, so there is no need for additional pumps to power the filter. The motor draws water directly from the tank via an intake tube, pumps it through the media, and then returns the water to the aquarium, usually through a waterfall-style chute.

Outside power filters are great and provide all three types of filtration: mechanical, biological, and chemical. Some are a little better than others, though. I recommend the models that use a sponge as one type of filter medium. The sponge collects debris, but also provides a place for helpful bacteria to colonize. When it gets dirty, you rinse it out and reuse it, retaining many of your helpful bacteria. Other models use disposable cartridges made up of a sandwich of polyester filter media and activated carbon.

Some recent versions include a gizmo called a Bio-Wheel. It looks like the wheel on a paddleboat and is suspended above the filter box. As water flows through the filter, it rotates the wheel, alternately wetting and exposing its surfaces to the air. Helpful bacteria grow on the wheel. Since there is 30,000 times as much oxygen in air as there is in water, and since these bacteria require oxygen to break down waste, they are quite efficient in this setup. Bio-Wheels can also be purchased separately for connection to the output of canister filters.

Outside power filters are mostly used on fish-only marine tanks but have some use in reef tanks, as well.

Fish and Tips

When purchasing an outside power filter, be sure to follow the recommendations of your dealer. Not only do you need to choose a model that is adequate for the size of your tank, but you also need to be sure you get one that will fit the frame of your brand of aquarium. Some tanks have thicker frames, requiring a slightly larger filter.

Canister Filters

Canister filters are similar to outside power filters in many ways. The major difference is that they sit beneath the aquarium and use hoses to draw and return the water, rather than hang on the back of the tank. Canister filters resemble miniature wet-vacs. Inside are various styles of filter media that provide all three types of filtration: mechanical, biological, and chemical. A built-in motor pumps the water through the filter.

Canister filters go beneath the aquarium. (courtesy of Rolf C. Hagen USA, makers of Fluval canister filters)

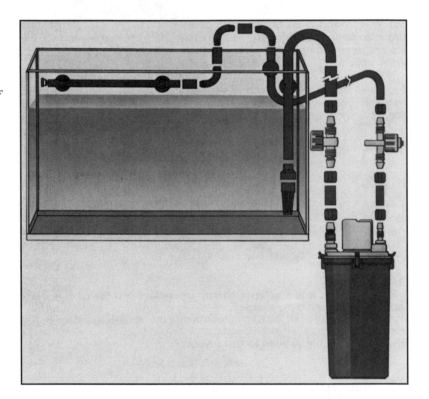

Canister filters have more capacity than outside power filters and are also more versatile. With an outside power filter, you have no choice where the output will be. With canister filters, you can install the output hose so that it pumps the water where you want it, and you can even tee it off so that it pumps to more than one location in the same aquarium. The output can be set up to spray the water back in a single large jet, or through a perforated spray bar that has many small jets. The output can be directed behind rocks or other large decorations to keep debris from collecting out of sight.

The brands I like best use three types of filter media and have separate inner compartments for them. Typically, the first compartment contains ceramic noodles. These noodles channel the water flow evenly, trap larger particles of debris, and provide space for helpful bacteria to colonize. The second chamber holds activated carbon or another chemical filter medium, and the third chamber contains a sponge. The chemical filter media are the only media that you replace. When dirty, the ceramic noodles and sponge get rinsed and reused, retaining helpful bacteria. Other brands of canister filters use polyester sleeves, pleated cartridges, and other types of filter media.

There is even a brand of canister filter on the market that is really a wet-dry filter. It has a built-in float valve that allows it to alternately fill with air and water to provide excellent bio-filtration. Unlike trickle filters (the typical style of wet-dry filter), it is a closed system, so it can't overflow and is easier to install.

One other consideration with canister filters is that some are easier to change than others. You may want to ask your dealer's advice on this topic.

I also should mention internal canister filters. These fit inside the tank instead of connecting with hoses. I don't care much for them. They use less efficient filter media and take up too much room inside the tank. I want to look at fish in my aquarium, not filters!

Something's Fishy

If you buy a canister filter, be sure that your model comes with shutoff valves for each hose, or you could have water back-siphoning onto your carpet when you disconnect the filter for cleaning.

Trickle Filters

Also called wet-dry filters, trickle filters are very popular choices for saltwater tanks—especially for reef tanks. The trickle filter is a large acrylic box (called a sump) that sits underneath your tank. An elaborate overflow system hangs on the back of your aquarium and siphons water to the sump below. (Or an overflow pipe can be plumbed directly through the glass bottom of the tank.)

The sump is usually divided into two side-by-side compartments. One compartment contains various types of filter media, suspended above the water level of the sump. The other provides space for a return pump and other optional equipment. Water trickles through the various types of filter media, which is where the name *trickle filter* derives. Since the media are suspended above the water, they are alternately exposed to water and air as the water trickles through. Hence, the other name for this filter: wet-dry. A water pump returns the filtered water from the sump to the aquarium above.

Several types of media are used in these filters. First is a sponge sleeve that fits over the intake port in the aquarium. It filters out large particles of debris and keeps fish and snails from getting washed down into the sump. Many models use a polyester filter pad in a tray atop the filter. This also filters out large particles and helps distribute the flow of water more evenly over the media below.

Trickle filters can use a hang-on-the-back over-flow, as Eric is modeling, or be plumbed through the bottom of the tank.

The wet-dry part of the filter uses more porous media. The most common type used is known as *bioballs*. There are several brands, but most are 1-inch-diameter spiny plastic spheres. Another type of medium often used is known as *DLS*, which stands for *double-layer spiral*. Two long sheets of filter media—a tight-weave white one and a loose-weave black one—are laid on top each other and rolled into a cylinder. The end product resembles a giant Ho-Ho snack cake!

Both bioballs and DLS are designed to be very porous so that lots of air can travel through with the water. The idea is to get the water to drip through the medium, rather than to pour through it. This allows for plenty of oxygen, so that bio-filtration can occur at maximum efficiency.

Bags of activated carbon or other chemical filtration media may be placed in special chambers at the bottom of the sump. This way, trickle filters will provide all three types of filtration: mechanical, biological, and chemical.

Trickle filters have a few unique features:

Fish and Tips

Some trickle filters are more complete than others. Be sure that the price includes the cost of the filter, the cost of the overflow box and fittings, and the cost of the return-pump and fittings. Some manufacturers include all three in the same package. Others sell them separately.

➤ They act as a reservoir for extra water, which can increase water quality by diluting dissolved wastes.

➤ They provide a place to mount heaters, protein skimmers, and other equipment out of sight. Wouldn't you rather look at your fish?

➤ They allow evaporation to occur without dropping the water level in your aquarium. (It drops in the sump instead.)

➤ Finally, the sump is an excellent place to administer various supplements, such as kalkwasser, which are too caustic to safely dose directly into the aquarium.

Something's Fishy

All filters should be installed as designed. Do not waste your time trying to hybridize them to make them better. Doing so could result in disaster. For example, do not try to replace the overflow system on a trickle filter with a siphon, or try to plumb a canister filter to run more than one tank. If you do, the result will be a flood, or a burned-out pump. Probably both.

Fluidized-Bed Filters

Relatively new to the aquarium trade, fluidized-bed filters are becoming popular. Most hang conveniently on the back of your tank, but there are also free-standing models available. Their design is simple: a sand-filled chamber with a water inlet at the bottom and an outlet at the top. A small powerhead pumps water through the filter (from bottom to top), keeping the sand in suspension.

Each particle of sand provides space for the colonization of helpful bacteria. There is a lot of surface area on that sand, so fluidized-bed filters do a great job of biological filtration. Unfortunately, that is all they do. They don't filter out debris (mechanical filtration), and they don't provide any chemical filtration. So you will need an additional filter to finish the job.

Many hobbyists use fluidized-bed filters to provide optimal biological filtration, while using a supplemental outside power filter for mechanical and chemical filtration. Fluidized-bed filters can be great substitutes for undergravel filters—particularly in aquariums where there are too many rocks to allow easy maintenance of an undergravel filter.

Protein Skimmers

A protein skimmer is one scum-sucking filter! I highly recommend having one on every saltwater tank. Protein skimmers come in a multitude of designs—some simple, some quite complex—but they all work on the same simple principle. If you have ever walked along a beach and seen foam building along the shore, you have seen protein skimming action in the wild.

Fluidized-bed filters provide only biological filtration.

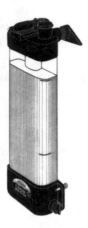

Protein skimmers (more accurately called *foam fractionators*) work by charging a column of water with jillions of tiny bubbles. It turns out that many dissolved organic molecules are attracted to water at one end but repelled by it at the other. So these molecules tend to collect anywhere that there is an air–water interface. Jillions of tiny bubbles make for a sizable amount of air–water interface!

As the tiny bubbles rise through the water column in the protein skimmer, they collect dissolved organics and carry them to the surface. At the surface, those waste products build into a thicker and thicker foam that eventually rises out of an open column at the top and drips over into a separate collection cup.

Protein skimmers are unique among filtration equipment. All other filters either trap waste until you clean the filter, or break it down into something else that stays in the water until you change some water. In other words, filters don't really remove waste, they just store it so that you can remove it. But not our scum-sucking protein skimmer. No, no, no! It actually removes waste and tosses it into a separate container, where it is no longer a factor in your system. Protein skimmers can even remove some things that other filters can't.

There are many designs of protein skimmers. Some are powered by air pumps, some have built-in motors that draw both water and air. Some hang on the tank (or sump), some stand in the sump, and others are freestanding models. The three major styles are:

➤ **Counter-current.** This style has been around the longest. Most are run by both an air pump and a small powerhead or water pump. The air pump forces air through a wooden airstone at the bottom of the protein skimmer. The powerhead pumps water into the protein skimmer near the top. The air rises to the surface and the water exits at the bottom. In other words, the air and water flow in opposite directions, and thus the name counter-current.

Counter-current protein skimmers come in all sizes, including models that are several feet tall. The taller the column, the more effective they are. Unfortunately, that means only the smallest sizes can be hidden from view.

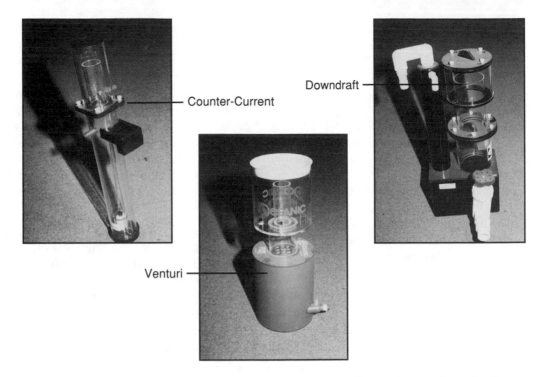

Protein skimmers are an excellent choice for the marine aquarium, and come in a variety of styles.

Another downside is that the wooden airstones used in counter-current skimmers place a lot of back-pressure on the diaphragm of your air pump. Many air pumps are not designed for this and quickly break down. Your dealer should be able to point you toward some models of pumps that can handle high back-pressure.

➤ **Venturi.** Many protein skimmers use the same pump to inject both air and water into the water column. This is accomplished via a device called a Venturi valve. The Venturi valve is really not a valve at all, but a T- or Y-shape pipe fitting with a special restriction inside. This restriction causes a low-pressure zone that draws air through the other strategically placed leg of the T-fitting.

Venturi protein skimmers tend to cost more, but they have a more compact design that lets them fit out of sight in the cabinet beneath your aquarium (usually in the sump itself).

➤ **Downdraft.** This style of protein skimmer has a compact shape, similar to Venturi protein skimmers. Instead of pumping the water-air mixture directly into the skimmer column, it is first injected into a smaller separate mixing column. It jets over a column of bioballs that whip the mix into a nice foam. The air and water separate in the main column, with the foam rising to the top.

Fish and Tips

If your protein skimmer uses an air pump and airstone to create the bubbles, do not use standard airstones. Instead, use special wooden airstones (limewood is most popular), because they produce bubbles that are much smaller than usual. This maximizes the air–water interface that makes your protein skimmer work.

Downdraft skimmers are fairly compact and many are small enough to hide in the cabinet beneath your tank. They tend to be the most expensive, but I also find them to be the most efficient.

Customers often ask which type of protein skimmer is best: downdraft, Venturi, or counter-current. Personally, I prefer them in that order, but the best skimmer is the one that is the right size for the job. A large counter-current skimmer can be as effective as a small downdraft skimmer, and it may be quite a bit cheaper, too. Buy the most powerful skimmer you can afford, and you should do well.

Here is a tricky question for you: Does a protein skimmer provide mechanical, biological, or chemical filtration? Because of the way it works, the correct answer is chemical filtration—even though no chemical compounds are used to make the device function. Adsorption is the process at work.

However, some small amounts of detritus will also become trapped in the foam and mechanically removed along with it. Additionally, a protein skimmer will remove some wastes that otherwise would have been acted upon by bacteria. So although a protein skimmer doesn't perform biological filtration, it will lessen your need for it.

Something's Fishy

Manufacturers usually claim that their protein skimmers are good for tanks "up to X gallons." Don't give too much thought to the numbers they use to fill in the X, because they are extremely arbitrary. I swear the manufacturers just make them up. Ask your dealer what he thinks is the real capacity.

Sponge Filters

Sponge filters have limited use in the marine aquarium. They come in very handy for use in quarantine tanks, though. Sponge filters do a very good job of biological filtration, and they collect some solid waste. They don't do chemical filtration at all. Also, they go inside the tank, so they are ugly to look at. There are models that stick to the side with suction cups and models that rest on the bottom. You need a small air pump to drive this filter.

How well do the various types of filters perform the three basic types of filtration? In the following table, I rate them from 0 to 5, with 0 being the worst and 5 being the best. Sometimes a range is given because it varies according to brand and model.

Rating the Filters

Type of Filter	Mechanical	Biological	Chemical
Undergravel	4	5	0–1*
Outside power	3–4	3–5	4–5
Canister	4–5	3–5	5
Trickle (wet-dry)	3–4	5	5*
Fluidized-bed	0	5	0
Protein skimmer	1	1	5
Sponge	2–3	4	0

If used with optional activated carbon

Filter Combinations That Work

As you have seen, there are many types of filters for saltwater aquariums and you need to make choices that provide all three types of filtration: mechanical, biological, and chemical. So which filters are right for you? Well, that will depend on your budget and on what type of a setup you want—fish-only or reef tank. Personal preferences will also be a factor. Don't be afraid to ask your dealer for advice.

Filters for Fish-Only Systems

Most saltwater tanks are fish-only systems, and there are a lot of ways to filter such a setup. The most common method is a combination of undergravel filter and outside power filter. The undergravel filter provides superior biological filtration, while the outside power filter provides mechanical and chemical filtration. This is one of the oldest methods of filtering a saltwater tank. Coupled with regular partial water changes, this method still works well. Add a protein skimmer and water quality will be even better.

If you want, you can substitute a fluidized-bed filter for the undergravel filter. It will provide ample biological filtration without trapping so much debris in the gravel. Likewise, a canister filter can be substituted for the outside power filter. In fact, a really good canister filter might be sufficient all by itself.

Trickle filters are becoming increasingly popular with saltwater aquarium enthusiasts. Besides providing all three types of filtration, they are excellent oxygenators of the water. Again, don't forget your regular partial water changes, and adding a protein skimmer is highly recommended.

Fish School

Adsorption is the process whereby substances are trapped by chemically bonding with the surface molecules of another substance.

Fish and Tips

When purchasing filters, first compare features. Then compare prices. Be sure to factor in the regular cost of any replacement filter media that may be needed. Sometimes cheaper filters use more expensive media and end up being more expensive in the long run.

Filters for Reefs

Reef aquariums are more advanced setups. Intense lighting and a good protein skimmer should be considered requirements. Filtration requirements are a bit different from those of the fish-only aquarium, too. All the various styles of filters I've mentioned can also be used on reef tanks—except for undergravel filters. You would not be able to perform the required maintenance of vacuuming the gravel beneath the mountain of live-rock and live corals.

The most common method of filtering a reef tank is to use a combination of trickle filter and protein skimmer. The trickle filter provides all three types of filtration and the protein skimmer increases water quality. This combination is a necessity for keeping live corals and invertebrates, which tend to be more delicate than most fish.

Be sure to read Chapter 20 on reef tanks, because it will contain some additional information that pertains exclusively to these aquariums.

Filters That Rock

There is one more type of filter that I haven't covered, and you won't believe what it is. It is the rocks. Live-rocks are tremendous biological filters. They are saturated with helpful bacteria that break down waste. Read Chapter 15 on cycling a new tank for full details on how biological filtration occurs.

Live-rocks are a necessity for reef tanks, but they are becoming increasingly popular for fish-only tanks and semi-reefs, too. And why not? They aren't just functional, they are also decorative.

Something's Fishy

Air pumps go outside the tank! Submersion will destroy them and could give you a serious electrical jolt.

Air Pumps

Air pumps come in many sizes and include not only varying degrees of power, but also varying number of outlets. They can drive undergravel filters or power decorative airstones and ornaments.

Picking the right size pump for the job can be difficult, because the packaging will often say "good for tanks up to X number of gallons." That information is fairly useless, because you should not pick your air pump based on the size of your tank, but rather, on what you want it to run. For example, it would take a large air pump to run the four outlets on the undergravel filter of a 55-gallon tank. But it would take a very small air pump if all you want to do is place one of those bubbling treasure chests in the very same tank.

Air pumps use a plunger-shape rubber diaphragm to pump air. Vibrating 60 times per second, it gets a thorough workout and may crack. If you find that your air pump only works in shallow water but not when you put the air line to the bottom of the tank, your pump has a cracked diaphragm. Your dealer sells replacement parts.

Clogged airstones and filter outlets cause excessive back pressure, which is the chief cause of wear and tear on air pumps. The built-up pressure is what stretches and cracks their diaphragms. Change airstones regularly to extend the life of your air pump.

You will need air line to go with your air pump and may also need gang-valves to increase the number of outlets that you can run. I'll talk more about those items in Chapter 9 on choosing supplies.

Powerheads

Powerheads are small water pumps that have many uses. The most common use is to power an undergravel filter, instead of using an air pump. The powerhead sits on top the undergravel filter lift tube and draws water directly. Many have adjustable flow, and some even let you mix in some outside air.

Personally, I prefer powerheads over air pumps for powering undergravel filters in saltwater aquariums. There are fewer bursting air bubbles, and so less salt spray. That means you will have less salt crust to clean away if you use a powerhead instead of an air pump.

Something's Fishy

Should the power fail, there are instances where the water can bounce up through the air line and back-siphon out through the air pump. To prevent this, either position your air pump higher than the water line in your tank or install a check-valve.

Powerheads are also great for stand-alone circulation. Suction-cup them to the inside glass or clamp them to the tank frame, and direct the flow where you want it. For current-loving critters, these take up where your filter output lets off.

Making Waves

If you are planning a reef tank, I highly recommend that you buy one of the wave-making devices. They aren't cheap, but live corals will do so much better when there is motion in the ocean. The back-and-forth surge and tidal action help circulate fluids through the bodies of the corals, help eliminate wastes, and also bring food to the feeding polyps. You can use wave-makers in a fish-only tank as well, but there is little need for doing so.

Air pumps (left) and powerheads can be used to power undergravel filters. (courtesy Tetra–Second Nature and Rolf C. Hagen USA)

The simplest wavemaking devices are timers that turn a single powerhead on and off throughout the day. The more advanced models control up to four powerheads and can be programmed in many ways to produce alternating, random, or cyclical currents. Many even have a special button for mealtimes. This button turns the powerheads off for a few minutes so that the food doesn't get washed under the rocks and out of reach.

Another design takes the water output from your main pump and oscillates it back and forth 90 degrees. This may be the best model, since there is no starting and stopping of motors, which does put a bit of wear and tear on a powerhead.

The Least You Need to Know

➤ Filters don't eliminate need for regular partial water changes

➤ You need mechanical, biological, and chemical filtration.

➤ For best water quality, use the proper filters and a protein skimmer.

➤ You may need an air pump or powerheads to drive your filter.

Chapter 6

Let's Heat Things Up

In This Chapter

➤ How to choose the right size heater for your tank

➤ Tips on evaluating common features of aquarium heaters

➤ Ways to prevent broken heater tubes

➤ How your heater's thermostat works

➤ Picking the proper thermometer

Almost all saltwater fish available at your local shop will be tropical fish. That means they come from warm climates. To keep them comfortable and healthy, you must be sure that their aquariums are warm enough. Thus, you will need to buy an aquarium heater.

Even if you keep your room warm enough that you think a heater isn't necessary, it wouldn't hurt to have one. Heaters have built-in thermostats, so they kick on only when necessary. If the furnace in your house malfunctions, it may become necessary. Heck, even Florida gets freezing spells sometimes.

Your dealer may carry several brands and styles of aquarium heaters. Price and features will help you make your selection.

Clamp-On vs. Submersible

There are two basic styles of aquarium heaters. One clamps to the side of the tank. The other mounts inside with suction cups and is fully submersible.

Clamp-on heaters are the least expensive and have the fewest features. If your budget is tight, a clamp-on heater may be the only choice. A thumbscrew clamps the heater to the top frame of your tank, with only the glass heater tube hanging in the water. The controls are above water. Don't knock the heater completely into the water, or you may ruin it. Never reach into the tank to retrieve any electrical devices that were knocked in! You could get a shock.

Economy heaters are always the clamp-on style and are usually available in sizes of 25 to 100 watts, which is big enough for tanks up to 20 gallons or so. Remember, I told you that a saltwater tank needs to be at least 29 gallons, so the economy models are not going to work for you. If you want a good clamp-on heater, look for ones that have magnetic thermostats. They are less prone to failure and come in sizes up to 200 watts.

With submersible heaters, you can place the entire heater underwater, including parts of the cord. You can even hide the heater behind some coral or rocks and hardly be aware that it is present. (Don't hide the pilot light, though. You won't be able to tell if the heater is working!)

Submersible heaters come with suction cups that mount them to the side glass. Both vertical and horizontal mounting is possible. If you don't want to look at your heater at all, you can place a submersible heater in the bottom of your trickle filter. This would not be possible with a clip-on heater. It wouldn't even reach the water.

Another advantage of many submersible heaters is that they have precalibrated temperature control knobs that make it easy to set them. Simply dial the temperature you want and you should be all set. Always check against a thermometer to be safe.

Most heaters, though, including all clip-ons, lack precalibrated control knobs and are calibrated using a separate thermometer. I'll talk about calibration in detail in Chapter 10 on assembling your aquarium.

Electronic Heaters

The best heaters are electronic. They have no moving parts, except for the temperature control knob. Most heaters have mechanical thermostats with parts that do move. I'll talk more about how thermostats work a little later in this chapter, but for now just remember that mechanical thermostats are more prone to failure than electronic ones.

Besides having no moving parts to fail, electronic heaters have some other advantages. They tend to have more accurate thermostats, which may even be mounted separately from the heater tube. While most heaters only have two phases—either they turn themselves on at full blast to add heat, or they turn themselves off to stop adding heat—electronic heaters often have smoother output. That is, some can run at a continuous low level of output to maintain the temperature more evenly.

Watts Hot

Aquarium heaters come in several lengths, typically 6 inches, 8 inches, 10 inches, 12 inches , and 15 inches. Be sure not to get a heater that is too long. The heater must usually be at least 2 inches shorter than the height of your tank; 3 or 4 inches shorter than the tank height is even better. That allows plenty of room for gravel and rocks at the bottom of the tank.

Standard wattages of aquarium heaters are 25w, 50w, 75w, 100w, 150w, 200w, 250w, and 300w. All wattages aren't available in all brands, and anything over 200 watts will be available only in submersible models.

The "5 watts per gallon" rule is most commonly used to determine the proper wattage of your aquarium heater. That is, a 20-gallon tank would take a 100w heater, and so on. Bigger tanks hold heat better, so 3 watts per gallon is usually enough once you get above 50 gallons.

Still, how much heat you need depends on other things besides the simple volume of your aquarium. If you live where the winters are cold, and particularly if you set your house thermostat low, you will need a more powerful aquarium heater to make up the difference. In warm climates, you may rarely need to heat your tank more than 5°F above room temperature, in which case a smaller heater will do.

You see, your heater is not really putting out, say, 78°F of heat. Rather, if the house is 70°F, your heater needs to heat the tank 8°F above room temperature. Likewise, if the room is 75°F, your heater need only heat 3°F above room temperature to warm your tank to 78°F. So to decide what size heater you actually need, you need to know what temperature you desire and how warm or cold your room will be.

Something's Fishy

Always unplug your heater and give it time to cool before removing it from your tank! Likewise, never plug in your heater before installing it. Aquarium heaters can get red-hot. Without water to dissipate that heat, they can start a fire or burn you. If the heater is already hot when you put it in the cooler water, it will shatter.

It always helps to have a little extra power, though. A bit too much is better than too little. If your heater is more powerful than you need, the only thing that should happen is it will turn itself off more quickly. In other words, it will heat faster, not more. The thermostat controls when it comes on and goes off. On the other hand, an undersize heater could kick on and run continuously during cold times without being able to produce enough heat for the job.

Some recent research produced the following charts. They give pretty accurate estimates of appropriate heater sizes. To use the first chart, find the size of your tank in the top row. Then follow the column down until you find the number of degrees above room temperature that your tank may need to be heated. (For example, if you want your tank to be 78°F, and the room is 70°, you need to add 10° of heat.) When you find the right figure, look at the wattage in the far left column to see what size heater you need.

Wattage Needed to Increase Water Temperature Above Room Temperature

Heater Watts	Aquarium Size, in Gallons				
	10	20	29	55	60
50	16°F	12°F	10°F		
75	19°F	17°F	15°F		
100	26°F	22°F	19°F	13°F	12°F
150		24°F	22°F	18°F	18°F
200			30°F	24°F	20°F
250			32°F	30°F	27°F
300			38°F	34°F	29°F

Table courtesy of Aquarium Systems, Inc., maker of Visitherm aquarium heaters.

To use the following table, find your tank size at the top. Then read down the column to see what size heater you need, based on the desired increase above room temperature, as listed on the left.

Heater Selection Guide

Desired Increase Above Room Temperature	Aquarium Size, in Gallons					
	20	25	40	50	65	75
9°F	50w	75w	100w	150w	200w	250w
18°F	75w	100w	150w	200w	250w	300w
27°F	150w	200w	300w	400w	500w	600w

Table courtesy of Aquarium Systems, Inc., maker of Visitherm aquarium heaters.

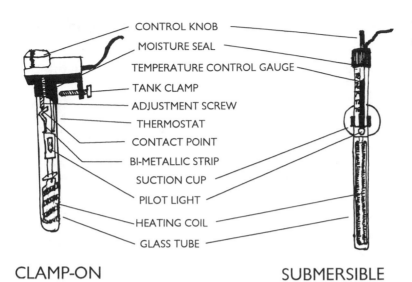

The parts of a typical aquarium heater.

CONTROL KNOB
MOISTURE SEAL
TEMPERATURE CONTROL GAUGE
TANK CLAMP
ADJUSTMENT SCREW
THERMOSTAT
CONTACT POINT
BI-METALLIC STRIP
SUCTION CUP
PILOT LIGHT
HEATING COIL
GLASS TUBE

CLAMP-ON   SUBMERSIBLE

Heater Elements

The following elements make up a typical aquarium heater:

➤ **Tank clamp.** Anchors the heater to the side of your tank. Submersible models use suction cups instead.

➤ **Control knob or dial.** Turns the adjustment screw, pushing on a bi-metallic strip in the thermostat.

➤ **Tamper-reducing peg.** Not all heaters have this feature. On the ones that do, you can find it beneath the control knob or dial. It matches with a tab on the underside of the dial and prevents you from turning the control more than one full turn at a time. To turn more, remove and reseat the control knob.

➤ **Temperature control gauge.** Some submersibles have this precalibrated scale. If so, merely dial the temperature that you want.

➤ **Moisture seal.** Keeps water away from electrical parts.

➤ **Thermostat.** Turns the heater on and off automatically, according to the temperature in the tank and the desired temperature, as set by the control knob.

➤ **Adjustment screw.** The extension of the control knob.

➤ **Heating coil.** Nickel-chromium wire that heats up when power is applied.

➤ **Bi-metallic strip.** Two types of metal back to back. Temperature changes make the two metals expand at different rates, causing the strip to bend.

➤ **Contact point.** When touched by the bi-metallic strip, it closes the circuit, allowing power to reach the heating coil.

➤ **Pilot light.** An orange light that glows when the heater is producing heat.

➤ **Glass tube.** Waterproofs the inner workings of the heater.

➤ **Electrical cord and plug.** Come on! I really don't have to tell you what this is for, do I?

Fish School

A **thermostat** is a device that controls temperature automatically. A **thermometer** is an instrument that measures temperature.

Look at That! A Thermostat!

You will better understand what your heater can do if you understand how it works. Aquarium heaters are somewhat complicated devices, but they work on very simple principles. Your heater needs to perform two functions. The obvious function is to produce heat. The built-in thermostat handles the less obvious function of deciding when to produce heat.

Your heater produces heat by passing electrical power through a coil of wire that glows red hot when current is applied. Controlling the output is the tricky part. You need your heater to kick on when the water cools and turn itself back off when the water reaches the desired temperature. This is the job of the thermostat.

Now, the thermostat works on a very simple principle, but it is a little complicated to explain. Without the thermostat, your heater would come on when you plug it in and never go off again until you unplug it. That's not a workable solution. You can't stand around plugging and unplugging your heater all day. Enter the thermostat. The thermostat replaces part of the electrical circuit with a couple of simple parts. One part is a stationary contact. The other part is usually a bi-metallic strip.

The Bi-Metallic Strip

The bi-metallic strip is made of two different kinds of metal sandwiched together. You may remember from physics class that metals expand and contract as the temperature changes and that different metals expand and contract at different rates. That is exactly what happens with the bi-metallic strip. Since each side of it expands at a different rate than the other side, the strip bends one way or the other as the temperature changes.

In your heater, when the bi-metallic strip gets cooler, it bends toward the stationary contact. When the bi-metallic strip touches the stationary contact, it completes the circuit. This allows current to pass to the heater coil, producing heat. When the strip gets warm, it will bend away and separate from the stationary contact. This disconnects the circuit and turns off the heater. When the tank cools down a couple of degrees, the bi-metallic strip will contract and turn the heater on again. It is all automatic.

Now, there are a couple of options to this process that determine the quality of your heater. Besides the bi-metallic strip and stationary contact, better heaters will have a small magnet on each. As the contacts get close together, the magnetic action takes over and snaps them together instantly. When the heater turns off and they separate, that happens quickly, too.

You may wonder what the big deal is about that. Well, the big deal is that as the two contacts approach each other, a spark can arise as the circuit completes. If the circuit closes slowly, more sparking will occur, and this causes carbon to build up on the contacts. Eventually this insulates them, and they no longer function. The other thing that happens is that the sparking may go on for several seconds, producing static that can interfere with your favorite radio program. So magnetic contacts are better than nonmagnetic.

Electronic Thermostat

Electronic heaters are even better. They eliminate the bi-metallic strip and stationary contacts. Instead, they have electronics inside that turn the circuit on or off. Also, they usually have a thermostatic sensor that mounts in a separate tube, away from the heater coil. Or the thermostat may read from a special sensor mounted directly on the heater's glass tube. Since glass conducts heat well, this method gets a more accurate measurement of true water temperature (as opposed to the bi-metallic strip, which monitors the air inside the heater, not the water).

The other nice thing about an electronic heater is that it stays on until it reaches the desired temperature, then kicks off. It's all one step. Since bi-metallic strip thermostats read air temperature inside the heater instead of true water temperature, heating becomes a staged operation. That is, the heater kicks on, and the air inside gets very hot. So the heater turns off before the water is quite warm enough. The air inside cools a bit, and the heater kicks on and heats some more. This process repeats a few times for each heating cycle. That is why you will often see the pilot light in some heaters flickering on and off a lot, rather than staying on for a couple of minutes and then staying off for a while.

Fish and Tips

An aquarium heater cannot function properly if there is no water circulating past it to distribute the heat. Your tank must have aeration or filtration for the heater to work. Without circulation, the water next to the heater will be heated and the thermostat will sense this and shut off before the rest of the tank gets heat.

Preventing Breakage

Aquarium heaters are electrical parts, sealed within a waterproof glass tube. Even a complete idiot knows that water and electricity don't mix safely. It is always wise to take steps to be sure that you don't break your aquarium heater. Always unplug a heater before putting it into or taking it out of the water! Heaters get very hot when they are on. You can get burned. You can start a fire. Also, if you take a hot heater and put it into cold water, you will crack the glass on the heater tube, getting water inside and potentially causing a shock to you or your fish.

Fish and Tips

When you use suction cups to mount your aquarium heater, be sure not to position them over the heating coils. The suction cups will melt.

Humans are not the only complete idiots when it comes to abusing heaters. Sometimes fish are pretty stupid, too. Large fish can break a heater by bumping it hard against the glass. A quick slap of the tail is all it takes. I've even known cases of fish that got so severely ticked off at the heater's pilot light blinking at them that they decided to give it a good bite!

To help prevent your fish from breaking the heater, I highly recommend that you install some suction cups to anchor it firmly to the side glass. Submersible heaters normally come with suction cups, but the hang-on-the-tank heaters don't. You should buy suction cups for those.

Shopping for Thermometers

Every aquarium must have a thermometer. How else are you going to know the temperature of your tank? Even if you have a heater with a temperature control gauge, you cannot trust it. You should always confirm the actual temperature with a thermometer.

Something's Fishy

Glass thermometers, including floating, standing, and stainless-steel models, are often quite inaccurate. I've seen a 10° range in the temperature readings of thermometers hanging on the same peghook! Check to be sure that the line of red indicator liquid inside has no bubbles. That will ruin the accuracy.

Your dealer sells several types of thermometers. All are quite inexpensive. Here are some typical ones:

➤ **Floating thermometer.** If you press this floating glass thermometer into a front corner of your tank, it will stay there for easy reading. Otherwise, the water current will carry it where it may, and you will have trouble finding and reading it.

➤ **Standing thermometer.** Like a floating thermometer, but with extra weight at one end, a standing thermometer sinks to the bottom. You could just drop it in the tank, but I prefer to wedge it in the gravel. Otherwise, the fish tend to knock it around, and it always seems to end up facing backward in some far corner when you want to see it.

➤ **Stainless-steel thermometer.** This is a glass thermometer attached to a metal bracket that hangs over the edge of your tank. I don't much like these, because the hanger interferes with the proper nesting of your glass canopy or full-hood on top of the tank. Also, it is not uncommon for the thermometer to slide in the metal holder that contains the temperature scale, ruining the accuracy.

➤ **Liquid-crystal thermometer.** These inexpensive thermometers can be found in many shapes, styles, and temperature ranges. They are absolutely the most accurate and easiest to read. While the cheaper glass thermometers may vary by several degrees, every liquid-crystal thermometer on the peghook gives the same reading. Liquid-crystal thermometers mount on the outside of the tank. The one disadvantage is that you really should not move them once they are installed. So they aren't much use for testing the temperature of a bucket of water that you've drawn for your water change.

Fish and Tips

My favorite liquid-crystal style is the horizontal. I like to mount it on the front of the tank, just below the gravel line. It gives a good, accurate reading there without obstructing my view of the fish.

➤ **Thermometer-hydrometer combination.** Sometimes, a thermometer comes inside your hydrometer. I'll talk about hydrometers in Chapter 9.

The Least You Need to Know

➤ Choose the proper-size heater. A typical rule is 5 watts per gallon for small tanks and 3 watts per gallon for tanks over 50 gallons.

➤ Don't buy a heater that is too long to fit your tank.

➤ Use suction cups to anchor your heater to the side of the tank.

➤ Never install or remove a heater that is plugged in.

➤ Liquid-crystal thermometers are the best choice.

Chapter 7

Bright Ideas in Lighting

In This Chapter

➤ How to determine your lighting needs

➤ Incandescent, fluorescent, and metal halide lighting

➤ Explore the color spectrum of light bulbs

➤ The relative advantages of glass canopies and full-hoods

➤ Find out how little electricity you will use

An aquarium without a light on it would be a lot less fun. If you couldn't see your fish, if you couldn't observe your invertebrates, what would be the point? The primary advantage of having a light on your tank is that it helps you see and enjoy what is going on inside that glass box.

Light has other functions, too, though. Your fish need light to help them find food and to help them spot predators. Light shows off their brilliant colors to prospective mates during courtship displays. A less obvious use of light is in the regulation of internal biological clocks. Circadian rhythms (*circadian* means *around a day*) regulate many life processes. They help determine when it is time to sleep and time to be active, and can even regulate the time to breed. Many marine creatures are known to spawn at certain times of day or only when the moon is in a certain phase. Your lighting system sets the time of day and season of year for your fish.

How Much Light Is Right?

In Chapter 2 I told you some things that would help you decide what kind of tank you want. Particularly, you need to know if you plan to concentrate on hardy fish in a fish-only aquarium or on more delicate corals and invertebrates in a reef tank. In Chapter 4 I also talked about how tall and shallow aquariums have different lighting requirements, with tall tanks requiring more light to achieve the same effect. All these things will be factors in deciding how much light you will need on your tank. So how much light is right?

A typical fish-only aquarium is the easiest and cheapest type to set up. The marine fish-only aquarium usually contains nothing live except the fish. The decorations are artificial corals, natural coral skeletons, and plastic macroalgae. Decorative rocks and perhaps even some live-rock are used, too. Invertebrates are avoided in the fish-only setup. Strong lighting is not necessary in this type of tank. In fact, it could be detrimental, contributing to an unsightly algae problem. Traditional full-hoods and strip lights are quite sufficient for the fish-only setup.

A reef tank, on the other hand, requires intense lighting, because most live corals are photosynthetic. Without strong light, they suffer and die. Don't even think of trying to set up a reef tank using a traditional full-hood or single strip light! I'll talk more about lighting a reef in Chapter 20 on reef tanks. For now, suffice it to say that 3 to 5 watts of full-spectrum light per gallon will be necessary to keep live corals.

Bright Choices in Light Bulbs

Before I discuss the various types of lighting equipment that your dealer may have available, I want to talk a bit about the bulbs themselves. The light unit you buy will house the bulbs, but it is the bulbs that produce the light. It can be difficult choosing, because there is a large array of styles, varying in color, intensity, and electricity requirements.

Incandescent Bulbs

Incandescent bulbs are old-fashioned bulbs with a screw-in base that fits standard household sockets. Incandescent aquarium bulbs, also known as *showcase bulbs*, are really poor choices for marine aquariums. They put out too much heat and too little light and are really designed for only the smallest aquariums. So for the purposes of a saltwater aquarium, let's just pretend they don't exist. OK?

Fluorescent Bulbs

Long glass tubes with pins at each end, fluorescent bulbs are commonly used as ceiling lights in commercial establishments. Internal phosphor coatings glow when electricity is applied to the bulb. The color of the resulting light will depend on the type of phosphor coatings used inside. Fluorescent lighting is a very cost-effective way to light your aquarium. It gives a bright, even flood of light and uses little electricity. Fluorescent bulbs come in many spectra, and I'll discuss that shortly.

Fish Tales

Light decreases with the square of the distance. This means that if one aquarium is twice as tall as the other, it will take four times as much light to illuminate its bottom equally. The taller the tank, the more light is required to achieve the same effect.

The high-frequency power needed to run a fluorescent bulb is generated inside a black box called a *ballast*. Usually you will be unaware of the ballast, because most manufacturers mount it inside the light unit, out of sight. However, some models have the ballast attached to the electrical cord.

Fluorescent bulbs come in standard lengths and wattages. The diameters of the bulbs do vary a bit, with 1-inch- and 1^1/$_2$-inch-diameter bulbs being the norm, but they are interchangeable. So don't concern yourself with the diameter of the bulb. Just be sure to get the right length and wattage. Particularly pay attention to the wattage (the F-number on the bulb), because bulbs of the same wattage will be the same length.

However, bulbs of the same length may be of different wattage! Here's why. There are three styles of fluorescent bulbs—SO, HO, and VHO—each using different types of ballasts and having different intensities of output. Normally, you will be dealing with standard output (SO) fluorescent bulbs. Standard aquarium full-hoods and strip lights use SO bulbs.

Fish and Tips

Your fluorescent bulb will usually have identification codes on the end. The T-number (such as T8 or T12) represents the diameter of the bulb in eighths of an inch. The F-number (such as F15 or F20) represents the wattage.

If you decide to set up a reef tank, however, you will likely find yourself becoming acquainted with high output (HO) or very high output (VHO) fluorescent bulbs and ballasts. These bulbs put out two to three times the light of a typical fluorescent bulb. While SO, HO, and VHO bulbs all come in standard lengths of 12, 15, 18, 24, 36, 48, and 72 inches, the bulbs should not be interchanged! Do not try to put an SO bulb in a VHO fixture, for example. You will ruin your bulb.

Power Compact Fluorescent Bulbs

Power compacts are relative newcomers to aquarium lighting. They are fluorescent bulbs folded upon themselves into a U shape, and they have higher output. You can squeeze more light into a smaller space with power compact fluorescents. The intensity of output is similar to that of VHO fluorescents, but with lower power consumption and less heat.

Color output of power compact fluorescents is rated on the Kelvin temperature scale. The Kelvin scale is a method of describing color, based on the changes of color that would occur "when an imaginary black body is heated" to a particular temperature. Anyway, degrees Kelvin is the scale and typical power compact bulbs are 5,400°K, 6,100°K, 6,700°K, 7,200°K, and 10,000°K. Bulbs with a higher Kelvin temperature produce more blue light.

Metal Halide Bulbs

Metal halide bulbs are usually shaped like household bulbs, but are larger and have a larger screw-in base called a *mogul* base. There are some versions on the market that are tubular with electrical contacts at both ends, though. Metal halide bulbs make a great choice for reef tanks. They have a high output of light that is capable of reaching deep into a tank. Typical sizes are 150w, 175w, 250w, and 400w.

Like power compact fluorescent bulbs, metal halide bulbs have a color rating in degrees Kelvin. Typical bulbs are 5,500°K, 6,500°K, 10,000°K, 14,000°K, and 20,000°K. Bulbs with lower numbers tend to be a bit more yellow, while those with higher numbers are more blue. Bluer bulbs are preferred for photosynthetic corals. Combinations of bulbs may be used to achieve a desired effect.

Here is something unique: Unlike fluorescent bulbs, metal halide bulbs provide a single-point light source. (Fluorescent tubes generate light from all points.) Do you know how moving water scatters sunlight, making it dance all over the bottom? Metal halides will do that, too! Surface ripples are necessary to cause the effect, though. It won't work in still water. Anyway, the effect is interesting, relaxing, and more natural.

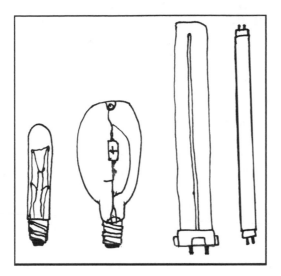

Common light bulbs (from the left): incandescent, metal halide, compact fluorescent, and fluorescent.

A Spectrum of Choices

Your aquarium will look its best, and your fish will stay healthiest, under white light. You probably remember from science class that white light is a mixture of all the colors of the rainbow. White light is composed of the entire visible spectrum of light.

In addition to visible light, sunlight includes wavelengths that cannot be seen by the human eye. Infrared (IR) light and ultraviolet (UV) light lie beyond the visible ranges of red and blue. All light bulbs produce some invisible infrared light, which our bodies detect as heat. Most bulbs give off little or no ultraviolet light, though. That is probably a blessing, because strong UV light causes sunburn or worse.

However, some ultraviolet light can be helpful. Many animals—humans, for example—require it to manufacture their own vitamin D. Some near-UV wavelengths are beneficial to photosynthetic corals, too. Light bulbs that produce both the full spectrum of visible light and small amounts of UV light are called *full-spectrum* lights. Full-spectrum bulbs cost a bit more but generally produce lighting that is more pleasing to the eye and more healthy for living things.

By tweaking the mix of inner gases or phosphor coatings, manufacturers can change the color output of a bulb for special purposes. For example, some bulbs are designed to highlight the colors of the fish, others to produce superior plant growth, and so forth.

Something's Fishy

People sometimes request pure ultraviolet lights (blacklights) for their aquariums, in an attempt to get Day-Glo colors. Don't do it! They won't give the effect you expect, and are unhealthy when not balanced with white light. Worse, the types of ultraviolet bulbs sold in aquarium stores are likely to be replacements for ultraviolet sterilization units. Incorrectly used, these bulbs can permanently blind you.

I've avoided using brand names in this book, but I could not find an easy way to describe the spectra of various common fluorescent bulbs without making it so general as to become confusing. So I am going to present a list of bulbs that are available from one popular manufacturer. There are many equivalent brands out there, but this company probably has the widest product selection and widest distribution, so its products may be easiest to find.

The following fluorescent light tubes, manufactured by Rolf C. Hagen Corp., are available in most pet stores:

➤ **Aqua-Glo.** A version of the Gro-Lux bulb sold for aquariums, this type of bulb tends to be least expensive and is commonly included in fluorescent full-hoods. It produces a pleasing white light with a slightly pinkish cast that accents the colors of the fish. Particularly, red fish will look red rather than orange. Aqua-Glo is a decent fish-only bulb.

➤ **Sun-Glo.** Designed to mimic the visible wavelengths of full-spectrum sunlight, these bulbs produce white light with a slight greenish tint that makes plants look superb. It's the color of sunlight on a warm day. Red fish look slightly orange under it, though. This bulb could be used on fish-only or reef tanks, but there are better choices to use on a reef.

➤ **Power-Glo.** These bulbs have a higher intensity than most fluorescent bulbs, but they are not HO or VHO. Some extra blue is mixed into the spectrum, making them good for saltwater corals and freshwater plants. They produce a nice bright white light and are great for reef tanks, as well as fish-only setups.

➤ **Life-Glo.** Similar to the Power-Glo bulb, but these have an internal reflector that directs the light downward, increasing the intensity of light delivered to your tank. This bulb is a great choice for reef tanks, as it provides even stronger light output per tube.

➤ **Marine-Glo.** This is Hagen's version of an *actinic* bulb, which I will describe in a moment. Actinic bulbs are blue and are not designed to be used alone. This bulb is often used on reef tanks, in combination with other full-spectrum bulbs.

➤ **Flora-Glo.** This bulb is good for freshwater plants but has a very orange cast to it. I don't recommend it for saltwater tanks.

A Little Extra Blue

With a fish-only tank, the light need only be pleasing to your eye. Almost any good aquarium bulb will do. With a reef tank, however, you must cater to the live corals.

Hobbyists do this by adding extra blue light to the spectrum. Many hobbyists use bulbs that produce blue, near-UV light. These bulbs are called *actinic* bulbs. (Some people also call them O3 bulbs after the model number of the original actinic bulbs, produced by Phillips.) The near-UV light encourages growth of live corals and even causes some to fluoresce slightly in brilliant red and green.

Actinic bulbs should be used in combination with other bulbs for best results. When used alone, they are way too blue to give a pleasing appearance to the eye, and they don't provide a balanced full-spectrum environment. One recipe you often hear is to use two daylight (or full-spectrum) bulbs with each actinic bulb. This gives a mix of light that pleases the eye and pleases the photosynthetic corals. Fluorescent actinic tubes are often coupled with 5,500°K or 6,500°K metal halide bulbs to achieve pleasing results, too.

Another common type of bulb is called a *50/50 bulb*. The phosphors inside have been tweaked to produce output that is half daylight and half actinic. These are good bulbs to mix for the right balance. In some ways, I like them better than using pure daylight bulbs in combination with pure actinic bulbs. They give a more homogeneous output. Tanks that have separate actinics tend to make the fish look blue when they swim directly under the actinic bulb. Their color changes when they swim under the other bulbs. In other words, mixing the light inside the bulb is more pleasing to the eye.

Does this really matter? Of course it does! You got your aquarium to look at, didn't you? So the color of the light matters a lot. Have you ever noticed how colors appear washed out in underwater documentaries—until the diver shines his light on his subject? As sunlight filters through seawater, colors filter out. First the reds are absorbed, then orange, then yellow, and so on. Blue light is last to go and penetrates deepest. Red fish only look red near the surface. Deeper down, they appear gray or black.

Got Your Tank Covered

Now that I've talked about the bulbs, let's discuss the light fixtures themselves. Most light fixtures also act as covers for your tank. Covering the tank is important for several reasons:

➤ **It reduces evaporation**, meaning you can refill the tank less often. Replacing evaporation is not a substitute for making a partial

Fish and Tips

Even though fluorescent bulbs from the hardware store will fit your aquarium's light fixtures, you should buy your bulbs from a pet store. The bulbs sold in hardware stores will be of a different spectrum and may cause algae problems for you.

Fish and Tips

Actinic bulbs have no benefit for fish. They are strictly for the live corals. If you have a fish-only setup, don't waste your money on actinic bulbs.

water change, though! And if you want a reef tank, check out Chapter 20 on reef tanks to see why you might want lots of evaporation.

➤ **It keeps the critters in.** A cover keeps the fish from jumping out onto the floor. It also helps keep crabs and other invertebrates from climbing out.

➤ **It keeps the rug rats out.** Your aquarium's top will help keep the kids and the cats from playing in the tank.

Let There Be Light

There are many ways to provide light for your aquarium. The range of styles and prices is quite wide, from inexpensive full-hoods to metal-halide pendant lamps that may cost several hundred dollars. The lighting system usually is the most expensive piece of equipment for your aquarium.

Full-Hoods

A full-hood is the most popular choice for covering and lighting a fish-only aquarium. It may work on a lagoon tank or semi-reef, too. It consists of a plastic chassis that has three basic sections:

➤ A lid in front that allows you to access the tank

➤ A glass section in the middle to protect the light strip from water damage

➤ Either punch-outs or a soft plastic strip at the rear of the hood, to allow for custom openings for installing heaters, filters, and air lines

A strip light (included with the full-hood) fits on top of the full-hood's chassis. There are two types of chassis. In one type (sometimes called deluxe), there are pegs on the underside that you snap off to make the hood nest perfectly on your brand of aquarium. There are also recessed versions of hoods. Rather than resting on top of the frame, they nest down inside, resting on the inner lip. The one disadvantage of these hoods is that not all aquarium frames have the same size inner lip, if any. So while the deluxe hoods should fit any brand, the recessed hoods may only fit the tanks of the manufacturer's brand.

Personally, I think full-hoods have the nicest appearance of the various choices to cover and light your aquarium, but they make it difficult or impossible to add additional lights. Because of this, full-hoods are not workable for reef aquariums.

Full-hoods are available in both fluorescent and incandescent models. Forget about the incandescent ones, though, as they are insufficient for a marine tank. Besides, fluorescent bulbs give off more light and less heat, and use less electricity. Each fluorescent full-hood has a bulb included—a bulb that is fine for fish-only aquariums but would be the wrong spectrum for a reef tank.

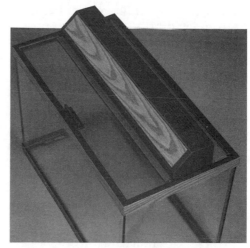

A full-hood light (left) and a glass canopy with a strip light (right). (courtesy All-Glass Aquarium)

Strip Lights and Glass Canopies

The glass canopy is a hinged glass cover for your tank. There is a plastic strip on the back that can be cut out to allow access for heaters, air lines, and other equipment. It functions similarly to the chassis on the full-hood. The long plastic housing containing the light unit is called a strip light and sits on top of the glass canopy. (If you thought that strip lights were mood lights for exotic dancers, then I'm sorry I got your hopes up!) Most strip lights are fluorescent models.

Although I believe the full-hood has a neater and more decorative appearance than the glass canopy/strip light combo, I've come to prefer the latter. Why? Because it is more versatile. You can pile a lot more lights on top of a glass canopy, and they can be of almost any style. Full-hoods greatly restrict the ability to add more light.

The glass canopy–strip light combination can be used for fish-only setups, for lagoon tanks or semi-reefs, or for full-blown reef aquariums. Even if you are setting up a fish-only tank, you may want to go with the glass canopy–strip light combination to make it easier to convert to a reef tank later.

Power Compact Fluorescents

With intense output and low energy consumption, power compact fluorescents can be excellent choices for the reef tank. They also have become quite popular for use in heavily planted freshwater tanks, which require intense lighting.

Fish and Tips

When you buy a fluorescent full-hood, the bulb is included in the price. With incandescent hoods, the bulbs are purchased separately.

Power compact fluorescent lights may be purchased mounted inside decorative wooden or ABS plastic boxes, or as retrofit kits in which the guts of the light units come mounted to a reflectorized aluminum sheet. Retrofit kits should be installed inside an existing wooden or acrylic canopy. Otherwise, you will be left looking at ugly wiring and exposed connectors.

One manufacturer recently added a line of power compact fluorescent lights mounted inside its standard strip light housings. Called SHO lights, I think these are wonderful! They can be used as replacements on the manufacturer's standard full-hoods, or you can install them atop a standard glass canopy. It's an easy way to increase the amount of light without changing the look of your setup, and it is the only way to make a full-hood usable on a reef tank.

Metal Halide Lights

These light units are usually sold as dome-shape hanging pendants. You hang them from your ceiling or from a wall bracket that you mount above the tank. By raising or lowering the unit, you can vary the intensity and dispersion of light in your tank. You also may find units that come preinstalled inside decorative wooden or metal canopies. Metal halide pendants can be hung over a glass canopy, but most aquarists prefer to hang them over open water.

Enhancing the Light

If you want to increase the output of your existing fixtures, there are ways to do so without buying new ones. Many stores carry polished aluminum reflectors that fit behind the bulb in your fluorescent light unit. These take light that normally comes out the sides and top of the bulb and direct it back toward the tank. It is not as good as adding another light, but it is an improvement.

A power compact fluorescent strip light (SHO light, left) and a metal halide pendant.

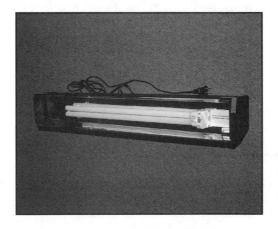

Also, some fluorescent bulbs come with either internal or external reflective coatings on the top half of the bulb. This directs more light downward. You may want to consider replacing your bulb with one of these.

How Much Electricity Can You Consume?

With all this talk of lights and pumps and heaters, you may be wondering what effect an aquarium will have on your electricity bill. Let me assure you that a typical fish-only aquarium setup will not have a noticeable effect. Your heater probably will be the item that pulls the most juice at any one time, but it will almost always be off. The added pumps and high-powered lights on a large reef tank will, of course, draw more power.

Electrical Consumption of a 55-Gallon Fish-Only Tank With a Fluorescent Full-Hood

Equipment	Watts	× Hours Per Day	= Watts Per Day
Powerheads (two) for undergravel filter	12	24	288
Outside power filter	6	24	144
Powerhead for protein skimmer	6	24	144
Light bulb(s)	40	12	480
Heater	200	.25	50
		Total watts per day	1,106
		× Days per month	30
		Total watts per month	33,180
		÷ Watts per kilowatt hour	1,000
		Total kilowatt hours per month	33.18
		× Cost per kilowatt hour	$.10
		Total cost per month	$3.32

The Least You Need to Know

➤ Reef tanks require much more light than fish-only tanks.

➤ Keep your tank covered to reduce evaporation, to keep the fish from jumping out, and to keep out small hands and paws.

➤ Full-hoods look a bit nicer, but glass canopies and strip lights are more versatile.

➤ Choose a bulb that provides the best color spectrum for the job.

➤ Turn off your aquarium light at night.

➤ Most aquariums will not drive up your electricity bill more than a few dollars a month.

Call in the Decorator

Whether you are setting up a fish-only aquarium or a reef tank, you should read every chapter in this book. Almost all the information applies to both types of setups. However, there are places where the information applies more to one than to the other. This chapter is one of those places.

This chapter is primarily about decorating a fish-only setup. In a reef tank, live-rock and live corals are the decorations. A fish-only tank gets decorated in an entirely different manner. Unless I specifically say *live* coral in this chapter, the word *coral* will be used to mean natural, but dead, coral skeletons or artificial corals. Still, even reef hobbyists should read this chapter, because I'll discuss many principles of decoration that apply to every kind of aquarium. There is important information to be found for all.

Your tank should have decorations. Your fish need places to hide and places to rest. Mainly though, you will find that a decorated tank is so much more pleasing to view. You can add natural rocks, corals, plastic macroalgae, and even some plastic or ceramic ornaments, if they fit your taste. This is your tank, so you get to be the interior decorator who decides what will make it look best. Be creative and have fun with it.

Gravel: Let's Get to the Bottom of It

The first decoration to go into your tank will be the substrate. If you like colored gravel, you will probably be disappointed to find that gravel for saltwater aquariums pretty much comes in only three colors: gray, grayer, and grayest. We use special calcareous (calcium-based) gravels in saltwater tanks to help keep the water hardness and pH high. (More about water hardness and pH in Chapter 16 on water chemistry.)

Saltwater substrates may be mined calcium carbonate rocks, including dolomite, aragonite, and crushed coral (which is not really crushed coral at all, but crushed fossilized coral rock). These may be available as gravel or sand. Various types of collected beach sand are also available, as well as some really coarse types that are composed primarily of broken bits of seashells and coral bits that have washed ashore. Chips of crushed oyster shell are sometimes used for substrate, as well.

Any of these substrates can be effective in a marine aquarium. Your choice will be based on local availability and the look you want for your tank. A pure sandy bottom can be very appealing and currently seems to be the preferred choice for reef tanks, but you cannot use sand with an undergravel filter—the sand will sift through the plate and clog the filter.

Likewise, the substrates composed of broken shells and other large pieces do poorly with an undergravel filter. The spaces between the bits are so large that food falls easily into them and becomes trapped, where it can pollute the tank. It is OK to mix this type of gravel in with something smaller, though. One-eighth- to 1/4-inch-diameter stones are best for undergravel filters.

Another reason not to pick pebbles that are too large is that pebble size affects your biological filtration. Smaller stones have more surface area per pound, providing more space to grow helpful bacteria. To illustrate this, think of an apple as representing a large stone. You have a certain amount of surface area, represented by the red skin of the apple. Now, if you take that apple and cut it in half, you will still have the original surface area plus the additional surface area of the two white faces that the cut created.

Fish Tales

The cute and hardy jawfish like to build burrows. If you mix some broken bits of coral and shells into your substrate, you will find that jawfish will collect all the large pieces from around the tank to build their homes. It's fun to watch the construction and antics of this fish.

Gravel in Depth

How much gravel will you need? Well, that depends a bit. You can get away with less gravel if you just want to cover the bottom. However, if you want to have enough for burrowing fish and invertebrates, you may need more. To make an undergravel filter function properly, you should create a layer of gravel that is 1½ to 2 inches deep.

Marine sand and gravel is usually sold in 10-pound, 20-pound, and 50-pound bags. It can be difficult to figure out how many pounds of gravel will be right for your tank. It will vary, depending on the type of filter you use, the look you want to achieve, and the number of large decorations in the tank. The habits of the critters that you intend to keep will also be a factor. There are many general rules you can follow to take a guess.

One popular method is to use 1 pound of gravel per gallon of aquarium. This rule works fine for most marine tanks that don't have undergravel filters. It takes closer to 1½ pounds per gallon for proper operation of an undergravel filter. If you plan to keep animals that like deep burrows, you may need even more. Sand packs down a bit more, so you may want to follow the 1½-pounds-per-gallon rule for it, as well.

An even better rule is to use at least 10 pounds of sand or gravel per square foot of bottom. This is a better guideline, because it considers the actual space that you need to fill. For example, there are three standard sizes of 20-gallon tanks on the market—20H, 20L, and 20XH—and they have bottoms that are 2.0, 2.5, and 1.4 square feet, respectively. You can see that using a pounds-per-gallon rule to choose your gravel will give quite varying results in depth for these three 20-gallon tanks!

Fish and Tips

Small size gravel is better than larger pebbles, but you also can mix them for pleasing effects. As the gravel settles, the smaller stones will sink to the bottom and the larger ones will rise to the top. When you use your gravel vacuum, they will be remixed.

Fish and Tips

If you choose sand for your sub-strate, be sure that you get a calcium-based sand for marine aquariums. Do not use silica sand (quartz), as it may contribute to diatom (brown "algae") growth.

Your dealer will probably give you an estimate of how much substrate to get for your size tank, based on a pounds-per-gallon rule. Feel free to ask him for the bottom dimensions of a tank if you'd rather use the more accurate pounds-per-square-foot rule, or use the following chart. It shows how much gravel I recommend for typical sizes of aquariums to achieve a depth of $1^1/_2$ to 2 inches. If I list a range, the first number fits the 10-pounds-per-square-foot rule, and the second number is the amount that I prefer to recommend—because I feel that the higher number gives an effect that's more pleasing to the eye. (Some tanks have deeper frames, so the gravel appears to be more shallow. The higher amount counter-acts that.) Don't forget that you really shouldn't try keeping a saltwater tank any smaller than 29 gallons.

Gravel Recommendations

Tank Size (in Gallons)	Tank Footprint (in Inches)	Gravel Needed (in Pounds)
20XH	20 × 10	15
20H	24 × 12	20–25
20L	30 × 12	25–30
29	30 × 12	25–30
30	36 × 12	30–40
40	48 × 13	45–60
50	36 × 18	45–60
55	48 × 13	45–60
70	48 × 18	60–75
75	48 × 18	60–75
90	48 × 18	60–75
100	72 × 18	100–150
125	72 × 18	100–150
135	72 × 18	100–150

A Behind-the-Scenes Peek at Backgrounds

One way that Mother Nature protects fish from predators is by darkening or fading their colors to better match their surroundings. A camouflaged fish is less likely to be spotted and eaten by another fish. Dark backgrounds and decorations will therefore tend to bring out darker colors in your fish, while lighter gravel and backgrounds may cause your fish to fade. This effect is more prevalent in freshwater tanks than in saltwater tanks, though. Most saltwater fish have colors that are intentionally gaudy.

Still, your aquarium will look best if you install a background, and darker backgrounds tend to display the fish better. A background will hide light-color walls behind the tank. It will hide electrical cords and air lines, too.

You can find many types of backgrounds at your aquarium store. Some are presized to fit the most popular sizes of aquariums, but the most popular types are cut from a roll and sold by the foot. Attach your background to the outside of the tank. Following are some types of backgrounds that you may find:

➤ Precut scenes are presized backgrounds, designed to fit specific popular sizes of aquariums. You merely tape them on the back of your tank.

➤ Scenes on a roll are the most popular choices. Your dealer sells them by the inch or foot and cuts them to fit the length of your tank. You may need to trim the top or bottom a bit to get a perfect fit. Be sure to buy a background that is tall enough for your tank. Ask your dealer if you are not sure. This type of background can easily be cellophane taped to the back of the tank. Many of them are reversible, too, so if you get bored with one scene you can flip the background over for another.

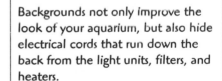

➤ Mirrored backgrounds can make a tank appear to have more depth. You can sometimes find reflective plastic backgrounds. Some aquariums even have a mirror built right into the back, but they are not really a good choice for saltwater tanks. If saltwater drips on the mirror, it tends to corrode.

Fish and Tips

Backgrounds not only improve the look of your aquarium, but also hide electrical cords that run down the back from the light units, filters, and heaters.

➤ Self-sticking backgrounds are solid-color backgrounds on a roll that include a self-adhesive backing. You peel the protective layer and apply the background directly to the tank. No cellophane tape is needed. This type of background should only be installed before the aquarium is set up, because the installation is more complicated.

Apply self-sticking backgrounds like window film. First take a cup of water and put a couple of drops of dishwashing soap in it. Do not get soap into your tank! It is deadly to fish. Wet the outside back of the tank with this solution. Then remove the protective backing from the self-sticking background and position it on the wetted back of the tank. Use a credit card or other flat object to squeegee out the bubbles. The result looks like a painted finish when dry.

➤ Speaking of looking like a painted-on finish, many people actually do paint the back of their tanks. Oil-based paint works best. Latex paints tend to degrade and peel if they get wet. A painted finish is very attractive but less versatile. If you want to change to a different background, you need to scrape off the old paint with razor blades or use a commercial paint-removing compound.

➤ You don't see dioramas very often, except maybe in public aquariums. A diorama is a 3-D display. Instead of mounting a background directly to the tank, you can build a little display behind the tank. Arrange rocks, corals, and so forth to give an added illusion of depth. To work best, you should put a separate light over your diorama. You can do some very novel things this way. I have heard of people building glass cages and putting birds behind their tank, so that it looks like birds are flitting through the water!

Solid Information About Rocks

Large rocks are super as stand-alone decorations, or they can make a great centerpiece for your tank. Rocks can be piled to build ledges and terraces to provide places for the fish to play hide-and-seek. Your dealer probably offers several varieties of decorative rocks. All should be safe for the saltwater aquarium.

Some people even collect their own rocks, but if you do, be very careful not to pick anything that has a high metal content or pesticide contamination. Remember that whatever was on the rock will now slowly leach into the water in your tank.

Rocks of any kind are usually limited in a fish-only aquarium. Most people prefer to use artificial corals to decorate their tanks. To my eye, most types of rocks sold by your dealer will look unnatural in a saltwater setup, anyway. There are some exceptions, though. Tufa, red lava, and lace rock are some common types that have rough porous textures that resemble natural coral rock. You can often buy these rocks with large holes drilled in them to help you form caves and hiding places.

Fish and Tips

When stacking rocks, try to place the bottom rock directly on the bottom of the tank or on top of the undergravel filter plate. Avoid putting the bottom rock on top of the gravel. If you do, fish digging beneath the rock, or even simple settling of the gravel, can cause the rocks to shift, falling against the glass and breaking it or crushing a fish.

Is That Rock Looking at Me?

Don't forget about live-rocks! Unique to the saltwater hobby are porous natural rocks called *live-rocks*. Harvested from the ocean, these rocks come with all kinds of living things attached. Leafy macroalgae, sponges, clams, snails, crabs, worms, starfish, and more can be found on the rocks. They add color and interest to any aquarium.

Live-rocks are starting to become popular in fish-only setups, and can be used to create the lagoon tanks and semi-reefs described in Chapter 2. I think they are a great choice to mix in, but you do need to be aware of their advantages and limitations. The advantages are

Fish Tales

Live-rock comes from around the globe. It is "wild" harvested in places like Fiji, Samoa, and Tonga. Each type has different shapes, textures, and organisms relative to the source. Caribbean rock is no longer gathered from the wild. Instead, there are rock farmers who build artificial reefs of mined limestone and then harvest the rocks after they've had a couple of years for organisms to settle and grow on them.

that the rocks look natural and add color, and the plants and animals on them can provide interest for you and food for the fish. Live-rocks are chock full of helpful bacteria that provide biological filtration, too.

The disadvantages are that most fish will eat the interesting and colorful algae from the rocks, and they'll eat most of the invertebrates that crawl out, too. The other downside is that if you ever need to medicate the fish, most medications used for fish will kill the invertebrates living on the rock.

Live-rocks reign supreme in the reef aquarium, though. In fact, live-rocks *are* the reef. They provide required flora and fauna, they provide biological filtration, and they are the platform upon which all else is built. Following are some common types of live-rock:

➤ **Base rock** is live-rock with little in the way of external life. In other words, it has a plain appearance, with little or no encrusted algae or sponges. It is the least expensive type of live-rock, but it is the type that you may use most. Build the inner layers of your reef with cheap base rock to save money. Put the fancier, more expensive stuff on the outer layer where you can see and enjoy it.

➤ **Fancy rock** is the good stuff. You will find several types, with various names based on the point of origin and the type of life growing on the outside. For example, algae rock or plant rock is harvested in shallow bays and is loaded with various types of macroalgae. It is like buying a rock with a green, red, and brown weed patch growing on it. Reef rock comes from farther out and has fewer plants and more animals. It will be

Fish and Tips

Live-rock is sold by the pound. To get the best value—that is, more "live" and less "rock"—avoid buying large spherical pieces. Besides being relatively cheaper, branchy pieces and flat pieces are easier to stack, lock together better, and make a more flow-through reef.

Fish School

Live-rock may be cured or uncured. **Cured** rock has been in your dealer's tank long enough to have stabilized. **Uncured** rock is the most recently acquired stuff. Some organisms become damaged and die in shipping. The rock will be cured when the dead tissue has finished rotting away.

coated with hard purple coralline algae, orange, black, and yellow sponges, assorted clams, and other goodies. It may even have some small coral colonies on it. Reef rock tends to cost more than algae rock.

Try to avoid buying your dealer's newest pieces of live-rock. Some of the organisms coating the rocks will have been damaged during the shipping process. Also, when collectors harvest the rock, they use wire brushes to scrape off some possibly harmful organisms—such as toxic chicken liver sponges. Bits of dead and dying organisms such as these can pollute your tank. Give the rock time to cure in your dealer's tanks. That is, don't buy the rocks until you are sure any damaged animals have fully rotted away.

I know this sounds bad. (It smells even worse!) But it is normal, and only a small percentage of organisms are lost this way. Most dealers cure their live-rock in tanks or vats that are separate from their fish and delicate invertebrates.

Picking Plants

When we talk about live plants in the marine aquarium, we are pretty much talking about algae—macroalgae. Vascular plants (plants with stems and leaves that circulate fluid internally) tend to grow either above the water or in freshwater. Still, while freshwater hobbyists think of algae as being a pest, marine hobbyists may think quite differently. Many types of marine algae look more like evolved vascular plants. For example, did you know that giant kelp, which can grow several hundred feet long, is a type of algae?

When it comes right down to it, though, you probably won't be able to keep much in the way of live macroalgae in your aquarium. Why? Because when most fish look at macroalgae, they say, "Oh, boy! Salad!" There are just too many things that like to eat it. The most popular species of fish in the fish-only aquarium will relish it, and in reef tanks, fish and invertebrates both may see it as food.

If you have your heart set on trying some live marine plants, give the following a try:

➤ There are several species of Caulerpa. Some have feather- or blade-shape leaves. Others look more like grapes or toadstools.

➤ Halimeda is made of branches of flattened plates.

➤ Penicillus (merman's shaving brush), and Udotea (mermaid's fan) get their names from their shapes.

However, if you want plants in your marine tank—especially your fish-only tank—you will probably be stuck settling for plastic plants. Any that are safe for freshwater aquariums are also safe for saltwater. Keep your eye out for the Marinescapers line, which is fashioned after real species of macroalgae.

You will find plastic plants in various heights, so be sure not to pick plants that are too tall for your tank. Likewise, if you pick all short plants, it will look like someone ran over your tank with a weed whacker. It is best to mix several sizes to give the tank a random and natural appearance.

Artificial Coral and Coral Skeletons

Fish School

Microalgae (*micro* means *small*) tend to be pests, while **macroalgae** (*macro* means *large*) may be quite desirable. There are many beautiful red, green, and brown macroalgae whose leafy or fingery fronds provide color and interest for you, and food and hiding places for your aquatic friends.

Corals are living organisms. Most are colonies of living organisms. Many types of coral (the stony corals) excrete calcium carbonate to build a supportive skeletal structure. With live stony corals, you don't see the skeleton at all, only the living polyps that coat the outer layer. They are jellylike, shaped like tiny flowers, and come in many beautiful colors.

When corals die, the skeleton is left behind. Skeletons of coral colonies come in a myriad of shapes, including ridges, fingers, tables, and ledges, or they may be round and brain-shaped. Except for a couple of varieties, all coral skeletons are white. Coral skeletons used to be the only choice for decorating a marine aquarium, and they are still widely used.

They are now falling out of favor, however. Coral populations are suffering and decreasing in the wild, due to pollution, climatic changes, silt runoff from agriculture, and other bad things caused by us humans. So why harvest live corals and kill them for their skeletons when artificial corals are now so widely available?

Artificial corals make a much better choice. No corals had to die to produce them, and they come in many colors besides the basic white. You can make a display that looks just as nice or better than one that uses dead corals.

Of course, the reef tank hobbyist will want to use live corals, and I'll talk about them in Chapters 13 and 20 on invertebrates and reef tanks.

Ceramic and Action Aerating Ornaments

While they are not especially popular in saltwater tanks, castles and other ceramic ornaments have been big sellers for ages. These days, manufacturers take them to a new level of sophistication. You can buy castle walls and cities that act as backgrounds

Fish and Tips

Action aerating ornaments can be fun to watch, but be aware that they can sometimes be tricky to calibrate. You must use a control valve, and you may have to adjust them with some frequency.

in your tank. You can find Roman ruins that are single, double, and triple columns, and entire rows of Greek goddesses to stand in the middle of your tank.

Ceramic "No Fishing!" signs are an old standby, and frogs, turtles, and mermaids are also still popular. Shipwrecks, sunken logs, skeletons on surfboards . . . you name it, somebody probably makes a ceramic or resin version of it.

Action aerating ornaments are also popular. In case you aren't familiar with them, you can find a huge range of these items. They are usually plastic, but sometimes are ceramic. When you hook an air line to them, these ornaments move! You will find treasure chests that open and close, a diver that battles an octopus, sunken ships with paddlewheels still turning, and even Goofy and Mickey Mouse in scuba gear. Kids especially like to have action aerating ornaments in the tank.

The Least You Need to Know

➤ A decorated tank is more pleasing to the eye and more comfortable for the fish.

➤ Dark environments help bring out the colors in your fish.

➤ Choose an appropriate marine substrate. Use calcareous sand or gravel.

➤ An aquarium background is attractive and hides unsightly air lines and electrical cords.

➤ Live-rocks are a must for reef tanks but can be used in fish-only aquariums, too.

➤ Use rocks, artificial corals, and macroalgae to imitate nature, and add ceramic or action aerating ornaments for fun.

What Else Can You Buy?

So now I've gone over choosing an aquarium, stand, and the three major systems for your tank: filter, heating, and lighting system. I discussed decorations as well. That covers the bulk of the items you need to set up your aquarium properly. Still, a few supplies remain to round out the setup, and I'll talk about those in this chapter. I'll also take time to tick off a few things you can live without, but may not want to, including some high-tech gizmos for you tinkerers out there.

Air to Spare

If you didn't buy an air pump as part of your aquarium setup, you can skip to the next section. If you chose an air pump, then you need a way to connect the air pump to the filters or ornaments and to regulate the flow. That is where air line and gang-valves come in.

➤ **Air line** is flexible vinyl tubing, about the diameter of a soda straw. Most dealers sell it by the foot, although some sell precut lengths. Use scissors to cut pieces of the desired length, and simply snug the ends over the valves and connections to hook everything up. Most air line tubing sold in stores is clear vinyl. You also may run across green silicone rubber air tubing. In most cases, it does not make any difference which you pick. The silicone tubing is more ozone-resistant, though, if you plan to buy an ozonizer. (I'll talk about ozonizers later in the chapter.)

➤ **Mini-tubing** is flexible tubing with a diameter about half that of regular air tubing. Do not use mini-tubing for most applications. In fact, you can't connect it to any fittings without using the enclosed adapters. The only use for mini-tubing is to connect to aerating ornaments. The smaller diameter and reduced buoyancy of mini-tubing makes it easier to hide from view inside the aquarium.

➤ **Air control valves** are necessary when you want to connect to extra outlets, combine into fewer outlets, control air flow, or vent excess pressure. The easiest type of valve to use is a **gang-valve**. A gang-valve is several valves connected and mounted on a plastic or metal hanger. You can buy two-gang, three-gang, four-gang, and five-gang valves, which can run two to five outlets, respectively.

Fish and Tips

Do not confuse two-way and three-way valves with gang-valves. A two-way valve inserts into an existing air line to control its output. It doesn't add outlets, only control. If you want to add an outlet, you must insert a three-way valve into an existing air line.

You hang the assembly on the back of your tank, attach the air line from your air pump to the side input connectors of the gang-valve. Then you connect air lines to the valves and run the output to your filters or ornaments. Remember that gang-valves divide the power of your air pump—they do not multiply it. So if you use gang-valves to run more outlets, first be sure that your pump is able to put out enough extra air to do so.

➤ **Check-valves** prevent water from back-siphoning through the air lines, should there be a power outage. The check-valve is a device that allows air to flow in only one direction. Ideally, you should put a check-valve on each outlet of your air pump (the outlets on the pump, not the outlets on the valve).

Chapter 10 on setting up your aquarium has diagrams showing the proper way to connect air pumps, check-valves, and gang-valves with air line.

Hauling in Your Catch

Normally, the only time you will ever want to net a fish is when it is dead and needs to be removed from the tank. However, you never know when you may need to catch a fish to move it to another tank to breed, to recover from a fight, or to be medicated. Or maybe the fish has just outgrown the tank and you want to give it to a friend. That is where a fishnet comes in handy.

Fine nets usually have a white mesh and a fine weave. The smaller holes make it more difficult for fins to become snagged. This may be helpful if you are catching marine catfish, lionfish, or other spiny species. The down side is that the tighter weave creates more drag, slowing the net down in the water. So fine nets are less maneuverable than coarse nets.

Coarse nets have a looser weave and are green. This is my favorite type of net. There is less drag, so the net is much quicker and more maneuverable in the water, making it easier to catch fish. Still, if you need to catch an easily snagged species, it may not be the best choice.

Marine fish can be particularly hard to catch. Many are quite good at burying themselves in the gravel or wedging into a coral head. Plus, the corals are very good at snagging a net, making it difficult to maneuver. Consider purchasing a clear plastic specimen container like the one your dealer uses to bag fish. You can place the clear container on its side inside your tank—the flat sides fit nicely against the glass—and then use a net to herd the fish into it. As soon as the fish is in, reach into the tank, stand the container up, and then lift it out. Be sure to stand the container up first, or the fish will swim out! Fish tend to flee sideways, so they will rarely swim out the top. Marine fish may be brightly colored, but they are not all that bright, if you know what I mean.

Aquarium fishnets typically come in sizes varying from 2 inches to 10 inches wide. You need to consider two things when selecting the size of your net:

➤ What size fish will you be catching?

➤ How big is the tank?

Obviously, you need to know what size the fish will be so that you can pick a size of net that is at least big enough for them to fit into. The reason tank size is a consideration is that you need to be able to maneuver the net when you stick it in there. If the net is too big, you will have trouble getting it into the tank and trouble moving it about without snagging every piece of coral or rock. If the net is too small, you will have a hard time catching fish. A 2-inch net is a very poor choice for a 55-gallon tank. I find that a 6-inch net comes in handy most often.

Fish and Tips

Sometimes the easiest way to catch fish is with two nets. Hold one in place, and use the other to herd the fish into the first. So you may want to buy one fine net and one coarse net. That way, you will have the right size mesh for the job and two nets when you need them.

Something's Fishy

Lionfish and other venomous spiny fish can be dangerous to catch. If you snag one in a net, it will be both difficult and dangerous to remove. Instead, use the net or other object to herd the lionfish into a clear plastic specimen container and then use the container to remove the fish safely.

Fish and Tips

Even if you draw water from a well, you may still want to use a water conditioner. You won't have chlorine to remove, but you may be able to use the other features provided by the water conditioner.

Avoid long-handled nets. While you may think a net with a longer handle will make it easier to reach the bottom of the tank, more often the long handle makes the net too difficult to maneuver. Remember that you will most likely be netting through a small lid at the front of the tank, and you will not just be netting fish at the front, but also at the top rear corners. A long-handled net makes this difficult or impossible.

Sea Salt

It probably goes without saying that you can't have saltwater without sea salt, but I'll say it anyway because, hey, I like to hear myself talk! Er . . . type. Sea salts come as a dry powder that you mix with tapwater to create seawater. Typical packages produce 5, 10, 25, 50, 150, or 200 gallons of seawater. The 200-gallon size comes packaged in a nice 7-gallon bucket that you can use for mixing seawater for water changes.

There are many brands of sea salt available. Some brands will claim to have extra trace elements, or more of this and none of that. You will find people who swear by one brand and swear at others. I like some better than others, too, but when it comes right down to it, all will do the job. Just be sure to keep up with your regular partial water changes.

Water Conditioners

Most aquarists need to treat their tapwater to make it safe for fish to live in. Your needs will depend on the condition of your local tapwater. (See Chapter 17 on water changes for help deciding which water conditioner you will need.) Following are some typical water conditioners.

Dechlorinators

Have you ever been swimming in a public pool? If so, you know the effect that chlorine has on mucous membranes, including a fish's gills. Municipalities add chlorine to the tapwater. If you have city water—that is, if you aren't pulling water from your own well—you will need to remove the chlorine before it is safe for your fish.

Your aquarium store will carry several water conditioners whose main purpose is to dechlorinate tapwater. Many brands also offer other benefits. For example, some will remove chloramines and heavy metals or buffer the pH a bit. Some brands even provide a "liquid bandage" factor that produces a temporary slime coat on fish that have had theirs damaged by being caught in a net.

Specialty Conditioners

If you have a reef tank, you will also want to pick up some kalkwasser and probably some kind of strontium-iodine potion for your live corals. You may need a jar of buffer as well. I'll talk about all of these later in the book, when I get more deeply into the topic of reef tanks in Chapter 20 and water chemistry in Chapter 16.

For fish-only tanks, you probably don't need any supplemental water conditioners. Your regular partial water changes should keep things under control. Sometimes a jar of buffer comes in handy, though.

Tests You Don't Want to Pass

Do not pass by the test kit aisle when shopping for your supplies, or you will regret it. You cannot tell the condition of your water by looking at it! If you think you can maintain a saltwater tank without using the proper test kits, you may as well spend your money in Las Vegas instead. The odds of success would be higher there. Chapters 15 and 16 on cycling a tank and water chemistry will fill you in on the details of what these kits test and why. For now, just add them to your shopping list.

The Indispensable Hydrometer

Pronounced *hy-DROM-et-er*, this device measures the density or specific gravity of your water—which is a roundabout way of saying that it can tell you whether or not you mixed the right amount of sea salt with your tapwater. You see, the more salt dissolved in the water, the higher the density of the water. You must buy a hydrometer.

Something's Fishy

Freshwater hobbyists can sometimes squeak by without testing their water. However, if you think you can operate a saltwater tank without test kits, you are destined to fail!

The most common type of hydrometer resembles a floating glass thermometer with a long glass neck on top, and is called a floating glass bulb hydrometer. The neck sticks up above the water and has a piece of paper inside with a scale of measurement. Where the water line of your tank falls on the neck of the hydrometer is where you read the scale. The denser the water, the higher the hydrometer floats. You can find small, inexpensive glass hydrometers and larger laboratory grade models that are more accurate.

A floating pointer hydrometer is a clear plastic box with a plastic pointer in the middle. You scoop some water into the box and then read the number at the end of the pointer. It's very quick and easy, and plenty accurate. Before taking your reading, though, give the device a couple of taps to be sure no air bubbles adhere to the pointer. Air bubbles will throw off the reading.

Fish and Tips

I prefer the plastic floating pointer hydrometer over the floating glass bulb type. The former gives a quick, accurate reading. With the latter, you have to wait for it to stop bobbing to take your reading, and then the scale always seems to end up turned away from you. The glass is more easily broken, too.

All the Test Kits

Always purchase a pH test kit. Be sure to get one designed for marine aquariums. A pH kit measures the acidity of your water. Besides needing to know the pH of the water in your new tank at any given time, your pH kit can be used to monitor trends. A declining pH is usually a sign of insufficient water changes.

Every saltwater hobbyist needs an ammonia test kit, too. It is especially critical to monitor ammonia levels in new tanks! This kit is a direct way to test the functioning of your biological filtration.

A nitrite test kit also tells you about the functioning of your biological filtration and is highly recommended for new tanks. You will see the part that nitrite plays in Chapter 15 on cycling a new tank.

An alkalinity test kit measures something called *buffering capacity* or *acid neutralizing capacity* in your system. This may also be sold as a carbonate hardness test kit. Do not confuse it with a pH kit—which tells you if water is acid or alkaline, or with a general hardness kit, which measures calcium and magnesium. This kit tends to be more popular with reefkeepers than with fish-only hobbyists, but both types should buy it.

You should definitely buy all of the test kits I've just mentioned. Here are some other kits that you may want but may not need:

➤ **Nitrate test kit.** Not to be confused with the nitrite test kit, this kit measures the next step in the biological filtration process. It is of most interest to reef hobbyists because of the role that nitrates play in algae growth, but fish-only hobbyists may find it useful, too.

➤ **Copper test kit.** Copper medications are used to treat saltwater protozoan infections. To properly dose the medication, you need to be able to monitor the amount of copper present in the water—too much kills the fish, while too little won't kill the disease. Copper is deadly to invertebrates, though, so this item is for a fish-only setup.

➤ **Low-range phosphate test kit.** Again, reef hobbyists will find this kit of particular use, as limiting phosphates can limit the growth of undesired microalgae.

➤ **Dissolved oxygen test kit.** Saltwater doesn't hold as much oxygen as freshwater, so dissolved oxygen levels can be more critical. If your fish are gasping, you may want to run this test. Still, if you have set up proper filtration and circulation, it is doubtful that oxygen levels will be below safe levels.

➤ **Strontium test kit.** Strontium plays an important part in the growth of live corals. Reef hobbyists may want this kit.

➤ **Iodine test kit.** Iodine also plays an important role in the growth of live corals. Reef hobbyists may want this one, too.

Isolation Tank

A quarantine or isolation tank is a smart idea—especially if you want a reef tank. Since the medications that kill the most common fish diseases also kill invertebrates, you should never add unquarantined fish to a reef tank. It will be impossible to treat them.

An isolation tank doesn't have to be fancy. A simple 5$^1/_2$- or 10-gallon aquarium, with a sponge filter, heater, and a couple of plastic plants for cover is all that you require. You can use a quarantine tank to medicate a single sick fish, rather than treating the whole tank (sometimes). A quarantine tank also makes a good place to allow an injured fish to heal. Of course, using it to quarantine new arrivals before they ever go into your main tank can help keep disease from getting there in the first place.

You also may want to have an isolation basket on hand. There are several styles of these, usually sold as net breeders, breeding baskets, breeding traps, or isolation containers. Some are clear plastic containers with perforations to allow water to flow through. They hang inside your tank, and you put the fish that needs protection inside. The best types are the ones made of a simple plastic frame with a net mesh all around. They allow water to flow through easily. There are coarse mesh and fine mesh models, but the coarse mesh is usually best. It allows droppings and uneaten food to fall out of the net more easily. Of course, if you want to use the basket to protect baby fish, then fine mesh may be required.

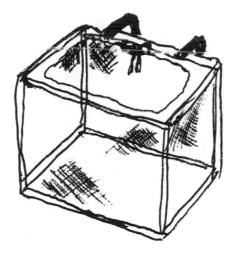

A net breeder can be used to isolate bullied fish.

Cleaning Supplies

There are a few items you will need in the routine maintenance of your aquarium. These items will make partial water changes and glass cleaning a snap.

Something's Fishy

Never use soap to clean your aquarium or any items in it. Soap is extremely toxic to fish.

Gravel Vacuum

If there is one item that will make your life easy, a gravel vacuum is it. Gravel vacuums are quick, easy, and cheap to use. They clean your gravel and make partial water changes at the same time, so you get rid of both dissolved waste and solid debris.

There is a fancier clean-and-fill version of this device that connects to your sink. It both drains the aquarium (while cleaning the gravel) and fills it back up—all without lugging buckets. You can buy models with 25- to 100-foot hoses, so that you can reach any aquarium.

A gravel vacuum makes life easy for you and your fish. (courtesy of Tetra-Second Nature, maker of Hydro-Clean)

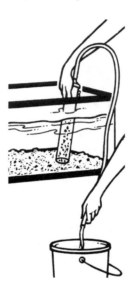

Algae Scrubber

Snails and other herbivores may help, but there is no getting around it—occasionally, you will have to wipe algae off the glass. There are many styles of algae scrubbers and scrapers on the market, but my favorite is the simple scrubber pad. You can buy coarse ones (usually blue) for glass tanks, or softer ones (usually white) for acrylic tanks. You can buy algae scrubbers on a stick, too, but they are much harder to maneuver than the hand-held pads. There are also razor blade scrapers for the really tough types of algae.

If you are the type of person who is afraid to dip your hand in the water much, then (1) you are a dweeb, (2) you may be in the wrong hobby, and (3) you should consider buying a magnetic algae scraper. This type of scraper consists of two magnetic parts. One part, which has either embedded blades or scrubber pads, goes inside the tank. The other part goes outside the tank. The magnetic attraction keeps the parts together. When you move the outer piece, the inner scraper portion slides around, too. These scrapers are kind of fun, and most do a fair job, but they don't get into corners or tight spots very well.

A Bucket to Lug It All

A 5-gallon fish bucket comes in very handy. You can use it for mixing or carrying water, for transporting fish, or for holding drippy filter media while you do maintenance. Turned upside down, it makes a decent step stool, too. If you ever break your tank, you may need a bucket to hold the fish while you go buy a new one. You can get a free 7-gallon bucket when you buy a 200-gallon portion of sea salt.

Something's Fishy

Do not use razor blade algae scrapers on acrylic tanks. You will scratch them.

Replacement Filter Materials

It doesn't hurt to have spare filter materials on hand for when you need them. It is definitely more convenient than making a special trip to the fish store. Then again, it is always nice to have a good excuse to make a trip to the fish store.

Buy a Book!

I can tell you right now that your chances of success with a saltwater aquarium will be quite low if you don't read up on it first. A good beginner's text is a must. Guess what? I recommend this book! So if you are standing there in the store reading but you haven't yet forked out the $16.95 for this little gem, what the heck are you waiting for? It can pay for itself by saving the life of one fish. Besides, it's for a good cause—I use all my royalties from this book to buy homes for homeless fish.

If you plan to set up a reef tank, this book will give you a very good start. However, reef tanks are at the most advanced end of this hobby. So, don't stop reading here. See my suggested reading list in Appendix C.

We Have the Technology

Hopefully, you won't end up with the six-million-dollar tank, but we do have the technology to make your tank better . . . stronger . . . faster! Or something like that. Following are some high-tech items that many people want but almost no one really needs:

➤ **Electronic test monitors.** These electronic devices mount outside your tank and have probes that hang in the water for continuous readings. You can buy them to monitor pH, salinity, oxygen/reduction potential (ORP), temperature, water level, and other parameters. The most sophisticated models can be set to activate alarms when the temperature or water level is out of range or to control dosing pumps that release chemicals to control pH or other parameters.

Something's Fishy

Don't use your household cleaning bucket for water changes in your aquarium. Soap residue may cause problems. Instead, keep a separate bucket, for aquarium use only, and make sure everyone in the house knows not to use it for other tasks.

➤ **Water purifiers.** I'll talk more about these items in Chapters 16 and 17 on water chemistry and water changes. Deionizers and reverse-osmosis units are the most common. These devices remove impurities from tapwater before you use it to mix seawater. In my opinion, almost no one needs these. However, if your tapwater is really nasty stuff, it may be a requirement. Also, some reef hobbyists are especially particular about their tapwater.

➤ **Denitrators.** These items are a waste of money, in my opinion. Live-rock will remove nitrates, and so will water changes. Spend the money on good rock and sea salt instead. Besides, denitrators can be tricky to operate properly.

➤ **Ozonizers.** Ozonizers are occasionally used with protein skimmers. Dosing the right amount of ozone can increase the skimmer's efficiency, but dosing it wrong can make things worse and can even be toxic to your animals. If I were you, I would save my money here. However, if you already sprang for the ORP monitor mentioned earlier, you will want this contraption to go along with it.

What About the Fish?

You cannot put any fish in your tank until you've had it up and running for a while. You need to get the water quality and the temperature just right. You need to make sure that all your equipment works and your tank doesn't leak. Besides, you've already bought enough stuff!

The Least You Need to Know

➤ If you bought air-operated filters, be sure to also buy an air pump and the proper valves and air line to connect it all up.

➤ A gravel vacuum is something you won't want to live without.

➤ Don't forget food, net, and water conditioner for your new tank. A fish-only bucket and algae scrubber pad are also recommended.

➤ You may want to set up a small quarantine tank.

➤ Buy a good beginner's book. I recommend this one because I know the author personally and I think he's really cool.

Some Assembly Required

In This Chapter

➤ Setting up your tank and stand

➤ Installing filters, heaters, and lighting systems

➤ Adding decorations to spice things up

➤ Getting everything ready for the fish

Let's assume for the moment that you just made your second trip to the aquarium store to pick up all the items you purchased for your new tank. (It's your second trip because you drove the new Beetle instead of the van on the first trip, and you forgot that you couldn't fit both tank and stand into that tiny car.)

Anyway, you finally got everything loaded up, and right now you are driving merrily toward home when suddenly you realize two things: (1) If, right now, you are driving merrily toward home, it is probably not a good time to be reading this book, and (2) if you make it home alive, you have no idea how to assemble all these boxes of cargo into a properly functioning aquarium.

Don't panic! It's not as scary as it might seem, and besides, I am here to help. That's why they pay me the big buck. We'll take it slow and assemble your aquarium in carefully ordered steps. I know it's your first time, so I promise to be gentle.

Fish and Tips

Don't buy fish until after the tank is fully set up and has been running for 24 hours. You need to make sure that all equipment is functioning and that the temperature is stable. Besides, you want to be sure you don't have a leaky tank. (It's rare, but it happens.)

Step 1: Pick a Spot

You really should have done this before you bought your tank and stand, to be sure that things fit. Remember what happened when you tried to fit the 55-gallon tank and stand in your Beetle? To avoid algae problems and overheating, it is usually best to place the tank away from windows.

Pick a location where you will have access to at least three electrical outlets—one each for the light, filter, and heater. Odds are you will need more, though. You may want to pick up a power strip or one of those six-outlet doodads that plug into the wall outlet.

While you are at it, you may want to have your wall outlet replaced with a *ground-fault [circuit] interrupter* (GFI or GFCI). This device, common in newer bathrooms and kitchens, shuts itself off if it detects current leakage—usually caused by splashed water. Saltwater and leaking current can be particularly nasty. A simple reset button turns the power back on once you are sure it is safe.

Try to set up your electrical outlets so that there is enough slack to form drip loops with the electrical cords. That is, the cord should dangle lower than the electrical outlet and then curve back up to be plugged in. That way, if any water runs down the electrical cord, it won't go into the socket. It will drop off the loop of cord at the bottom instead.

Choose a location near the electrical outlets and away from windows.

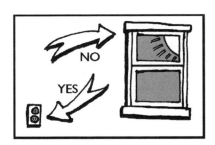

Step 2: Position the Stand

As you position your aquarium stand, make sure you allow enough room behind the tank for electrical cords, filter hoses, and any hang-on-the-back filters, overflow boxes, or protein skimmers that you plan to install. If necessary, use shims under the bottom corners of the stand to make sure it is flat and level. A twisted stand can crack your tank.

If necessary, use wedges to level the stand.

Step 3: Clean the Aquarium Glass

When you get your aquarium, use paper towels and plain water to clean the glass inside and out. It may be a bit dusty or grimy from sitting on your dealer's shelf or in the distributor's warehouse. Never use soap on your aquarium or any items that go into it. Soap kills fish.

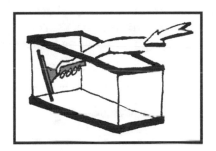

Clean the glass with plain water.

Step 4: Test the Tank for Leaks

A leak test is optional. Leaky tanks are fairly rare but not unheard of. So if you don't want to live dangerously, here is an easy way to test a tank. Lay out some dry newspaper on a flat, level surface. It can be on the floor of the garage or on your aquarium stand—wherever is convenient. Place the tank on top of the newspaper, and carefully fill it with water. Fill to the bottom of the top plastic frame on glass tanks, or within an inch of the top for acrylic tanks. Be very careful not to spill a single drop of water on the newspaper or outside the tank.

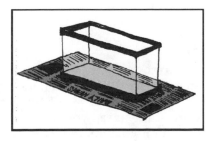

You may want to test for leaks before adding decorations.

Something's Fishy

Never try to lift an aquarium that is full of water. The stresses on the tank could easily break it. Always drain the tank first.

Watch for water welling up inside the bottom plastic frame, leaking from any seam, or soaking the newspaper and making it dark. If you do see water welling up in the bottom frame, are you positive that you didn't splash any water down in there? If you did, when the tank is full and settles it may squeeze out some water that dripped there before, making you think you have a leak when you really don't. Give it a few hours, and if everything is still dry, it is safe to proceed. You will need to remove the water from the tank before proceeding, and if you want to get the newspaper out from underneath.

Step 5: Attach the Background

You will find it much easier to do this now, rather than after the tank is installed and filled with water. Attach the background on the outside of the back, facing into the tank. Most glass aquariums do not have specific fronts or backs. You can face either side out. Not so with acrylic tanks. Special cutouts for hanging heaters and outside power filters must face the back.

Use cellophane or plastic electrician's tape to attach your background.

Step 6: Position the Aquarium on the Stand

Center your tank on the aquarium stand. Make sure it is seated flat, with no wobble, and that no bits of gravel or other obstructions are lodged between the tank and the stand. These objects could easily break a tank once you add the weight of the water. Check again to be sure that you left enough room behind the tank for outside power filters, filter hoses, electrical cords, and so forth.

Step 7: Install the Filter(s)

There are too many brands of filters for me to cover every possible scenario for installing them. That subject alone could fill an entire book (although not one that's really fun to read). So I'm going to stick with the basics. I will cover all popular styles, but just because I list a style of filter doesn't necessarily mean you should have purchased it. Your filter choices will have been based on information in earlier chapters and on

Center the aquarium on the stand.

advice from your dealer. Be sure to read the manufacturer's instructions that come with your brand of filter.

The main thing to note for now is that the instructions in this step only include directions for assembling and positioning the filter systems. You won't actually start the filters until later. Do not plug in any electrical devices until I specifically say to do so. Do not add water until you're told. Doing so could cause fire, flood, or permanent damage to the equipment. Worse, everyone will call you a bonehead, and we can't have that.

Undergravel Filter

Position the perforated undergravel filter plate inside your tank on the bottom, and install the large-diameter filter lift tubes. (Lift tubes should be at the back.) These days, most brands use 1-inch-diameter tubes. I usually use two tubes per filter plate for air-operated models, or one tube per plate for models run by powerheads. You may need to cut the tubes to the right length. Cap unused filter stem ports.

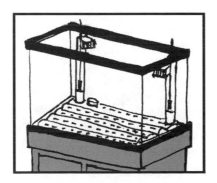

Install the undergravel filter system.

Something's Fishy

Besides following the steps in this book, be sure to take time to read all instructions and warranties that come with each piece of equipment. Do this *before* you try to assemble the equipment.

Fish School

An **airstone** is an air diffuser, usually made of cemented sand grains (although sometimes made of wood) that is porous enough to allow air to pass through it, thus splitting the airstream into tiny bubbles.

If you chose an air pump to power your undergravel filter, attach an airstone to the smaller rigid air line tubes and place them inside the larger outer tubes, with the airstones at the bottom. The exhaust spouts go on top, with the air lines protruding through the small hole on top. Point the exhaust spouts at the front middle of the tank for best circulation.

Install the airstones for your undergravel filter in a position as low as possible, but above the filter plate. The lower the airstone, the better the water flow it will generate, but if you put it too low, air will go under the filter plate instead of up the lift tube. If bubbles burp out from under your filter plate, you have installed the airstones too low.

If you plan to use powerheads to run your undergravel filter, you can discard the exhaust spouts, small-diameter rigid air line tubes, and airstones. Instead, you will position the powerheads directly on top of the 1-inch-diameter lift tubes. Make sure they are snug. Most powerheads come with brackets that clip over the tank frame. Some use suction cups to anchor the powerhead instead.

Outside Power Filter

Hang the filter on the back of the tank and adjust the leveling device on the bottom. The leveling device makes sure the filter hangs level, so water can't spill over the back. Some leveling devices are snap-off tabs. Others adjust by turning. Make sure the impeller seats properly in the motor. Install the intake tubes and strainers. Go ahead and rinse the filter medium, and install it according to the manufacturer's directions. If there is a lid to the unit, you can leave it off for the moment.

Install the outside power filter on the back of the tank.

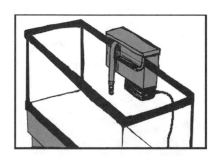

Canister Filter

Rinse the appropriate filter medium and fill the canister with it, according to the manufacturer's directions. Connect all filter hoses and valves. The candy cane-shape intake tube with the strainer on the bottom should be connected to the hose that connects to the input side of the canister filter.

Now it's time to snap the top onto the unit. Be sure to follow the manufacturer's directions here. Some units require you to position a rubber O-ring or gasket and may require you to lubricate it first with a bit of petroleum jelly. Some units must be filled with water before closing them up, or they won't start. But most will be difficult to start, unless you leave the water out for now. Remember, don't plug anything in until I say so.

Fish and Tips

You may need to trim the length of the lift tubes on your undergravel filter to get a proper fit. A hacksaw will cut them, or you can cut them with a heavy razor blade. On air-operated models, the exhaust spout should be completely or mostly submerged. With powerheads, make sure the exhaust spout is completely under water. If you mount the exhaust too high, you may get water shooting out of your tank.

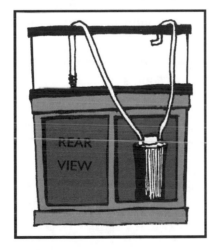

Install the canister filter.

Trickle Filter

When it comes to trickle filters, there are too many styles and options to describe them all here. So follow the manufacturer's directions, and ask your dealer for further assistance in assembling and positioning the filter. I will give you the basic steps, but be sure you get all the advice you need. And do not plug anything in or put any water in the filter yet.

115

Fish and Tips

Canister filters are more complicated to assemble than most other filters. A common error is to reverse the input and output hoses. Most canister filters will have "in" and "out" clearly marked, but it may be unclear if "out" is out of the tank into the filter or out of the filter into the tank. "In" is into the filter from the tank. "Out" is out of the filter and into the tank.

1. Install the sump beneath the tank. You may now discover one reason why you have not yet put water in the tank. Sometimes, the only way to fit the sump into the stand below is to lower it through the top of the stand or to slide it in from behind. Go ahead and put the bioball or DLS trickle filter medium in place, and install the filter lid.

2. Now install the overflow system on the tank. If you bought a reef-ready aquarium, you only need to take the enclosed overflow pipes and thread them through the holes in the bottom of the tank. Otherwise, assemble the overflow box according to the manufacturer's directions and hang it on the back of the tank. If you have an overflow box, loosen the wingnut or thumbscrew that lets you move the inner notched compartment to its highest possible setting (for now).

3. Install the water return pump. Depending on the model you bought, this will either set inside the sump, or set outside the sump, and connect through the side with PVC pipe fittings.

4. Connect the overflow system to the sump. A large hose attaches to the bottom of the overflow box (or overflow pipe on reef-ready systems). Run this hose down under the stand. Cut it to the proper length, and connect it to the fitting on top of the filter portion of the sump. This hose will bring the water from the tank down to the trickle filter.

Install your trickle filter.

5. Connect the return hose to the pump. Then run this hose back up to the tank, attach it to the gooseneck fitting, and hang it on the tank. This hose will spray filtered water back into the tank.

6. Drill a small hole in the return gooseneck fitting, just at or below the water line in your tank. If there is a power outage, air drawn through the hole will act as a siphon break and prevent water from back-siphoning into the sump of the trickle filter.

Fish and Tips

When connecting the hose between the overflow box and the sump on a trickle filter, try to keep a gentle downhill slope. Any U–shape sections of hose can trap water and cause a toilet–flushing effect when the hose fills.

Fluidized-Bed Filter

If you purchased a fluidized-bed filter, install it according to the manufacturer's instructions. Most are hang-on-the-back models. Hang the unit on the back of your tank and use the enclosed piece of tubing to attach the input to a small powerhead, which sits just inside your tank. The output nozzle or hose on the fluidized-bed filter should point back into the tank. Be sure to connect the hose from the powerhead to the inlet port of your fluidized-bed filter, so that water will flow up through the sand when it is started.

Some fluidized-bed filters stand on a base instead of hanging on the tank. If you have one of these, either connect it to draw and return water from the sump, or set it above the aquarium and connect it as I just described.

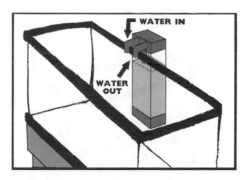

WATER IN

WATER OUT

Install your fluidized-bed filter.

Protein Skimmer

Again, there are too many designs to go into detail here, so be sure to follow the manufacturer's instructions—which, unfortunately, are usually quite meager. Better yet, ask your dealer to show you how to install the protein skimmer before you leave the store. Have him complete as much assembly as possible in the shop. In the case of

117

hang-on models, you can leave the store with the unit completely assembled and ready to hang on the tank. Stand-alone models may require some simple plumbing on your part. I'll talk about how to calibrate the protein skimmer a bit later in this chapter.

Install your protein skimmer. A counter-current model is shown.

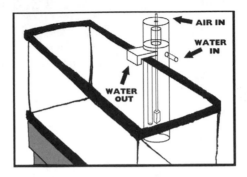

Step 8: Add the Substrate

Before putting gravel, sand, or other substrate in your aquarium, you will need to wash it. Place a few pounds in a bucket and use a garden hose to run water through it. Stir with your hands to put dust and sediment into solution, and then pour off the dirty water. It will take several washings to get off most of the dust. Still, no matter how much you wash the gravel, the rinse water will never come off perfectly clear. So give it a few good rinses and then be satisfied.

A layer $1\frac{1}{2}$ to 2 inches deep is usually about right. You may want to slope the substrate so that it is higher in the back. That way, sediment collects at the front where it can be easily siphoned away.

Add gravel to the tank, sloping toward the front.

Step 9: Add Decorations

Rocks (but not live-rocks), artificial corals, coral skeletons, and most ornaments can now be set in place. Be careful not to drop heavy objects into the tank. If you have action aerating ornaments, you may want to position them now. It's easier to hide the air lines under decorations before there is water to make them buoyant. If you bought plastic plants for your tank, we'll get to them in a bit.

Fish and Tips

If you make piles of rocks, it's a good idea to make sure there is no substrate beneath the bottom rock in the pile, so the pile doesn't settle and shift. Rocks could fall against the glass and break it. Falling rocks can also hurt your fish.

Position rocks, artificial corals, and other ornaments.

Step 10: Install Your Thermometer

If you bought the stick-on liquid crystal thermometer, it goes on the outside glass at the place of your choosing. Try to put it somewhere innocuous, though. Other styles of thermometers go inside the tank.

Liquid crystal thermometers go outside the tank. Other thermometers go inside.

Step 11: Fill the Aquarium with Water

Mix hot and cold water to achieve the desired temperature of 75° to 78°F (24° to 26°C). If you lay a coffee saucer on the substrate, you can pour or spray water onto it without disturbing the substrate. When the tank is full, remove the saucer.

Fill the tank by pouring water onto a coffee saucer. Premix hot and cold to achieve correct temperature.

Fill glass aquariums to the bottom edge of the top frame. Fill acrylic tanks to within an inch or so of the top. As discussed in Step 4, be sure not to slop water on the outside of your tank, or you may have difficulty telling if you have a leak.

Step 12: Add Water Conditioner

Use your dechlorinating water conditioner to remove chlorine from your tapwater. The package will tell you how much to dose, usually given in drops per gallon or teaspoons per 10 gallons.

Add water conditioner to remove chlorine from your tapwater.

Step 13: Add Sea Salt

You can start mixing in your sea salt. Add a little at a time, and stir to help it dissolve. Take regular readings with your hydrometer to reach a specific gravity of 1.023. Better yet, work toward bringing the level up to only 1.019 or 1.020, then let the tank sit overnight. Salt can get trapped in the gravel, where it cannot easily dissolve. So you may find your reading goes up overnight as that "lost" salt eventually finds its way into solution. Tomorrow, you can add a bit more salt to achieve the desired salinity if you need it.

Something's Fishy

If you fill your tank with a garden hose, run some water to rinse it out before use. The plasticizers that keep a hose flexible are toxic to fish. Water that has been sitting in the hose may be unsafe.

Slowly add sea salt. Stir to help it dissolve.

Step 14: Install the Aquarium Heater

If you bought a hang-on-the-tank model, the glass tube hangs in the water and the main body clamps to the back top frame of the tank. Turning the side screw knob tightens the clamp.

If you bought optional suction cups to keep the heater from being bumped against the glass and broken, slide them over the heater tube before placing the heater in the tank. The suction cups anchor the heater securely to the tank wall. Position the suction cups so that they aren't over the heater coils, or they will melt. Do not plug in the heater yet.

Fish and Tips

Always add the salt in steps, and always start out with less than you think you will need. It is much easier to add a bit more salt to increase the reading than it is to remove saltwater and replace it with freshwater to dilute the salinity.

If you have a submersible heater, use the suction cups that are included to mount it inside the tank or inside the sump. You can mount it horizontally, vertically, high, low—it's up to you. Sometimes it's convenient to mount the heater vertically, with the control knob sticking out of the water for easier access. Mainly, be sure to mount it where you can see the pilot light so you can tell if it is working. If you bought a model with a preset temperature scale, go ahead and dial up the desired temperature before installing the heater. Do not plug in the heater yet.

Install your heater, but don't plug it in yet.

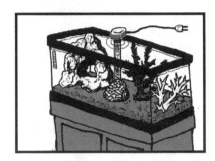

Step 15: Add Your Plants

If you bought plastic plants for your tank, now is a good time to add them. Some hobbyists prefer to add plants before filling the tank. I prefer to add them after the water is in the tank, because without the water to hold the plants up, you can't really judge how they will look. Besides, if you are afraid of getting your hands wet, you are in the wrong hobby. Taller plants usually look best toward the back of the tank. Be artistic.

Arrange your plants. The tallest plants look best at the back.

Step 16: Install the Lights

Before installation, check to be sure that all bulbs are properly seated. Then, continue by choosing the directions in the following sections for the appropriate lighting system.

Full-Hood

Most of you will choose a full-hood for fish-only setups. If so, follow the manufacturer's instructions for mounting it. Some brands have pins that snap off the bottom to get a custom fit, others have plastic strips that snap off the edge for a perfect fit, and still others sit recessed into the aquarium's top frame without modification. Trim the plastic strip on the rear of the hood to fit around heaters, outside power filters, and other equipment that hangs on the back of the tank.

Something's Fishy

Never plug in a heater that is out of the water. You could get burned or cause a fire.

Install your full-hood or other lighting system.

Glass Canopy/Strip Light Combo

Glass canopies sit recessed inside the top aquarium frame, resting on the inner lip. Not every brand fits every tank, so if yours doesn't seem right, you may have purchased the wrong brand. The strip light then sits on top of the glass canopy. Add as many strip lights as you want. Again, a rear plastic strip can be trimmed to allow heaters and other equipment to hang on the back of your aquarium.

Metal Halide Lights

The pendant style of metal halide lights is most popular. Install a ceiling hook or a wall-mounted bracket, and hang the lights from that. Metal halide lights also come in metal and acrylic enclosed hoods that can be hung above your tank or set on top of it.

Power Compact Fluorescent Lights

The easiest of these come installed in a standard strip reflector housing. Use them with a glass canopy or to retrofit a full-hood. Usually though, power compact fluorescents will be purchased in a custom plastic hood. You can hang it above the tank or set it directly on top.

You may now plug in your light unit.

Step 17: Start the Filter System

Choose the instructions that apply to the type of filter system(s) you purchased.

Undergravel Filter

If you have an air-operated undergravel filter, position the air pump outside the aquarium, preferably on a shelf above the water level of the aquarium. This will prevent the possibility of water siphoning back into the electrical portion of the pump during a power outage. If you are going to position the pump lower than the water surface, install check-valves in the main air lines for added safety. Be sure to install them facing in the right direction— narrow end away from the pump.

To connect an undergravel filter system, (A) first connect air lines to the top of the filter stems or to an optional gang-valve. Then (B) use check-valves to prevent water from siphoning during a power outage.

Cut air line tubing to the appropriate lengths, and use it to connect the air pump outlets to the top of the undergravel filter stems. You may need to run the air lines through the holes in the back of your full-hood. Air should flow from the air pump to the check-valves (if any), to the gang-valves (if any), to the lift tubes of the undergravel filter. If you use a gang-valve, hang it on the back of your aquarium and connect the air lines coming from the air pump to the side fittings of the gang-valve. Then connect air line from the top fittings to the undergravel filter stems. Simply snug the tubing over the fittings, leaving enough slack to prevent kinks.

Adjust your gang-valves, if any, so that they are all wide open. Plug in the air pump. Bubbles should now be flowing out all filter outlets. If the flow of air in all outlets is not equal, decreasing flow to the stronger

Something's Fishy

Never allow an air pump to get wet. If you purchased an air-operated filter system, the air pump always goes *outside* the tank.

outlets will divert air to the weaker ones. Adjust as necessary to get strong equal flow from all outlets. If the flow is not equal, your filter may not be working properly—even though it has a strong flow of bubbles. This is because the stronger flowing lift tubes can pull water down the weaker tubes, rather than pulling it through the gravel, where the filtration takes place.

You may need a gang-valve to connect a filter and ornament to the same air pump. (A) air in from pump; (B) air out to filters and other devices; (C) control knobs.

If you use a powerhead instead of an air pump, you will not have to worry about connecting air lines and valves. Since you already installed the powerheads in an earlier step, go ahead and plug in the powerheads. Most powerheads have two adjustments. One controls the amount of water output, and the other controls the amount of air mixed into that water. It is usually best to turn off the air mix in saltwater tanks. This will reduce the amount of salt spray you have to clean.

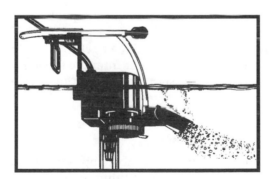

A powerhead can be used instead of an air pump. (courtesy of Rolf C. Hagen Corp., maker of AquaClear powerheads)

Outside Power Filter

Prime the filter by filling the filter box at least half full of water. Then plug in the filter. Give the filter a minute to expel any air remaining in the filter intake tube. It should then begin pumping and filtering the water. The filter will be a bit noisy at first but will quiet down once it expels the remaining air. If your filter has a lid, you can put it on now.

*Fill the outside power filter
with water before plugging
it in.*

Canister Filter

There are as many ways to start canister filters as there are brands, and I certainly don't have room to cover all the options here. So be sure to follow the manufacturer's directions. Here is the method I use, and it works with most brands. I usually find that I have the best luck by starting with no water in the canister and connecting all the hoses. Then I disconnect the output hose near the top of the tank and suck on it to start water siphoning into the unit. Draw hard to remove any air bubbles from the intake side of the hose, or they will break the flow. Keep the hose disconnected until the canister fills with water and water starts coming up the output hose. Then reconnect the output hose.

At this point, plug in the filter and hope for the best. Most filters will start right up. Some will spit and sputter for a minute as they expel trapped air (tilting the unit may help speed the process). Other times, the unit may stall if air gets trapped in the wrong place. If that happens, you may have to empty the water from the filter and start over. Although some canister filters are a bit tricky to start, once operating they tend to be excellent filters.

Fish and Tips

For best circulation, point the exhaust from your undergravel filter stems at the front top center of the tank.

Trickle Filter

"Tricky filter" may be a more appropriate name for this device, because if you set things up wrong, you can get a flood, a burned-out pump, or both. However, here are some general steps for getting a properly installed trickle filter running while allowing a margin of safety. These directions also assume that you have filled the aquarium to the desired water level.

1. Fill the sump with water to within 1 or 2 inches of the top.

2. If you have a hang-on-the-tank overflow, loosen the wingnut or thumbscrew, and lower the slotted skimmer box until water just starts to flow from the tank, through the slots and into the box. Tighten the wingnut. You have just set your desired water level in the tank. Any additional water will overflow into the box and be siphoned back down to the filter.

   If you have through-the-glass plumbing, make sure the top of the overflow tube is right at water level. If you have a reef-ready setup, the height of the divider compartment presets your water level. (Your tank should be filled to this point.)

3. If you have a hang-on-the-tank overflow, fill the outer box with water—but only the empty half of the chamber, not the half with the prefilter sponge. Remove the U-shape siphon

tube and thread an air line into it all the way to the center of the bend. Without removing the air line, replace the siphon tube so that one end is underwater in the notched inner skimmer box and the other end is underwater in the chamber of the outer box. Suck on the other end of the air line to draw the air out of the siphon tube, then remove the air line. Once you're done, water will siphon from the inner box to the outer box. Be sure to leave no air bubbles in the tube.

4. Plug in the pump (the one down in the sump). As water pumps into the tank above from the sump below, it will spill over the slotted skimmer box, be siphoned to the outer box, and then overflow through the prefilter sponge, where it will return to the sump below. As water pumps from the sump to the tank above, two things happen. First, the water level in the tank will increase slightly —by perhaps a quarter inch. Second, the water level in the sump will decrease by several inches.

5. Keep an eye on this process for a few minutes to be sure all is well.

Fish and Tips

Air pumps should be quiet. If yours hums too loud or rattles, you may be restricting the output too much. Also, be sure the pump is not bumping against other objects, creating sympathetic vibrations. Finally, remember that water acts as the muffler for your air pump. So all pumps are noisy when disconnected from their air lines, valves, and outlets.

Something's Fishy

If your water pump is too powerful for the job, use a valve to restrict flow on the output side of the pump. Restricting the intake can cause extra wear on your pump's impeller. It can also cause **cavitation**, which is the formation of air bubbles in a low pressure zone. Cavitation makes the pump noisier, and can cause a buildup of calcium carbonate within your pipes.

Fish and Tips

Your aquarium will never be cooler than room temperature. So if your room is 80°F and you calibrate your heater for 75°F, the tank will still be 80°F, and the heater won't turn on unless the temperature drops below 75°F. Lights and pumps add heat, too. So your tank may be warmer than room temperature, even when the heater is off.

Be sure that the tank doesn't overfill. If it does, your overflow box is probably hooked up incorrectly and the water can't get out. Be sure the siphon tube has no bubbles, and be sure the slotted skimmer box is dropped so that the slots are just below the desired water level.

Be sure that the pump doesn't run dry. This would only happen if the overflow box isn't properly installed or if you have a very large tank and a very small sump. If you have a submerged pump, it should stay submerged at all times. Without water to cool it, it will burn out.

Properly done, your pump will not run dry, and in the event of a power outage, the sump will have safe capacity to handle the small amount of water that backflows.

Once equilibrium is established and you are confident that the tank won't overflow and that the pump won't run dry, take a marker and draw a safety line at the current water level in the sump. Label it "maximum level." (This level should be somewhere between the top of the pump and the level you filled the sump to—before you turned on the pump.) Draw a line at the top of the pump and label it "minimum level."

As evaporation occurs, the water level in the sump will drop. Check daily, and add water to keep the water level in the sump between minimum and maximum. As long as you don't adjust the output of the pump or the level of the notched skimmer box

above, you can safely refill the sump to the marked maximum level without worrying that the sump will overflow in a power outage. Remember, though, that these maximums and minimums apply while the pump is running.

Step 18: Calibrate the Heater

Some of you will have selected a model of submersible heater that has a built-in temperature control scale. If so, you simply dial the temperature you want, plug in the heater, and then check a bit later to make sure everything is functioning as expected.

Fish and Tips

Some hang-on-the-tank heaters have a safety device that prevents the control knob from rotating more than one complete turn at a time. It reduces the amount of damage that can be done if the kids tamper with it. However, if you need to turn more than that, remove the control knob, turn the knob underneath, and reinstall the control knob.

Most of you, though, will need to calibrate your heater by looking at the pilot light and coordinating with your thermometer. The process is a little complicated but straightforward, and once the heater is properly set, it should automatically maintain the proper temperature.

1. First, be sure that your heater has been hanging in the water for about 15 minutes (unplugged). That way, you can be sure the heater parts are the same temperature as the tank water.

2. After the heater has spent at least 15 minutes in the water, plug it in and look for the orange pilot light. If the light is off, the heater is off. If the light is on, the heater is on.

3. If the pilot light is on when you plug in the heater, turn the control knob down (usually counterclockwise) until the light just kicks off.
   If the light is off when you first plug in the heater, turn the control knob up (usually clockwise) until the light just kicks on. This point where the pilot light just kicks on or off is the point that calibrates the heater for the current water temperature.

4. Now take a look at your thermometer and see what the current water temperature is. If the temperature you want is higher or lower than the current temperature, you need to adjust the heater up or down slightly. Check it in an hour to see how you've done, and adjust further if necessary. As an estimate, a one-eighth turn of the dial will usually give a 2° change in temperature.

Use the pilot light to help calibrate your heater.

Step 19: Final Check

At this point, you should be able to clean up your mess. I know you are excited, but give yourself at least 24 hours before buying fish, invertebrates, or live-rock. Patience! Meanwhile, check to make sure that there are no leaks, that the temperature is stable, and that all equipment appears to be working normally. Most important, retest your salinity before you buy livestock, because your last reading may have been taken before all the salts were dissolved. And don't be concerned if the water is a slightly cloudy at first.

Wait 24 hours before buying fish.

The Least You Need to Know

➤ Always read and follow manufacturers' instructions and warranties.

➤ Do not plug in filters and heaters until they are fully installed in water.

➤ Proper temperature is 75° to 78°F (24° to 26°C).

➤ Assemble all equipment and let it run at least 24 hours before buying fish, invertebrates, or live-rock.

➤ Use your hydrometer to retest salinity before you buy any livestock. Your last reading may have been taken before all the salts were dissolved.

Part 3
Your Denizens of the Deep

Get ready for the real fun! No more talk about boring equipment. It was the fish and plants that drew you to the hobby, not the heaters and filters, right?

I start by teaching you how to select compatible species. Then I'll talk about common varieties of fish and invertebrates that can be found in most shops. Finally, you'll end Part 3 by learning how to transport your animals safely home from the store and how to acclimate them to your home aquarium.

Tank A: Clown Fish

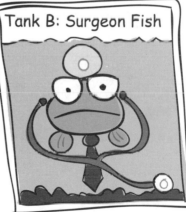

Tank B: Surgeon Fish

Chapter 11

The Principles of Picking Fish

In This Chapter

➤ Considering compatibility

➤ Picking species to fit the environment

➤ Rules to prevent overcrowding

➤ Spotting a healthy animal

I don't know about you, but it wasn't heaters, filters, lights, or air-operated treasure chests that got me interested in keeping an aquarium. No, it wasn't the gadgets. It was the fish. Dazzling, colorful, beautiful fish. You might call me a grouper groupie. So let's stop talking about equipment for a while and get into the fun stuff—the animals. This chapter is all about how to choose fish and invertebrates for your saltwater tank.

There is nothing more fun that going fish shopping. Hundreds of species are available, and your dealer will likely offer so many choices that you will feel like a kid in a candy store. But, like the kid in the candy store whose eyes are bigger than his stomach, you are going to find that your eyes are bigger than your tank and, perhaps, your pocketbook. Yes, shopping for fish is fun, but it is not all that easy. Your tank has so little room and there are so many fish!

There are some things you need to consider before you buy your first batch of animals. You cannot walk into a store and just pick out every cool fish and invertebrate you see, throw them in your tank, and expect success. Well, you could expect that, but you would have to be . . . ahem . . . a complete idiot. I can tell you horror stories about novices who found out the hard way that all fish don't mix. In fact, I think I will tell you one now.

A Horror Story

Recently, I had a customer who was complaining about the quality of livestock he had purchased at another store. So far, he had lost all his fish, replaced them, and lost them again. All this happened in the span of a week. Saltwater fish aren't cheap, so you can understand that he was not in a very good mood.

He was new to the hobby, had never had an aquarium before, and had just set up his first 20-gallon saltwater tank. The man told me that he bought eight fish for his tank the first day—three domino damsels, two maroon clownfish, a yellow wrasse, a Meyer's butterfly, and a lionfish. The clerk at the other shop had happily netted any fish the customer pointed to, without offering any advice.

The man took his fish home, poured them in the tank, and they seemed to be OK. Some swam around, others rested, but nothing seemed out of line—at least, not the first day.

But tomorrow was another day. It started with the maroon clowns. With the exception of mated pairs, they don't like having their own kind around, so one began to bully the other. Whenever it came into sight, it was chased and nipped by the other. Eventually, the poor fish found a spot out of sight behind a piece of artificial coral. But how was poor Mr. Clownfish supposed to know that the domino damsels had claimed that coral head for their home?

So, Mr. Clownfish's badly beaten body was found later, lying dead on the bottom, its eyes eaten out by. . . well, by just about any fish with lips. (I don't know why it is, but the eyeballs of a dead fish seem to be something of a delicacy to most live fish. Go figure. Probably they look like little fishy candies or something. Come to think of it, they look a bit like maki sushi, which I can personally attest is deliciously good stuff.)

Soon, evening came. If you check Webster's Dictionary, you'll see that *evening* is defined as "the time when yellow wrasses become active, and lionfish discover that yellow wrasses are even tastier than a dead fish's eyeballs." What? You don't believe me? Well, go look it up. Anyway, poor Mr. Wrasse soon discovered what the inside of a lionfish's stomach looks like and was never seen again.

Noticing that the wrasse was missing and that the lionfish seemed unusually fat, the customer realized his mistake. He decided to feed everyone heavier to try to prevent it from happening again. Maybe if everyone was well fed, they'd leave their tankmates alone.

The following day, the remaining clownfish disappeared, and on the third day, a damsel turned up missing. Of the eight original inhabitants, only one lionfish and two damselfish were left.

The lionfish died for no apparent reason on the fourth day, and even the two remaining damsels didn't look well. Their fins were clamped, and they were gasping in a corner at the surface. They were damsels in distress.

The remaining damsels died on the fifth day. You see, even without predators present, eight fish was way too many for starting a 20-gallon tank. They excrete too much ammonia for an aquarium that size, and the extra-heavy feedings made things worse.

Frustrated, but undeterred, the customer went back to the store, bought four replacement fish, and lost them all within a day—victims of the same high ammonia levels. So he decided to give us a try, and here we are.

Enough of this horror story. It is easy to see that these problems could have been prevented if the customer had taken time to educate himself before buying fish, and if the dealer had taken time to be sure the customer knew the basics. Compatible species would have been chosen, and the tank wouldn't have been overcrowded. OK, so how can you pick fish that will mix?

Something's Fishy

Never buy an animal until you know what it eats, how large it grows, and whether or not it will get along with tankmates.

Be Prepared

Do your homework. Before you buy any species of fish or invertebrate, read up on it. Learn its quirks. Does it have a special diet? Does it get along well with others? In the next chapter I'll talk about some popular species that will normally mix. The more you know, the fewer mistakes you will make.

A good dealer will ask about your tank before he sells you anything to go in it. If he doesn't ask, tell him anyway. Let him know what size tank you have, how long it has been established, and what species (if any) are already present. Take full advantage of your dealer's expertise. Before the salesperson nets each fish for you, be sure that he takes a moment to describe its nature and considers if it will be compatible with its future tankmates. Also, don't forget to ask what diet is appropriate.

Remember, though, that the best your dealer can do for you is give an educated opinion based on the norm for that species. He cannot guarantee compatibility. Ultimately, it is up to the fish to decide if they are compatible or not. Even a peaceful species will have the occasional criminal individual. Be sure to check out Chapter 23 on dealing with aggression.

Can't We All Just Get Along?

Unfortunately, no. We can't. Neither can fish. While most marine species carried by your dealer will mix, you can't just throw every fish that interests you into the same tank and expect them all to get along. Fish sometimes fight, and when they do, they usually have good reason. They may be protecting their home territory from intruders, protecting their young from predators, driving off mate-stealing rivals, or just reserving a favorite sleeping spot.

Fish and Tips

Sometimes, your dealer will tell you if a fish is peaceful or aggressive right on the price tag stuck to the tank.

While there is no way to list easy rules for choosing compatible species, I will cover some general concepts. I'll also try to cover more species-specific compatibility traits in the next two chapters. Don't be afraid to ask your dealer for guidance, and check out the recommended reading list at the end of this book for some titles that carry more details on individual species.

Little Fish Equals Big Snack

It is a basic law of nature that big fish eat little fish. Even big peaceful fish eat little fish. Choosing tankmates of similar size is usually sufficient to guard against this—but not always. Don't just look at the overall size of the fish. Consider the size of the fish's mouth, too. Squirrelfish, anglers, and others can eat a tankmate that is almost the same size as themselves. Very few of the animals sold in the local shop are adult size, either. So be sure to allow for growth. An inch-long clown trigger can grow to a foot in length.

Likewise, fish prey on invertebrates and invertebrates may be dangerous to fish. A longnose butterfly fish may happily snarf down your featherduster worms, and a sea anemone can sting a longnose butterfly to death without even thinking about it. Drop an attractive new snail into your tank and a wrasse may make escargot out of it before it ever hits the bottom. Everybody likes seafood.

Big fish eat little fish. Even big peaceful fish eat little fish.

Smart Fish Stay in Schools

While some fish are territorial, many are fin-loose and fancy-free. They go where the currents take them, and home is where they hang their . . . uh . . . well, not their hats. Fish don't have hats. Not even the highhat or black-cap basslet.

Hanging out in gangs is a natural form of protection. When fish form a school (some people call it a shoal), it's because they know that it's hard for a predator to single out and track a particular individual. The individual has a better chance of going unnoticed by blending into the crowd. Fish that are in schools are almost always on the go. Schools of fish add action to your tank, yet schools of fish are relaxing to watch.

Fish Tales

Basslets of the genus *Pseudanthias* live in large groups, with a single male dominating a harem of females. Interestingly, all *Pseudanthias* start life as females. The largest, most dominant fish becomes a male, and if it dies or disappears the largest female will change into a male to replace him.

But fish behave differently under different circumstances. For example, a school of yellow tangs can come drifting by the reef, peacefully nibbling algae and bothering nary a soul. But yellow tangs don't always live in schools. Sometimes they split off and travel as pairs. In the aquarium, we usually just keep a single yellow tang in a tank. In that situation, the fish tends to settle down and stake out a territory, and may defend it readily. Without the protection of the group, the fish takes charge of its own defense and, indeed, may become aggressive.

Fish that like to school will be happier when kept that way. Unfortunately, it is a rare aquarium that is large enough to keep a school of anything but the smallest species. You just can't fit 50 yellow tangs in a household aquarium. For a school to function as designed, you need a large group. When the group is large, everyone depends on safety in numbers, and aggression is limited. Just as the predator cannot easily pick out an individual, neither can the other individuals.

However, when those numbers diminish—when the group is small—a pecking order develops. If you put three yellow tangs in an aquarium, you will likely see just that. One fish will be at the bottom of the pecking order and will eventually die of harassment. Then the next fish in the chain becomes the new guy at the bottom. The same thing repeats until one fish is left. And that is why we usually keep just one yellow tang per tank.

Are You Calling Me Yellow?

Some fish just don't like others of their kind. One lemonpeel angel may continually harass another lemonpeel angel that is placed in the same tank. It may also harass yellow angels, yellow tangs, or yellow longnose butterflies. Why? Because their color patterns are similar enough to elicit a territorial response.

Many species will challenge other individuals of their own species or species with similar markings. It is usually safe to mix several species of butterfly fish in a tank—as long as they don't look similar and as long as you have only one per species. A vagabond butterfly and a long-nose butterfly look quite different and will usually mix. A vagabond and an auriga butterfly look more similar and may not.

It Eats What?

Diet is an important consideration when buying marine tropical fish and invertebrates. Almost all these animals are wild-caught, and many have diets that consist solely of specific organisms—organisms that may not be available for you to feed them. For example, Moorish idol butterfly fish feed almost solely on live coral polyps and sponges. The rock beauty angel prefers a diet high in sponges. Many colorful sea slugs eat only specific species of hydrozoan, sponge, or gorgonian. Your dealer may receive animals in his shipment whose diets are completely unknown and even impossible to achieve in the aquarium. Those animals are doomed to death by starvation.

Besides ensuring that you can provide the right diet for new additions, be sure that they don't eat critters you already have in the tank. This is especially true of aquariums that mix fish and invertebrates. The species of fish that are safe to mix in a reef tank are more limited because of this.

Dig That Crazy Fish

When you choose fish and invertebrates, you must also consider their habits. Many like to go underground. Jawfish build burrows, and it is entertaining to watch them poke out their big heads. Flounders not only bury in the sand but also can change the color of their skin to match it. This makes them nearly invisible, even when they're above ground. When wrasses are frightened or when they want to sleep, they often dive into the sand and go underground. It seems like there ought to be a joke here about your wrasse and a hole in the ground.

Your aquarium's tenants don't just need to be compatible with one another—they also need to be compatible with your decorations. Many invertebrates dig, as well. Serpent stars may come out at feeding time, but the rest of the time they will be hiding unseen beneath the rocks and decorations. Be careful, because many lobsters and crabs can excavate to the point that your reef structure collapses. Anyway, if you pick too many animals of this type, you may have a very boring tank because everyone will be hidden from view.

Day Shift and Night Shift

You can have a tank full of peaceful, beautiful fish, but if they are never out when you are around, how much fun would that be? The answer is not much, unless you are really easily entertained. When choosing species, consider whether they are diurnal or nocturnal. Fortunately, most marine fish species available are active during the day. Even the species that are nocturnal in the wild tend to adapt to daytime feeding schedules.

How Many Pesos for That Pisces?

Believe it or not, a brand new, sparkling clean tank is rougher on fish than an established, dirty aquarium. (Check out Chapter 15 on cycling your aquarium to see why.) Because of this, I recommend that you start with cheaper, hardier species to cycle your new tank. You can add the more delicate or pricier fish a bit later.

If you are wondering why saltwater fish cost more than freshwater fish, it is because almost all are wild-caught, as opposed to being farm-raised. Most species are quite adept at diving into holes in the reef to avoid capture, too. Fish collecting is not easy. Some species come from deep water. A diver may have to spend hours decompressing as a result of spending only a few minutes collecting in deep water. This adds to the cost of the fish.

Fish School

With **diurnal** animals, lights out means time to zonk out. **Nocturnal** animals party all night and sleep all day.

Fish and Tips

Damsels are inexpensive, hardy fish that are ideal for cycling a new tank. There are many colorful choices, and most run around $5 each.

Don't Pack Them Like Sardines

Assuming that you purchase only compatible species, how many fish will fit in your tank? That's a tough question, and you may get many different answers. Here are some common guidelines that often make the rounds:

➤ You need 24 square inches of water surface for each 1-inch length of fish.

➤ Don't keep more than 1 inch of fish per 2 gallons of water.

➤ One typical size fish needs 3 to 5 gallons of water.

If you look at that first guideline, you will see that an aquarium that is 12 inches wide by 24 inches long by 16 inches high would give you 288 square inches of water surface (length times width). Take 288 and divide by 24 (as stated in the rule), and you will see that you could keep 12 inches of fish in that tank. So 12 1-inch fish or 6 2-inch fish would be about right. Either way, it's a total of 12 inches of fish.

Fish School

There are two ways to measure fish length. **Standard length** is the length from tip of nose to base of tail (excluding the tail fin). **Total length** is measured from tip of nose to tip of tail. Use standard length to determine how many fish will fit in your tank.

The second rule is more commonly quoted. According to it, you could put 10 1-inch or 5 2-inch fish in a 20-gallon tank. The dimensions of the tank that I quoted in the previous guideline happen to be for a tank that size, so you can see that both rules give similar numbers.

However, the third rule is my favorite. Allowing 3 to 5 gallons of water per fish—3 gallons for 1-inch fish and 5 gallons for 2- to 3-inch fish—means that a 20-gallon tank would hold 4 to 6 typical marine fish. I think this is a more reasonable number. Rules based on surface-area-per-inch-of-fish don't account for the difference in volume between tall tanks and short tanks, and an inches-per-gallon rule doesn't account for the mass of the fish.

However, even the 3- to 5-gallons-per-fish rule has its limitations, as you are about to see.

Broken Rules

All the guidelines I just gave you assume that you are keeping small fish. The larger the fish, the less accurate those guidelines become. Here is why. The rules only consider the length of the fish, but when a fish grows, its height and breadth change, too. In fact, when a fish doubles its length, it is increasing its mass and volume about eight times. Technically, any change in length will cube the change in mass or volume of the fish. Following is a conversion chart to illustrate this for you. Notice how rapidly the change occurs.

Fish Tales

Dealers usually keep their tanks a lot more crowded than the rules allow. Most dealers can do this safely, though, because they have central filtration systems on their tanks. These systems connect each tank to a larger volume of water that is out of sight. This water circulates, via plumbing to each tank, 24 hours a day. The central filtration system also allow the dealer to do *daily* partial water changes on every tank. In other words, your dealer is a skilled professional. Don't try to crowd fish like this at home.

Fish Mass

Fish Length	Equivalent In 1-Inch Fish	How Many Gallons Per Fish This Size?
1 inch	1	2
2 inches	8	3
3 inches	27	5
4 inches	64	8
5 inches	125	10
6 inches	216	15*
7 inches	343	20*
8 inches	512	30*
9 inches	729	35*
10 inches	1,000	40*
11 inches	1,331	45*
12 inches	1,728	50*
24 inches	13,824	Are you crazy?

* These figures assume that you will make weekly partial water changes. Otherwise, waste will build up too quickly.

If you compare the difference between the mass of 24 1-inch fish (24) and 1 24-inch fish (13,824), you can see why an inches-per-gallon rule may not work. You may need to allow for the shape of a fish in making your calculations, too. For example, a 24-inch eel probably has the mass of an 8- or 10-inch fish that's shaped more like a fish.

By the way, don't forget to allow for growth. A fish that is 1 inch long today may be 4 inches long in a month or a foot long in a year.

Hold Your Seahorses

Despite all that talk about how many fish you can put in your tank, there is just one more small detail. Those guidelines don't apply. . . yet. Your tank won't hold that many fish when you first set it up. In fact, you should not put more than 1 inch of fish per 10 gallons in a new tank. That's because the tank is not yet cycled. The helpful bacteria that break down ammonia and other fish waste are not yet present. See Chapter 15 on cycling your new tank for full details. It's *very* important.

That's Sick!

It's important to pick compatible fish, but it's even more important to pick healthy compatible fish. It only takes one sick fish to infect a whole aquarium, and if that aquarium is a reef tank you are in double trouble—because the most common medications are not safe to use with live corals and invertebrates.

Don't overcrowd. Allow 3 to 5 gallons of water for a typical 3-inch fish. Cycle a new tank with only 1 inch of fish per 10 gallons.

Tip-Top Fish

So let's look at some signs that indicate a fish is healthy. In Chapter 22 on stress and disease, I'll tell you how to spot a fish that is sick.

➤ **Clear eyes.** These are a good sign. Note, however, that I am talking about the cornea of the eye. Some species, such as boxfish and puffers, have a reflective membrane inside the pupil, which may make the eye look cloudy inside. That is normal for those species.

➤ **Bright, even colors.** Healthy fish display full colors. There should be no unusual discoloration or bloody patches.

➤ **Good body weight.** Avoid fish with hollow bellies and bent spines. Before you buy a fish, ask to see it eat.

➤ **Erect fins.** Watch the way fish hold their fins. Healthy fish usually keep their fins fairly erect. They'll spread them even more when courting a mate or displaying to mark territory. This doesn't always hold true for inactive species, though.

➤ **Smooth, untorn fins.** These are also a sign of a healthy fish. Ragged edges may be a sign of disease or a sign that the fish has been bullied. Split fins are usually the results of fights. A split fin or two is not usually a big deal. Split fins heal quickly.

➤ **Behavior and coloration that is normal for the species.** For example, if a species likes to school, avoid the specimen hanging in the corner away from the rest of the group.

➤ **Level of activity.** Does the fish show an interest in life? Avoid lethargic specimens of normally active species, but be aware that it is normal behavior for many fish to sit there and do nothing most of the time.

You know your tank is too crowded when . . .

. . . you toss in just one more fish and it bounces.

. . . you toss in just one more fish and the others toss it back.

. . . you toss in just one more fish and the floor sags.

. . . you can turn the lights on and the bottom is still dark.

. . . you remove all of the fish and the water level drops 75 percent.

. . . sardine cans begin to look roomy.

. . . you can't do a 25 percent water change without the fish on top getting dry.

. . . all of the fish swim to one side of the tank and the other side rises an inch.

. . . only a filter made by Boeing can handle the job.

. . . you can do a 50 percent water change with a thimble.

. . . your ammonia-eating bacteria have grown to 5 pounds each.

. . . your fish beg you to flush them down the toilet.

. . . the cat walks across the top of the aquarium and you have no lid on it.

If fish show signs of stress or illness, avoid them. You may not want to purchase healthy looking fish from that tank, either—in case they are already infected. Particularly, avoid tanks that contain dead fish. Note the color of the water in the tank. Discolored water probably means that the fish are sick and that the tank is under medication.

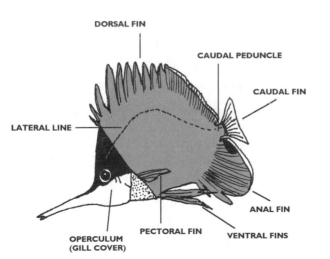

Anatomy of a fish.

Healthy Invertebrates

The same basic rules apply to choosing healthy invertebrates, except that you won't be checking fins for signs of damage. Instead, you'll be inspecting legs, claws, antennae, shells, tentacles, and other appropriate body parts.

➤ Starfish with sores should never be purchased. Infected animals seldom survive. A missing bit of leg on a serpent or brittle star is not usually a problem, though. They grow back readily.

➤ Clams and scallops should have no large gaps between the meaty part of the body and the shell. The animal should be able to close up quickly and tightly.

➤ Crabs and shrimps with a leg or two missing are probably not a big deal. Legs will regenerate when the crab sheds its shell.

➤ Sea anemones should show no damage. One small tear or infection can rapidly kill them. When anemones die, they melt into a smelly ball of mucous that is no fun to remove. Anemones should display fully and retract on contact.

➤ Corals should show no signs of infection, and tentacles should be freely displayed. Polyps should contract on contact.

Enough about how to pick fish and invertebrates. Let's move on to the next chapters, where you can decide which ones to pick.

The Least You Need to Know

➤ Big fish eat little fish. Even big peaceful fish eat little fish.

➤ Be sure you know if a species is compatible with the other fish you have before you buy it. Ask your dealer for advice.

➤ Don't forget to ask if the fish needs a special diet.

➤ Consider whether the species is active at night or during the day.

➤ Keep species that like to school in small groups.

➤ Allow 10 gallons of water for each inch of fish while you cycle your new tank. After the tank cycles, 3 to 5 gallons each will be right for most fish.

Chapter 12

Popular Fish for Beginners

In This Chapter

➤ The difference between common and scientific names

➤ Brief descriptions of popular, hardy species

➤ Recommended algae-eaters and scavengers

There are hundreds of species of fantastic marine tropical fish available to the aquarium trade, but it is not within the scope of this book to show you all of them. There are entire atlases of marine species available. These books are not cheap, but they are loaded with color photos and detailed information about individual species. See the recommended reading list in Appendix C for suggestions on further reading.

For now, though, let's focus on species that are readily available, relatively easy to keep, and usually compatible. I'll discuss the major groups of marine aquarium fishes, and I'll even give you a list of popular varieties that are good choices for the beginning marine hobbyist.

Name That Fish

Before I tell you about some good choices of species for your new tank, I want to fill you in on the difference between common names and scientific names.

The *scientific name* is the standardized Latin name for a species. It is a name that has been agreed upon by the scientific community and is universal. In every country and every language, educated people will know what species you mean when you use the standardized Latin scientific name. For example, the scientific name *Paracanthurus hepatus* belongs to a fish sometimes called the blue surgeonfish. Normally, the scientific name will never change, but as science progresses there are a few instances where fish get reclassified.

Fish School

The scientific name consists of two parts: genus and species. The first part of the name is the **genus** and usually represents a group of related fish. For example, the common varieties of dwarf angels are of the genus **Centropyge.** The genus is followed by the **species** name, which is unique for that variety of fish. For example, **Centropyge heraldi** is the yellow angel and **Centropyge loriculus** is the flame angel.

The *common name* or *trade name* of a fish is the name it will go by in the local stores. It is the name you are more likely to know the fish by and the name most people will use. In the United States the common name will be in English. Elsewhere it may be French, Spanish, or whatever. The thing about common names is that they are not standardized. For example, the blue surgeonfish that I just mentioned is also known as the blue tang, the yellowtail tang, the flagtail surgeon, the hippo tang, the liver tang, the palette tang, and probably some other names that I have overlooked. Worse, there is another, unrelated species that is also called the blue tang. Common names vary by country, region, dealer, and local custom.

Normally, you only need to concern yourself with the common name. However, if you get to a point where you want your dealer to find something exotic for you, it may help to know the scientific name. To make things even more confusing (or maybe less), you will sometimes find that the scientific name is part of the common name—for example, gold anthias, auriga butterfly, and navarchus angel. In all those cases, the word that's hard to say is part of the scientific name.

Anyway, in the descriptions of individual species, I will list both the scientific name and as many common names as pop into my mind. I'll even be sweet and give you the pronunciations of the more difficult common names. If you want to learn proper pronunciation of the scientific names, though, I suggest you take a course in Latin.

Fishes for the Community Tank

Here are some popular fishes for the marine aquarium. Unless I state otherwise, these species will fare quite well in a fish-only setup. I'll make note of species that are also safe for reefs.

Angelfish

Marine angels are always popular, particularly the dwarf angels of the genus *Centropyge,* which rarely grow over 4 inches long in the aquarium. (Many other angelfish species can easily reach more than a foot in length.)

As angels are territorial and fight amongst themselves, it is best to keep no more than one of any particular species. If you do mix angelfish species, pick ones that look quite different from one another to decrease the likelihood of your angel turning into a devil.

Angels will take most foods offered, but there are some "angel formula" frozen foods on the market that are especially good choices because they contain marine sponges—an important component of the angel's diet in the wild. Angelfish are usually poor choices for the reef tank, as they eat most invertebrates.

➤ **Coral beauty angel** *(Centropyge bispinosus)*. This is probably the most popular angel, due to its bright colors, hardiness, and low price. Colors vary greatly in individuals, but general coloration is a dark background ranging from blue to violet to black, with a foreground vertically striped in orange or yellow-orange. These fish are native to the Indo-Pacific.

A coral beauty angel.

➤ **Half-black angel** *(C. vrolicki)*. Pearl on the front half, black on the back half, this is an inexpensive, hardy fish. It's also native to the Indo-Pacific.

➤ **Flame angel** *(C. loriculus)*. This is one of the most beautiful fishes. The body is bright red-orange. The sides have a large yellow field with vertical black stripes. This fish hails from Hawaii and the Indo-Pacific. A few aquarists have reported success keeping flame angels in a reef tank. Others have seen them nip bits off corals and anemones.

➤ **Yellow angel** *(C. heraldi)* and **lemonpeel angel** *(C. flavissimus)*. These two fish are quite similar in appearance and care. The cheaper yellow angel tends to be a bit more mustard-yellow in color, while the lemonpeel is a brighter yellow with a blue eye ring and a blue edge to the gill plate. These two are Indo-Pacific natives.

147

➤ **Cherub angel** *(C. argi)*. This Caribbean angel is one of the smallest of the dwarf angels. Most specimens available are only about an inch in length. This fish has a yellow face and a blue body. Also called the pygmy angel, it is one of the few angelfish that is safe for a reef tank. The similar **resplendent angel** *(C. resplendens)* of the Indo-Pacific has a yellow dorsal stripe and a blue body.

➤ **French angel** *(Pomacanthus paru)* and **gray angel** *(P. arcuatus)*. These two Caribbean species are quite similar. The juveniles are of special interest, due to their unusual shape and striking coloration—black with yellow vertical stripes. Adults lose the stripes and turn more gray. Adults grow to over 12 inches and are too large for most tanks.

Something's Fishy

The Caribbean rock beauty angel *(Holacanthus tricolor)* and the similar Indo–Pacific bicolor angel *(Centropyge bicolor)* are commonly seen but are poor choices. They require a diet rich in marine sponges and rarely survive long in captivity.

➤ **Blue angel** *(Holacanthus isabelita)* and **queen angel** *(H. ciliaris)* are two more Caribbean species that resemble each other. Juveniles have a fair amount of yellow in the body and light blue vertical stripes, which will disappear in adulthood. Adults are blue-gray with yellow scallops on the scale edges. Adults can be more than a foot long.

➤ **Emperor angel** *(Pomacanthus imperator)* and **koran angel** *(P. semicirculatus)*. As juveniles, these two Indo-Pacific species are similarly, and spectacularly, marked with rounded blue, white, and yellow stripes against a black background. Adults look quite different. The adult koran angel doesn't impress me much, but the adult emperor has a spectacular pattern of its own, with a black mask and chest band, yellow tail, and horizontally striped body. These fish can grow to 16 inches.

Although lovely, this rock beauty angel would probably not survive very long in your tank.

Angels to avoid: The regal angel *(Pygoplites diacanthus)*, the rock beauty *(Holacanthus tricolor)*, the bicolor angel *(Centropyge bicolor)*, and Potter's angel *(C. potteri)* are species that are often available in shops, but their specialized dietary requirements usually doom them in the aquarium.

Basslets

Dottybacks, also known by their scientific name *Pseudochromis*, are highly colorful and stay small (under 4 inches, in most cases). They fare best in a reef tank with lots of hiding holes. Dottybacks mix with most species but are vicious to one another. Never keep more than one dottyback of any species per tank.

They come from the Indo-Pacific, but a few species are now tank-raised. Dottybacks eat all foods, but a varied diet is required to keep colors from fading.

➤ **Diadema dottyback** *(Pseudochromis diadema)*, pronounced *sue-doh-KROH-mis dye-uh-DEE-muh*. Also called the purple-and-yellow pseudochromis, it has a magenta stripe down the back and a yellow body.

➤ **Magenta dottyback** *(P. porphyreus)* and **orchid dottyback** *(P. fridmani)*. Both of these are bright magenta. The magenta has clear fins, while the orchid has purple fins. Both sometimes sell under the name purple pseudochromis.

➤ **Royal dottyback** *(P. paccagnellae)*. The front half is purple, and the rear half is yellow. It's also known as the bicolor pseudochromis.

Grammas are similar to dottybacks, but are from the Caribbean. Care is the same, although they are a bit less aggressive.

➤ **Royal gramma** *(Gramma loreto)*. One of the most popular aquarium species, this fish resembles the royal dottyback. The change in color from purple to yellow is more graduated, though.

➤ **Black-cap basslet** *(Gramma melacara)*. This bright purple fish with its black forehead comes from deep water. That makes it harder to collect, and therefore, pricier.

Fairy basslets, which are usually sold as anthias (pronounced *AN-thee-us*), are planktivores. That means that in the wild they eat plankton—a collection of microscopic orgamisms, including algae, that drift in great clouds in the ocean. Hovering above the reef, they dart out for any foods that pass by. Frequent feedings are important. While they accept most foods, regular inclusion of live and frozen foods will get the best results. Anthias are best kept as a single male with a small harem of females (two or three, at least). Most grow to around 5 inches in the aquarium. Please do not try to keep these spectacular fish unless you are willing to keep them in groups and give them some room. Anything under a 55-gallon tank would be a poor choice. They

Royal gramma basslet.

can be kept in reef or fish-only setups. Some popular choices, both from the Indo-Pacific, are:

➤ **Lyretail anthias** *(Pseudanthias squamipinnis).* The males are pink overall, with a lyretail and a couple of extended rays at the front of the dorsal fin. Females are golden. This sexual dimorphism often causes them to be sold as separate species, with males being called pink or lyretail anthias, while the females are sold as gold anthias.

➤ **Square anthias** *(Pseudanthias pleurotaenia).* Color varies in this species, but males are usually pink with a large purple square on their side. Females are more solid yellow and may be sold as gold anthias.

Batfish

There are several species of batfish available, but only the **orbiculate bat** *(Platax orbicularis)* fares well in the aquarium. Beginners should avoid the other species. Juvenile "orbic" bats are common and inexpensive. Their leaflike colors and winglike fins make them tempting. Too bad they turn plain gray, get short stubby fins, and grow to 20 inches as adults. So unless you want to end up with one big ugly fish, avoid these.

Blennies

This delightful group of fish tends to be quite peaceful and stays small. Most are great choices for the reef aquarium and tend to be happier there. Being on the small side, blennies are often reclusive. Except when food is near, a head peeking out of a hole in the rock may be all you see.

Most aquarium species are Indo-Pacific. Blennies accept most foods. Some species are excellent algae-eaters.

➤ **Forktail blenny** *(Meiacanthus atrodorsalis)*. Most blennies kept in the aquarium are sedentary, but not this one.

➤ **Algae-eating blenny** *(Salarias fasciatus)*. Especially popular in reef aquariums, this mottled brown fish is fine for the fish-only tank, too—as long as you provide enough food.

Something's Fishy

Boxfish, cowfish, and trunkfish can excrete a toxin into the water when they are stressed. This toxin is capable of killing everything in the tank, including the fish that excreted it. I've never seen that happen, but is it worth the risk?

The algae-eating blenny is popular in reef aquariums.

Boxfish, Cowfish, and Trunkfish

Found in both the Caribbean and the Indo-Pacific, these species resemble puffers and porcupine fish, but have hard, noninflatable bodies and tiny mouths. The beginning hobbyist should probably avoid these, as they don't take flakes well and will starve if not offered enough small live foods.

This is a Boston bean boxfish (Ostracion cubicus).

Butterflyfish

Marine butterflies tend to be delicate. Many have highly specialized diets that cannot be met in the aquarium. For example, many species feed almost solely on live corals. Even the hardiest butterfly species may not be the best choice for beginners.

In the wild, butterflies tend to be found in pairs or large schools. In the aquarium, keeping more than a single specimen of a species tends to result in territorial disputes. Often, other nonsimilar-looking species of butterflies will be tolerated in the same tank.

Butterflyfish are poor choices for reef tanks, as they prey on many of the invertebrates. If you try butterflies, use lots of live and frozen foods. Flake foods will not suffice. Here are the hardiest species:

➤ **Yellow longnose butterfly** *(Forcipiger flavissimus)*. Hardy, attractive, popular, these fish are great choices, although their long noses make it easy for them to decimate tubeworms in a reef aquarium. They hail from the Indo-Pacific.

➤ **Heniochus butterfly** *(Heniochus spp.)*, pronounced *hen-ee-OH-kuss*. The common names bannerfish or wimplefish come from the long trailing dorsal fin, but these names are rarely used in the aquarium trade. These are very hardy Indo-Pacific fish. The black and white striped heniochus *(H. acuminatus)* is often called "the poor man's Moorish idol" for its resemblance to the Moorish idol *(Zanclus canescens)*—a beautiful fish that is very difficult to keep in captivity. The brown heniochus *(H. varius)* is also sometimes available.

➤ **Spotfin butterfly** *(Chaetodon auriga)*. Also called the auriga butterfly, this is a hardy Indo-Pacific species. The base color is crosshatched white with a yellow back and a prominent dorsal spot. Adults have long tips on the dorsal fin, which also earns them the common name of threadfin butterfly.

➤ **Raccoon butterfly** *(C. lunula)*. One of the hardiest butterflies, this Indo-Pacific species is yellow with a black band through the eye.

The raccoon butterfly.

➤ **Punctato butterfly** *(C. punctatofasciatus)*. Also called the dot-dash butterfly, this Indo-Pacific fish is yellow overall, with black spots and banding. The base of the tail is orange.

Beginners should probably avoid any butterfly not mentioned in this list, as most are difficult fish to keep. The blue-stripe butterfly *(Chaetodon fremblii)*, the ocellate butterfly *(C. ocellatus)*, the ornate butterfly *(C. ornatissimus)*, and the blue-spot butterfly *(C. plebeius)* have extremely low survival rates in captivity, due to dietary requirements that cannot be met.

Cardinalfish

The large-eyed, wide-mouthed cardinalfish tend to be more active at night. During the day they like to hide in caves. However, they are quite hardy and adapt to a daytime feeding schedule. Most will eventually learn to take flakes, but live and frozen foods are still a requirement.

Cardinals are mouthbrooders and commonly spawn in the aquarium. If your fish seems to have a distended chin and lower jawline, it is probably incubating eggs. They will not eat while incubating. Cardinals work well in both fish-only and reef setups.

➤ **Pajama cardinal** *(Sphaeramia nematoptera)*. When you see the unusual markings on this Indo-Pacific fish, you will see where it got its name.

➤ **Flame cardinal** *(Apogon maculatus)*. An attractive red Caribbean species.

➤ **Banggai cardinal** *(Pterapogon kauderni)*. A relative newcomer to the trade, this strikingly marked fish was popular from the start. These fish are Indo-Pacific, and many aquarists have reported breeding them. Kaudern's cardinal is another name used in the trade.

This is the banggai cardinal.

Catfish

Only one species of marine catfish is typically seen in the trade—the boldly striped **coral cat** *(Plotosus lineatus)*. It is an inexpensive and hardy fish, best kept in groups. The spines are venomous, so be very careful handling this fish. Although schools of coral cats hang out near the bottom of the tank, they are not scavengers.

Clownfish

Clownfish, also called anemonefish, are amongst the most popular of marine fish. They have bright colors and are quite hardy. Tank-raised specimens are readily available, too. Clowns are specialized members of the damselfish family that take up residence with host sea anemones (pronounced *uh-NEM-uh-nees*). The stinging tentacles of the sea anemone are dangerous and deadly to most species, but the clownfish is able to live safely among them. In exchange for the protection, the anemone benefits by eating bits of food retrieved by the fish.

In the wild, clowns are never found far from their host anemone. In the aquarium, they are best enjoyed in a reef tank with a host anemone, but will work in a fish-only tank, too. Be careful, though. The little devils like to guard their homes and will often nip your hand when you are working in the tank. One clownfish where I work often has fibers of algae scrubber pad stuck between its teeth from attacking the algae pad during maintenance.

Clowns accept all foods readily. Never mix more than one species of clown per tank, and of that single species, keep only one or two fish. Clownfish come from the Indo-Pacific.

If you buy two small clownfish of the same species, you will be guaranteed to end up with a mated pair. Juvenile clowns are sexually immature and are hermaphrodites. In a group, the most dominant fish grows largest and becomes a female. The second most dominant fish grows a bit less and becomes a male. The rest remain small immatures. Now here's where it really gets wacky. If the female dies, the male will change into a female and the most dominant immature fish will become the new male. Clowns can change from immature to male to female, but the path is not reversible.

Fish School

Clowns are **protandrous hermaphrodites,** which means "first male, both sexes." It is a fancy way of saying that all young clownfish mature first into males but can later change to females.

➤ **Tomato clownfish** *(Amphiprion frenatus)* and **cinnamon clown** *(A. melanopus)* are similar species. The background color ranges from orange to red. There may be a central black patch. Tomato clowns will accept most Indo-Pacific anemones as hosts.

This male tomato clownfish carefully guards his eggs, which have been laid neatly at the base of his host sea anemone. The white dots in the egg mass are the eyes of the soon-to-hatch fry.

➤ **Percula clownfish** *(A. percula)* is less commonly seen in the aquarium trade, but a similar and very common species, *A. ocellaris,* is often mistakenly sold as the percula clown. These fish have bold vertical orange and white stripes. Percula

155

clowns will accept most Indo-Pacific anemones as hosts. By the way, I've heard this fish's name pronounced several ways, but *per-KOO-luh* seems most popular.

➤ **Clark's clownfish** *(A. clarkii)* is commonly sold as the sebae clown, but the true sebae clown, *A. sebae,* is rarely seen in the aquarium trade. Colors range from mustard to brown to black with white vertical stripes. The mustard or brown specimens are often sold as sebae clowns, while the black specimens are usually correctly marked as Clark's clowns. These clowns will accept most Indo-Pacific anemones as hosts.

➤ **Maroon clownfish** *(Premnas biaculeatus)* are the most aggressive of the clownfish—particularly toward one another. Only mated pairs will tolerate each other. Others of the same species will usually be killed. Maroon clowns are also the pickiest when it comes to choosing a species of host anemone. The bubble-tip anemone, *Entacmea quadricolor,* is the only species readily accepted, although I have in rare instances seen maroon clowns choose other Indo-Pacific anemone species.

Chromis and Damselfish

Closely related to the clownfish, some species of damselfish have symbiotic relationships with anemones, too—but only as juveniles. Damselfish are the hardiest of marine fish and are inexpensive, making them ideal starter fish for cycling a new aquarium. They are often a bit aggressive, though.

Damsels are usually not good choices for the reef tank, as they may bother corals and other invertebrates. Chromis, however, are usually quite safe for the reef. They live more of an open water existence and tend to hang out closer to the surface. Chromis and damsels accept all foods readily. All species listed in this section are Indo-Pacific unless specified otherwise.

➤ **Three-stripe damsel** *(Dascyllus aruanus)* and **four-stripe damsel** *(D. melanurus)* are similar species, both with bold black and white vertical stripes.

➤ **Domino damsel** *(D. trimaculatus).* Also called the three-spot damsel, this fish is black with white spots. The spots shrink and may disappear as the fish matures. The similar **Hawaiian three-spot damsel,** *(D. albisella)* is occasionally offered.

➤ **Blue devil** *(Chrysiptera cyanea).* Several species are sold as blue damsels or blue devils. Their ornery temperament is the origin of the name. The fish are an overall iridescent blue. Some have blue color in the fins; some don't. The Fiji blue devil is of special interest, as the males are solid blue, including fins, and have a yellow edge to the tail. I've had success keeping them in reef tanks, too.

This is a three-stripe damselfish.

➤ **Yellow-tail blue damsel (Pomacentrus caeruleus).** Again, several species are sold under this name. They have blue bodies and yellow tails, and some have yellow undersides. They are not as aggressive as the blue devil.

➤ **Blue chromis** *(Chromis cyaneus).* Also called blue reef chromis, this is a gentle Caribbean species. They are royal blue with black edging on the top and bottom of the tail. Blue chromis are best kept in groups and are safe for reef tanks.

➤ **Green chromis** *(Chromis viridis).* The reflective coloration of this fish changes according to the angle of light striking them. They may look green from one angle and blue from another. You may see them incorrectly labeled as blue chromis because of this. Again, small schools are best, and they are safe for reef tanks.

Dragonets

These unusual fish are very popular. However, they really should only be kept in a reef tank. Their small mouths and love of tiny crustaceans, such as copepods, makes it difficult to prevent them from starving in a fish-only setup. In a reef tank, there are always microscopic critters to munch off the live-rocks. Unless they are pair-bonded, dragonets fight a bit with one another. So it is usually best to keep only one per tank.

➤ **Mandarin dragonet** *(Pterosynchiropus splendidus).* Usually called the mandarin goby, this fish is not a goby at all. It is also goes under the name of red or psyche-delic mandarin. The body is red with green reticulations. Another species, *Synchiropus picturatus,* is light green with large black, orange, and green concentric spots. It is sometimes called the target, green, or bullseye mandarin.

Dig this psychedelic mandarin dragonet.

➤ **Scooter dragonet** *(Neosynchiropus ocellatus)*. Like the misnamed mandarin, this fish is usually sold as a scooter blenny, but it is not really a blenny.

Eels

Moray eels are popular in large, fish-only aquariums. Eels grow large and are predatory, so they are not good choices to mix with small community fish. Keep them only with tankmates that are too large to be eaten.

Eels do not like open spaces. Always have plenty of hiding places to keep them comfortable and to keep them from trying to escape. You can build caves out of live-rock, large shells, and coral skeletons. Lengths of PVC pipe also make great hiding holes for eels—if you can stand an ugly piece of pipe lying in your tank.

Something's Fishy

Eels are skilled escape artists. Keep your tank well covered, or you will find them dried up and stiff on your carpet the next morning.

Eels do not eat flakes, and only the smallest will touch live brine shrimp. Be prepared to offer krill, fish, ghost shrimp, crayfish, squid, and other seafoods. Eels will readily learn to take food from your hand, but this may not be a good idea. Use a feeding stick instead. Besides the chance of getting accidentally bitten, you'll find that you can no longer do maintenance in your tank without your eels following your hand around, looking for food. It is rather nerve-wracking.

➤ **Snowflake moray** *(Echidna nebulosa)*. The body pattern resembles a sprinkling of black and cream snowflakes. This eel grows to around 30 inches long.

➤ **Zebra moray** *(Gymnomuraena zebra)*. Zebra morays are covered from head to tail with bold alternating white and reddish-brown bands. They grow to around 3 feet.

A black-edged moray eel.

The banded snake eel *(Myrichthys colubrinus)* and the ribbon eels *(Rhinomuraena quaesita)* are nearly impossible to get to eat in captivity and should never be purchased. The ribbon eel is sold as blue ribbon eel, black ribbon eel, or yellow ribbon eel, but all are the same species. The black ones are juvenile, the blues are male, and the yellows are female.

Filefish and Triggerfish

Filefish get their name from their tough skin, which the Polynesians once used as sandpaper. Triggerfish get their name from the mechanism of locking spines on the dorsal fin. Once cocked, the fins won't fold until the fish is good and ready to let them. Both filefish and triggerfish use their fins to lodge tightly into coral crevices when frightened.

There are species from the Caribbean, but most species sold are from the Indo-Pacific. These fish generally accept all foods readily. However, they are opportunistic— particularly the triggers—and sometimes will take after tankmates or become vicious. Files and triggers should not be kept in a reef tank.

➤ **Clown trigger** *(Balistoides conspicillum)*. Probably the most prized species, it commands the highest price. The fish is black with white polka dots and some yellow patches on the mouth and back.

➤ **Redtooth trigger** *(Odonus niger)*. A pure black fish with red teeth, it also sells as the niger trigger (pronounced *nye-JEER,* as in Nigeria). All triggers move by undulating their fins in a way that resembles flying more than swimming. The redtooth trigger's opaque black fins make this motion even more apparent and beautiful.

➤ **Picasso trigger** *(Rhinecanthus aculeatus).* The "modern art" markings of this fish appear to be painted on or patched together. You may see this trigger sold as the humu-humu trigger, which is short for the Hawaiian name for it, humuhumu-nukunuku-apua'a (there will be no pronunciation guide for this name).

➤ **Orange-tail filefish** *(Pervagor spilosoma).* The red-orange tail contrasts nicely with the silver, black-spotted body.

The orange-spotted filefish *(Oxymonacanthus longirostris)* is one to avoid. It's a tempting beauty with its orange spots against an emerald background. However, it feeds almost solely on live coral polyps and rarely survives long in captivity.

Flounders

Here is a group of fishes that is both often and rarely seen—all at the same time. Stores commonly offer them for sale, but their camouflage is so good that you can be looking right at one and not know it. Flounders are strictly bottom dwellers and like to bury themselves. Use sand or fine gravel for a substrate. Caribbean species are the ones usually seen in the shops.

Frogfish or Anglerfish

When you look at fish from this group, you can practically see evolution in action. The fins have evolved to form shapes that more closely resemble legs and hands. You rarely see these guys swim. More likely, you will see them walk or crawl. They actually grasp onto rocks with their handlike fins. Their bodies have colors, frills, and appendages that make them mimic blobs of sponge or seaweed sitting in your tank. Some are beautiful reds and yellows.

Frogfish are not active animals. They sit. And they wait. When a fish or shrimp wanders by, the huge mouth gapes open and vacuums in the prey. Those of the genus *Antennarius*—the anglers—are even more sinister. On top of their head they have a fleshy fishing pole with a wiggling worm shape on the end. When prey comes near, the pole folds out and the worm wiggles to tempt the prey closer to the angler's mouth.

Be careful what you mix these fish with. They will eat any prey that fits in their mouth, which is anything the same size or smaller than the predator. Think of them as stomachs with fins, and you will be set. They require live foods, and since they don't chase their prey, you may want to keep them in a tank by themselves to avoid competition from other fish. Specimens come from both Caribbean and Indo-Pacific sources.

Goatfish

They get their name from the whiskers on the bottom lip, but pigfish would have been a better name. One goatfish is a cleanup crew all by itself. They are super scavengers, using their whiskers to stir food out of the gravel, but they will not hesitate to go where the food is. Expect your goatfish to be first in line at the feeding trough when you put food in the tank. Anyway, they are hardy and peaceful but grow too large for most tanks. Keep them in a fish-only aquarium.

This is a bar-tail goatfish (Upeneus tragula).

Gobies

Another delightful group of fishes with a large array of varieties, gobies are excellent fish for the reef tank. Most do well in a fish-only tank, too. The main concern is to be sure their dietary needs are met. Some gobies do not readily accept flakes. Unless noted otherwise, the species here are Indo-Pacific.

➤ **Clown goby** *(Gobiodon spp.)*. Several species are sold in stores. They come in assorted colors, ranging from pure yellow to black to brick. Some are green with red markings in the face. Clown gobies stay under 2 inches, and due to their tiny size are best kept in reef tanks away from larger fish.

➤ **Watchman goby** *(Cryptocentrus leptocephalus)* and the **yellow watchman goby** *(C. cinctus)* are my favorites. *Amblyeleotris* and *Valenciennea* species are also sold as watchman gobies. These fish build burrows beneath the decorations in your tank and sit at the entrance, watching. In the wild, these fish live in pairs, often sharing their burrows with commensal shrimp.

➤ **Engineer goby** *(Pholidichthys leucotaenia)*. This fish is also called the eel-tail goby or the Asian neon goby. Young fish are black and white striped, resembling the Caribbean neon goby. Adults, however, are tan with large black spots. Engineer gobies like to hang out in groups. They get their name from their propensity for digging.

➤ **Bar goby** *(Ptereleotris zebra)*. A hardy fish, they are light blue with thin pink vertical stripes.

➤ **Firefish** *(Nemateleotris magnifica)*. This fish and its cousin, the **purple firefish** *(Nemateleotris decora)*, are hardy and popular, but shy. Juveniles fare better in small groups, but adults pair off and drive away other firefish.

➤ **Neon goby** *(Gobiosoma oceanops)*. These tiny 1- to 2-inch fish set up cleaning stations. When other fish come by, they will dart out to pick off any parasites that can be found. Sometimes they explore your hand for parasites when you have it in the tank to do chores. Neon gobies are from the Caribbean.

These neon gobies set up cleaning stations for other fish.

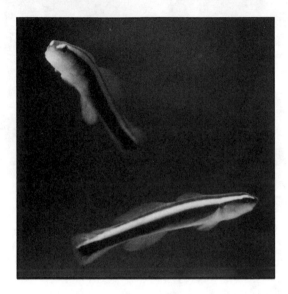

Avoid the Catalina goby *(Lythrypnus dalli)*. This is a small bright red fish, beautifully striped in blue. It comes from cold waters off California and tends to fare poorly in the tropical marine aquarium.

Groupers

See the big grouper. See the big grouper's big mouth. See the big grouper's big mouth eat the poor little fish. That is pretty much all you need to know about groupers. Actually, they can be great choices for fish-only setups containing other large fish—as long as you don't mix them with anything small enough to eat. Groupers are hardy, and some are quite pretty, too. The species listed here are Indo-Pacific, but Caribbean species also appear in stores.

➤ **Panther grouper** *(Cromileptes altivelis)*. Many hobbyists buy this fish without thinking about how large it will get. The 2- to 3-inch juveniles, with their prominent black spots against a white background and undulating butterflylike fins, make a tempting selection. But this fish grows to nearly 30 inches, and a good portion of that is mouth. Adults are a bit more tan, with smaller black dots.

The panther grouper grows into a big fish.

➤ **Strawberry grouper** *(Cephalopholis miniata)*. Also called the miniata grouper, coral trout, and coral rockfish, this is my favorite of the groupers. The bright red color, covered with blue seedlike dots, is how it came to be known as the strawberry grouper. This fish grows to 18 inches.

➤ **Saddleback grouper** *(Plectropomus lacvis)*. White body, black saddles, and yellow fins make this a striking fish. It grows to 40 inches.

Hawkfish

The popular hawkfish gets its name from its habit of perching on a branch of coral or on top of a rock and watching. They actually turn their heads to get a good look. Here and there, they swoop out to nab food or maybe just to rattle some other fish's chain. Hawkfish are hardy, but most get quite large. The species listed here are usually safe for both fish-only and reef tanks.

➤ **Spotted hawkfish** *(Cirrhitichthys spp.)*. Several species are sold under this name. Red or brick spots against a white background are typical coloration. The tips of each dorsal spine have smaller fingerlike spines called cirri. Adult size is 4 inches or so.

➤ **Arc-eye hawkfish** *(Paracirrhites arcatus)*. Color varies, but the fish is usually pink with an orange semicircle near the eye and a white stripe down the side. The arc-eye grows to 6 inches and may be kept in a reef or fish-only setup.

➤ **Flame hawkfish** *(Neocirrhites armatus)*. These are quite popular for reef tanks, growing to only 4 inches or so. The fish is solid red with a black dorsal stripe.

The spotted hawkfish.

➤ **Long-nose hawkfish** *(Oxycirrhitus typus)*. The long-nose hawkfish has a different body shape than the others in this group. The color pattern consists of red lattice against a white background. Collected in deep water, they cost a bit more than other hawks. Adult size is around 5 inches, with an inch of that being the slender snout.

Fish and Tips

Jawfish will often become quite tame, learning to take food from your fingers. However, they are shy fish that, even when tame, will not stray far from their burrow for food. So if you keep jawfish, monitor their food intake to be sure they get their share. Use a turkey baster to get food to them, if necessary.

Jawfish

If you can picture Jabba the Hutt in a state of anorexia, then you've got a pretty good idea what a jawfish looks like—big head, big eyes, big mouth, and a skinny little body.

These comical fish build burrows in the substrate. Then they gather larger bits of shell and gravel from around the tank to build their homes. The jawfish is never far from its burrow. Often, you see only the cute little heads poking out. Other times, they hover above the burrow with their tails aimed to dive back in.

Jawfish are good choices for both reef and fish-only aquariums. However, if you put them in a reef, be sure your rocks are sitting squarely on the bottom without gravel underneath. Otherwise, the jawfish's tunneling may collapse the structure. Be sure to supply a substrate that is deep enough to allow jawfish to dig a proper burrow.

➤ **Yellow-head jawfish** *(Opistognathus aurifrons).* This 4-inch Caribbean fish is light blue with a yellow head. Some populations lack the yellow and are sold as pearly jawfish.

➤ **Dusky jawfish** *(O. whitehursti).* Dusky jaws are substantially larger than yellow-heads, growing to 9 inches. The coloration is mottled brown. I find them to be highly comical and interactive. They have personality. These fish hail from the Caribbean.

This yellow-head jawfish stays at the entrance to its burrow.

Lionfish

Also called turkeyfish, even most nonhobbyists recognize this group. They are well-known for their spectacular venomous spines. Lionfish are hardy residents of the fish-only setup. Be careful not to mix them with anything small enough to eat.

Most lionfish will only accept live foods at first. Feeder goldfish and ghost shrimp can be offered. You should wean them over to frozen krill, silversides, squid, and other marine foods as soon as possible, though. Lionfishes are not a good choice for the reef tank.

Always be careful when you have your hand around a lionfish. They are normally not a danger, but rare instances have been reported of fish that charged their owners, impaling them with their venomous spines. It may be that the fish was defending a territory, or maybe it had learned to associate the owner's hand with the arrival of food. Who knows? So be careful.

➤ **Volitans lionfish** *(Pterois volitans)*, pronounced *VOH-lih-tanz*. This species is probably the most commonly offered. Related species, including the **antennata lion** *(P. antennata)*, the **radiata lion** *(P. radiata)*, and others are also readily available. Lionfish of these species may grow to 18 inches.

The venom from the spines of this red volitans lionfish can be dangerous.

➤ **Dwarf lionfish.** At least a couple of species sell as dwarf lions—*Dendrochirus zebra* and *D. brachypterus* are two. They have shorter fins and only grow to around 6 inches. The **Fu Manchu lion** *(D. biocellatus)* is less commonly seen, but is my favorite of the dwarf lionfishes.

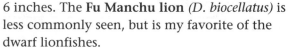

Something's Fishy

Lionfish are dangerous. If you get stung by one, immerse the wound in water as hot as you can stand for 20 minutes. Heat breaks down the toxin. You may want to seek medical attention, too.

Parrotfish

A parrotfish's teeth are fused into a beak and have the ability to bite off bits of coral head, skeleton and all, and grind it to dust. They extract food from the polyps and algae and excrete the ground-up bits of coral skeleton as sand. This behavior obviously precludes you from keeping them in a reef tank with your live corals, but parrotfish are really a poor choice for the fish-only marine tank, too. They are too large and active to be happy. Beginners should avoid them.

Puffers and Porcupine Fish

Puffers and porcupine fish are related to the boxfish, cowfish, and trunkfish that I discussed earlier in this chapter, but with an added feature. These fish are famous for their ability to use water to inflate themselves to several times normal size. It is a defense that not only surprises a predator, but also makes it less likely that the victim will fit down its throat.

The porcupine fish takes it a step further by covering itself with spines that distend as it swells. If that weren't enough, these fish are poisonous, too. Needless to say, predators tend to leave them alone.

➤ **Dogface puffers** *(Arothron spp.)* have adorable faces. Several species are available, ranging from solid colors to striped or spotted. Adults' sizes range up to 20 inches. All are Indo-Pacific.

➤ **Sharpnose puffers** *(Canthigaster spp.)* are another Indo-Pacific group. The saddled or **valentini puffer** *(C. valentini)* is the species most commonly seen. It is a white fish with a yellow tail and black saddles.

➤ **Porcupine fish** inflate into a spiny ball when threatened. Several species are available, usually from the Caribbean. Uninflated *Diodon spp.* have folded spines, while the spines of *Chilomycterus spp.* are permanently erect.

The porcupinefish at rest. Those spikes turn it into a spiny ball when the fish is threatened.

Rabbitfish

Their propensity to munch algae is what has given this group of fishes its name, but only one species is commonly seen in the trade—the foxface *(Lo vulpinis)*. The shape of the snout gives this fish its name. It is a yellow fish with a black face, and closely resembles the long-nose butterfly. Foxfaces are peaceful additions to an aquarium, but be careful handling them. The fish's dorsal spines are somewhat venomous.

Seahorses and Pipefish

The seahorse may be the most readily identifiable saltwater fish. Its unusual shape is the source of its name. Pipefish are related. Picture a seahorse stretched into a straight horizontal line, and you can envision a pipefish.

Seahorses and pipefish come from grassy bays—not from the reef. *Keep pipefish and seahorses **only** in a tank dedicated to them.* They are slow swimmers and cannot compete for food with faster-moving fish. Nor can they survive the stings of corals and anemones.

An elegant seahorse (Hippocampus *spp.*).

Seahorses and pipefish require copious quantities of small live foods. A single specimen can eat hundreds of brine shrimp per day. Do not expect them to eat flakes. Nor should you expect brine shrimp alone to be a satisfactory diet, and that is one of the problems of keeping these animals. Many hobbyists don't even have access to live brine shrimp, let alone ghost shrimp, blackworms, baby fish, and so forth, so they are unable to keep the animals alive for long. In other words, seahorses and pipefish are not for beginners.

A banded pipefish (Doryrhamphus dactyliophorus).

Sharks and Rays

Neither sharks nor rays should be considered by most hobbyists. Most get too big for the aquarium. There are a few species of dwarf shark that may do well in a large aquarium, though. These are sometimes sold as bamboo, cat, or epaulet sharks. These animals are particularly sensitive to stray voltage in an aquarium and may be sensitive to copper-based medications, too.

The banded cat shark (Chiloscyllium plagiosum) can do well in a large aquarium.

Squirrelfish

I love these fish. They are colorful and hardy. Also called big-eyes and soldierfish, squirrelfish tend to be solid red, or red and white striped, with large eyes. During the day, they prefer to hide in groups under overhangs.

Squirrelfish have really big mouths—so don't trust them with smaller fish, and don't tell them any of your secrets. Keep them in a fish-only setup, and use lots of krill and silversides to keep them fat and happy. These fish are happiest in groups.

This is a squirrelfish (Myripristis spp.).

Tangs and Surgeonfish

Both these names are interchangeable, although species with a more elongated body tend to get the surgeonfish label. All have an extendible spine on both sides of the base of the tale. They whip it at adversaries or predators. It is sharp like a scalpel—hence the name *surgeon*.

These fish are found mostly in schools in the wild, but in the aquarium one per species per tank is all you should have. Do not mix similar looking species, or fights will likely result.

Tangs are largely herbivores. They will nibble continuously at algae in the tank, but be prepared to supplement with frozen or dried algae, too. Sometimes, these guys become territorial and aggressive. Tangs are generally safe for both reefs and the fish-only aquariums. All the species listed here are Indo-Pacific unless noted otherwise.

➤ **Pacific blue tang** *(Paracanthurus hepatus)*. Alias hippo tang, yellow-tail blue surgeon, liver tang, palette tang, and flagtail surgeon, these popular fish are bright blue with a yellow tail and black edging. Some hobbyists report this fish is more susceptible to saltwater ich infection than most fish.

➤ **Yellow tang** *(Zebrasoma flavescens)*. This fish is a pure bright yellow. At night, though, its color fades, and it develops a bright white lateral stripe.

➤ **Sailfin tang** *(Z. veliferum)*. The sailfin tang has vertical brown, orange, and white stripes and a yellow tail.

➤ **Brown tang** *(Z. scopas)*. Here is a hardy fish with subdued coloration.

A sailfin tang.

The following tangs have a very low survival rate in captivity and should be avoided: clown tang *(Acanthurus lineatus);* powder blue tang *(A. leucosternon);* powder brown tang, also known as gold-rim tang *(A. glaucopareius);* and Achilles tang *(A. achilles).* Unfortunately, this list includes some of the most beautiful species.

Wrasses

The wrasse (pronounced *rass*) family is a highly diversified group. They come in all shapes and sizes—up to 10 feet long. So not all make good choices for the aquarium. Most are highly active, like to bury themselves when frightened or tired, and love to munch on tiny crustaceans and other invertebrates that they might find. Consequently, many are poor choices for the reef aquarium.

➤ **Yellow wrasse** *(Halichoeres chrysus).* This bright yellow Indo-Pacific fish is also sold as the yellow coris wrasse.

A yellow wrasse.

➤ **Red coris wrasse** *(Coris gaimard).* Juveniles are bright red with white and black markings that make them resemble clownfish. Adults are solid blue with green specks. This is an Indo-Pacific fish.

➤ **Bird wrasse** *(Gomphosus varius).* Highly active, with a birdlike snout, the Indo-Pacific bird wrasse is an interesting addition to the fish-only tank. You may see three varieties sold (brown, black, and green), but they are all the same fish. Adult males are green, females are black, and juveniles may be more brown.

➤ **Cleaner wrasses** *(Labroides spp.).* These fish are often sought after for their desire to pick parasites off other fish. However, these Indo-Pacific fish are poor choices for the aquarium, and most starve in short order. Please do not buy these fish. (The hardy Caribbean neon goby is a better choice.)

➤ **Blue-head wrasse** *(Thalassoma bifasciatum).* Only the males have a blue head. Females and immatures are more yellowish overall. In the wild, they live in groups, with a male guarding his harem of females.

171

➤ **Six-line wrasse** *(Pseudocheilinus hexataenia)*. An attractive orange and purple striped fish, six-line wrasses stay under four inches. They make a good addition to reef aquariums and are noted for their ability to prey on the small pyramidellid snails that are parasites of giant clams.

➤ **Flasher wrasses** *(Paracheilinus spp.)*. Also good choices for the reef aquarium, flasher wrasses tend to hover in schools above the rocks and feed on passing zooplankton. Indeed, their appearance and behavior is similar to the anthias basslets, which fill the same type of ecological niche. The **filament-fin flasher wrasse** *(P. filamentosus)* and **Carpenter's flasher wrasse** *(P. carpenteri)* are varieties that are often seen.

➤ **Fairy wrasses** *(Cirrhilabrus spp.)* are occasionally available. Care and behavior is similar to flasher wrasses. They may be kept in reef tanks.

➤ **Spanish hogfish** *(Bodianus rufus)*. A yellow fish with a purplish patch in the top front, the Spanish hogfish is a hardy variety from the Caribbean. They grow to 20 inches in the wild.

Well, there you have it. If you can't find fish that are safe for your tank and exciting to keep in that list, it's just too bad—because I am ready to move on to the chapter about invertebrates.

The Least You Need to Know

➤ Pick species that are compatible.

➤ Pick species that won't outgrow your tank.

➤ Be sure that you can provide the correct diet.

➤ Inexpensive and hardy, damselfish are an excellent choice to cycle a new tank.

➤ Avoid difficult species. If other hobbyists can't keep them alive, chances are you can't, either.

A pajama cardinalfish (Sphaeramia nematoptera) on patrol. These fish prefer a tranquil environment.

Artificial corals add color to a fish-only aquarium.

This flame angelfish (Centropyge loriculus) is not too aggressive, and lives well in a community tank.

You can see where the zebra moray eel (Gymnomuraena zebra) gets its name.

Hawaiian featherduster worms (Eudistylia polymorpha) are hardy filter feeders.

The yellow longnose butterflyfish (Forcipiger flavissimus) in flight.

This royal dottyback (Pseudochromis paccagnellae) is a member of the basslet family.

The graceful heniochus butterflyfish (Heniochus acuminatus) readily accepts a variety of foods.

The bold and beautiful koran angelfish (Pomacanthus semicirculatus) changes color when it reaches adulthood. This is a juvenile.

The live-rock in this reef has been colonized by many soft corals, including button polyps, mushroom anemones, star polyps, and a large leather coral.

This clown triggerfish (Balistiodes conspicillum) can use its fins to wedge itself tight into a rock crevice.

A pair of percula clownfish (Amphiprion percula) nestle in close to their protective sea anemone.

This magnificent adult emperor angelfish (Pomacanthus imperator) does look regal.

The clown grouper (Pogonoperca punctata) is also called the bearded grouper because of the extra piece of skin on its bottom lip.

The square anthias (Anthias pleurotaenia). Anthias are sub-members of the grouper family.

This purple reef lobster (Enoplometopus debelius) is a colorful character. It stays small, but is a voracious predator.

Chapter 13

20,000 Legs Under the Sea

In This Chapter

➤ Little shrimp, big crabs, and other crustaceans

➤ Happy clams, sluggish snails, and other mollusks

➤ Christmas tree worms for all year round

➤ Sea cucumbers, sea apples, and chocolate chip starfish

➤ Corals and sea anemones: animals that sting

Legs, claws, eye stalks, tentacles, suckers, tube feet, shells, siphons, arms, branches, and spines are features you wouldn't expect to find on a fish. Festively colored fish are what draw most of us to the aquarium hobby, but the oceans are filled with countless interesting life forms. The saltwater aquarist has access to multitudes of species of those inveterate invertebrates. Invertebrates, of course, are animals without backbones. You could say they are the spineless choices for a marine aquarium.

However, invertebrates are more delicate than fish, and indeed, many fish consider them to be tasty snacks. Also, the most popular medication for treating saltwater fish is lethal to invertebrates. So most invertebrates make poor choices for the fish-only marine aquarium.

In addition, unless you have the backbone to set up a full-fledged reef tank, the specialized requirements of most invertebrates will make them off limits to you. I've noted some exceptions, but in general only hobbyists with reef tanks should consider keeping any of the following species.

Crustaceans

Legs, claws, and segmented exoskeletons are hallmarks of the *Crustacea*. Members of this diverse group range in size, form, and behavior. Many are harmless scavengers, while others are vicious predators. One interesting feature of these animals is that they can regenerate legs and claws when they molt.

Fish School

Crustaceans are a class of aquatic animals with a segmented body, a continuous exoskeleton, and paired jointed limbs. Lobsters, shrimp, and crabs are members of this class.

Crabs

➤ **Arrow crab** *(Stenorhynchus stenicornis)*. Picture a daddy longlegs spider with an upward-pointing, carrot-shape body, and you have an idea of how unusual this creature is. Arrow crabs are quite hardy. They eat almost anything, and have even been noted for their propensity to munch on bristleworms. Unfortunately, they may be too aggressive to keep with other small invertebrates, and some hobbyists have reported that their spindly legs can damage corals. So the arrow crab probably fares best in a seahorse tank or a semi-reef.

➤ **Sally Lightfoot crab** *(Percnon gibbesi)*. Looking like a crab that somebody stepped on, this flattened crustacean is a scavenger noted for its ability to eat hair algae. The flat body allows it to slip into some tight spots to feed. The Sally Lightfoot crab is even a candidate for the fish-only aquarium, assuming that you don't keep crab-eating species of fish. However, these crabs may grab small sleeping fish.

➤ **Horseshoe crab** *(Limulus polyphemus)*. Although it's not a crustacean, this arthropod is often sold as a crab. Juveniles make interesting additions to tanks with open sandy bottoms, scavenging along the bottom and burying themselves to rest. Adults grow to a foot across (plus tail) and would be too destructive to keep in the aquarium. Some aquarists consider horseshoe crabs to be hardy, but most don't live long in captivity. Perhaps they are badgered by other inhabitants of the aquarium, but I've always found them to be picky eaters. If you try one, be sure that it gets its share of food. You may have to tuck a piece of krill under its shell now and then.

➤ **Hermit crabs.** Many species of hermit crabs are offered for sale. Hermit crabs have soft rear bodies, which they protect by tucking them into an uninhabited shell. Some, such as the tiny **blue-leg hermit** *(Clibanarius tricolor)* or the half-inch **red reef hermit** *(Paguristes cadenati),* are popular algae grazers for reef tanks. Other hermit crabs can be large and predatory, but they sometimes fare well as scavengers in fish-only aquariums. One interesting hermit crab, the **anemone** hermit, has a symbiotic relationship with a species of sea anemone. The anemone lives on the crab's shell, and when the crab changes shells, it moves the anemone to its new home.

A large hermit crab of unknown species makes its home in this conch shell.

➤ **Porcelain crabs** *(Neopetrolisthes spp.)*. These creatures are often sold as anemone crabs (not to be confused with the anemone hermit crab). They live among the tentacles of sea anemones. These animals are a flat china white with brick mottling. Despite the large and threatening claws, they are filter feeders.

Avoid predatory crabs, including large hermit crabs, swimming crabs, and box crabs. These are poor choices for most marine aquariums. Decorator crabs are an especially poor choice for the reef tank. They pinch off bits of sponge, coral, anemones, algae, and so forth—usually destroying your most prized specimens—and cement them to their backs for camouflage.

Lobsters

Lobsters are generally unsuitable for the aquarium, due to their predatory and destructive nature. They will feed on almost anything organic, including your fish. Lobsters may

Fish School

Filter feeders are animals that filter microscopic life and nutrients from the water. Most filter-feeding organisms do poorly in aquariums and should be avoided, because the water in most tanks is just too clean to keep them alive for long.

collapse your rock structure with their digging. If you really want to keep lobsters, do not try them in a reef. Instead, try keeping them in a semi-reef with larger compatible fish. There are three basic types of lobsters:

➤ **True lobsters,** like the ones you eat, are too large and would never do in the marine aquarium. However, there are a few species of **dwarf lobsters** *(Enoplometopus spp.),* also called reef lobsters, available. They are similar in size to freshwater crayfish and are quite colorful, marked with patterns of red or purple. Both Caribbean and Indo-Pacific species are available, and both grow to around 5 inches.

➤ **Spiny lobsters** have no large claws and two large sweeping antennae. The variety most often seen in the trade is the Indo-Pacific **blue spiny lobster** *(Panulirus versicolor),* which can grow to a foot long—plus antennae.

➤ **Slipper lobsters** *(Arctides spp.* and *Scyllarides spp.)* are the most peaceful of the lobsters. They have a very flattened shape, and the two front antennae are modified into flat shovel-like appendages that enable them to dig rapidly. Some hobbyists have even had success keeping them in reef tanks.

Shrimp

Shrimp are more delicate than crabs and lobsters, and so there is less worry about them eating something else than about something else eating them. Shrimp eat most any food and are good scavengers, too.

In fact, there are several popular species of what are known as cleaner shrimp. These are species that set up a little drive-through. . . er, swim-through. . . operation on the reef. A fish stops by and the shrimp swims out to inspect it. The shrimp removes and feeds upon any parasites and dead tissue that it finds. Part of the routine includes a thorough inspection inside the fish's gills and mouth. In return, only the hungriest or most criminal of fish would ever consider eating a cleaner shrimp. Look for the white antennae on the various species of cleaner shrimp.

➤ **Skunk cleaner shrimp** *(Lysmata amboensis).* Also called the eel cleaner shrimp because it is commonly found in association with moray eels, this small Indo-Pacific shrimp has a yellowish body with red and white dorsal stripes and the characteristic cleaner shrimp white antennae. These shrimp are commonly found in pairs. They are simultaneous hermaphrodites. Any two can form a pair, and they fertilize each other's eggs.

➤ **Fire shrimp** *(Lysmata debelius).* This animal is bright blood red with white dots and antennae. It comes from deeper waters, so the price is higher. Unfortunately, I find that they usually hide during the day—although they will come out at feeding time. Fire shrimp are Indo-Pacific.

A skunk cleaner shrimp mans its cleaning station.

➤ **Banded coral shrimp** *(Stenopus hispidus)*. Also called the coral-banded shrimp or boxer shrimp, this larger Caribbean species is quite hardy but can be more aggressive to smaller tankmates. Some hobbyists have noticed it eating valuable soft corals, so it may not be the best choice for a reef tank.

➤ **Camel shrimp** *(Rhynchocinetes durbanensis)*. This Indo-Pacific species is one of my favorites. They like to be kept in groups and remain visible during the day. The shrimp is red with white stripes and has a humpback that gives it its name. However, they have been noted to eat corals. The similar Caribbean **peppermint shrimp** *(Lysmata wurdmani)* is a safer choice for many reef tanks.

➤ **Anemone shrimp** *(Periclimenes spp.)*. Several species are sold under this name, with the most common probably being *P. pedersoni* from the Caribbean and *P. brevicarpalis* of the Indo-Pacific. All are small species, under 1 inch, that are as transparent as glass, with a few brown or white spots. They live within the tentacles of sea anemones and scavenge for food but often act as cleaner shrimp.

Shrimp of the genus *Saron*—known as saron shrimp, monkey shrimp, horsehead shrimp, or marble shrimp—have larger, heavier bodies and may feed on soft coral polyps. They should be avoided in the reef but may do well in a semi-reef or seahorse tank. Also avoid the harlequin shrimp *(Hymenocera picta* and *H. elegans)* unless you are willing to provide the only thing they eat—live starfish.

Mantis shrimp are predatory shrimp, also known as *thumb-splitters* for their ability to damage any human being silly enough to handle them. They are another group to avoid. Mantis shrimp have modified appendages on the front that allow them to either skewer their prey (those are classified as *spearers*) or give it a sudden powerful punch (classified as *smashers*). Large specimens (I've seen 10-inchers) have been known to break the aquarium glass with a single blow.

Echinoderms

Starfish and sea urchins are the best-known members of this group, whose name means *spiny skin*. All have radial symmetry, most obvious in five-armed species of starfish, and internal skeletons. Another feature shared by echinoderms are their tube feet, which resemble tiny tentacles with suction cups on the end.

Sea Stars

Everyone is familiar with starfish, though of course, they are not fish at all. Many species grow too large for the aquarium or have special feeding requirements. For example, the crown-of-thorns starfish eats live coral polyps. Other stars, particularly heavy-bodied varieties, feed on clams, mussels, and other bivalves. They feed in an unusual way, too. Using their many tube feet to slightly pry open the hapless clam, the starfish simply inserts its stomach inside the clam's shell and digests it right there.

Something's Fishy

Never buy a starfish that is showing any kind of sore or decay at the point of a wound. Infections kill them rapidly. However, if a leg is missing and the end seems to be healed, there is no reason to avoid that animal.

Sea stars have an amazing ability to regenerate. Not only will a missing leg regrow, but the broken-off piece may also grow into a whole separate sea star.

➤ **Brittle stars and serpent stars** *(Ophiocoma spp., Ophioderma spp., and others).* These sea stars have a central body disk and five thin snakelike arms. The brittle stars have spiny arms, while the arms of serpent stars are smoother. Brittle stars and serpent stars are excellent nighttime scavengers, hiding under rocks or corals during the day. They quickly learn to come running at feeding time, as well. A scuttling motion of the long arms allows them to move quite quickly. Caribbean species are most readily available, but brittle and serpent stars are found worldwide.

➤ **Blue starfish** *(Linckia laevigata)* is a bright blue Indo-Pacific species with tubular arms. They scavenge the rock surfaces for anything edible, including algae and microbes.

➤ **Red starfish** *(Fromia elegans).* This small Indo-Pacific starfish has a flattened shape and is a scavenger. It is bright red-orange.

➤ **Chocolate chip starfish** *(Protoreaster spp.).* A tan body with large dark brown knobs gives this Indo-Pacific star its name. Yes, they look like big five-armed cookies. Although this sea star does scavenge to some extent, it is more predatory than the other species I've included here. Offer it pieces of krill or other seafood to keep it from eating tankmates. There are reports of chocolate chip stars eating corals and other invertebrates that can't run away. That's why this is a better candidate for the semi-reef than for a reef tank.

A scavenging chocolate chip starfish.

Sea Urchins

Sea urchins are the pincushions of the sea. They have spherical skeletons and are covered with sharp spines. Some are even poisonous. All should be handled carefully.

Sea urchins are primarily vegetarians but they scavenge for other foods, too. They are excellent scavengers and algae-eaters, but larger specimens can overturn rocks. Some species don't stop at eating the undesirable macroalgae—they also eat the desirable purple coralline algae. The following species are all Caribbean, but Indo-Pacific species are sometimes sold, too:

➤ **Pincushion urchin** *(Lytechinus variegatus),* also sold as the variegated urchin, has multitudes of short sharp spines. The color varies—usually white or greenish. This species is also sold as the carrier urchin, due to its habit of carrying around bits of shell, rock, or food for camouflage.

➤ **Black sea urchin.** Several species may be sold under this name, including the rock-boring urchin *Echinometra lucunter* and the reef urchin *E. viridis.*

➤ **Long-spine urchin** *(Diadema antillarum).* Watch out for the needlelike spines on this devil. They can be up to 8 inches long. This urchin is another that is usually black.

➤ **Pencil urchin** *(Eucidaris tribuloides).* Here is a species with thick blunt spines, which may be brown or gray. There is virtually no chance of getting poked by this critter.

Be careful handling the long-spine sea urchin!

Sea Cucumbers

The sea cucumbers are an unusual lot. Most are long and fairly thin (like the vegetable), and they have feathery appendages at one end for gathering food. Some use the appendages to filter food from the water column, while others actively pick up bits of detritus from the bottom or ingest the substrate, digesting the useful bits within before excreting it.

The innocuous sea cucumber is a dangerous addition to your aquarium. When disturbed, it can intentionally eject its internal organs, releasing a toxin capable of poisoning the entire aquarium. Sea cucumber eggs are poisonous to fish, as well. Other species exude sticky threads, which are like thick versions of spider silk, to teach their prey a lesson. Finally, the occasional specimen that is accidentally drawn into a powerhead can turn into poison puree.

Something's Fishy

Sea cucumbers are interesting and even useful animals, but when unduly stressed, they can poison your aquarium. Is it worth the risk?

➤ **Black sea cucumber** *(Holothuria mexicana)* is a Caribbean species often sold as the donkey dung sea cucumber. One look at it and you will know why. This species is popular in reef tanks because it swallows sand, which helps clean the substrate. It can grow to over a foot in length. If you have to handle it, do it very quickly. After a couple of seconds of handling, the animal is likely to shoot you with a stream of sticky threads that are amazingly tacky. Spiderman has nothing on this critter.

180

This black sea cucumber is using its tentacles to pick up and ingest sand.

➤ **Yellow sea cucumber** *(Colochirus robustus)* is a small Indo-Pacific species, rarely over 2 inches in length. It is a filter feeder and spends its time attached to rocks or the aquarium glass, usually in a spot where the current is strong.

➤ **Sea apple** *(Pseudocolochirus tricolor).* This attractive creature is the size and shape of an apple, with feathery feeding appendages at one end. Colors vary greatly from one individual to the next, but reds, yellows, and blues compose the mix. The sea apple is a filter feeder, and will position itself in the current. Regular meals of assorted small bits of seafood should be offered to prevent this Indo-Pacific animal from starving and shrinking away. Remember that a dead sea cucumber can poison your whole aquarium.

➤ **Medusa worm** *(Amphitrite spp.).* This Hawaiian animal is so disgusting to look at that it is just too cool. Think of a 2-foot-long writhing piece of large intestine with some feathery appendages at one end, walking and climbing all over the tank, and you've got it nailed. The Medusa worm actively scavenges for detritus. However, many consider it to be the most toxic of the sea cucumbers, so proceed with caution.

Fish Tales

Did you know that some species of sea cucumber are harvested in commercial quantities for consumption by humans? Many Asian cuisines consider sea cucumber to be a delicacy.

Mollusks

A diverse group, these soft-bodied animals with hard shells come in many forms. The gastropods (*gastropod* means *stomach foot*) have a single shell. This group includes snails, cowries, and cones. The bivalves have two shells that come together to protect the animal. This group includes clams, oysters, mussels, and scallops. The most advanced mollusk—the octopus—has no shell at all.

Clams

Many bivalves make their way into reef tanks as accidental hitchhikers on live-rock. However, hardly a reef tank is assembled without the addition of at least one giant clam from the Indo-Pacific. The undulated opening of the shell and colorful mantle (the meaty part that extends outside the shell) make them attractive additions to any reef.

➤ **Giant clams** *(Tridacna spp.)*. The mantle of Tridacnid clams (which resembles a pair of rubbery lips) contains zooxanthellae *(zoo-zan-THEL-ee)*—symbiotic photosynthetic organisms that produce sugars for the clam. The clam's waste feeds the zooxanthellae, and the sugars from the little critters feed the clam. Clam colors vary widely by individual and species. The mantle may be mottled tan or green, bright blue, turquoise, iridescent green, or even orange. Giant clams make excellent aquarium centerpieces. They require intense light and calcium supplementation.

Fish Tales

Even though the movies portray giant clams as man-eating predators, the truth is that they are not predatory. In fact, they are primarily photosynthetic. They extend their fleshy mantles—their "lips"—to soak up rays of the sun. They also filter nutrients and microscopic organisms from the water.

Giant clams were not available to aquarists a few years ago. Overharvesting for the food and seashell curio trades nearly wiped them out in the wild, and they became a protected species. Since then, clam farming has turned into big business, and although most farmed clams are still sold as food, the smaller and most colorful specimens are offered for sale in the aquarium trade. Several species are available. Some have the potential to grow to 3 feet, but it is rare to see specimens in the aquarium that are more than a foot across.

➤ **Bear claw clam** *(Hippopus hippopus)*. Compared to the Tridacnid clams, this species has a small and unattractive mantle. It makes up for it with a shell that is marked in brick-color striations.

Mussels

Similar to clams, but with more elongated shells, mussels are probably best avoided in the aquarium. While they are quite hardy—often found above water on rocky beaches at low tide—mussels are filter feeders. They are likely to starve very quickly in an aquarium. On the other hand, you may want to grab some live ones at the seafood counter of your grocery store and crack them open for your fish to eat.

Scallops

Picture the logo of Shell Oil, and you will know what a scallop shell looks like. True scallops are rarely seen in the aquarium trade, although some specimens may come attached to live-rock.

The invertebrates normally sold as scallops in the trade are actually the similar file clams. They are filter-feeding bivalves with an array of tentacles protruding from the shell. They tend to anchor themselves with threads to rocks or even the tank wall, but when frightened, scallops can close their shells rapidly, expelling water. The jet action of this expulsion allows them to swim jerkily about the tank to avoid predators. Indeed, some varieties are sold as flying scallops.

Other common varieties include the Caribbean flame scallop *(Lima scabra)*, which comes with either a red body and tentacles or a red body and white tentacles, or the Indo-Pacific electric scallop. The latter is especially interesting. Upon first inspection, it appears to be a typical flame scallop—but look closer. The edges of the mantle are rimmed with a bright blue line that flashes on and off like a flickering neon sign.

Something's Fishy

Please do not purchase scallops for your aquarium. They are strict filter feeders and will starve in short order.

Snails

Now, here is a mollusk you can sink your teeth into. Ever heard of escargot? Come to think of it, you can sink your teeth into most mollusks. I've personally eaten some of every type, although not necessarily the species listed here. Seriously, though, several species of snail make excellent aquarium guests and ideal scavengers.

➤ **Astraea snail** *(Astraea tecta)*, also called star snail, is a great algae-eater. They are highly recommended grazers for the reef aquarium.

183

An astrea snail cleans algae from the aquarium glass.

➤ **Turbo snails** *(Turbo spp.),* also called turban snails, are also excellent algae eaters, but are larger and more expensive than the astraea snails. Many hobbyists find them to be less hardy, too.

Something's Fishy

Occasionally, dealers will offer colorful species of sea slugs, alias **nudibranchs** (pronounced *NEW-dih-brank*). The name means **naked gills.** Never buy them. Although exceptionally beautiful, these shell-less snails have diets that are too highly specialized to provide in the aquarium. They inevitably starve. Some species have the unique ability to eat sea anemones, incorporating their stinging cells into the nudibranch's body without digesting them.

➤ **Cowries** *(Cyprea spp.)* have shells that are exceptionally smooth and shiny. Some primitive cultures have used them as money, and there is a small green one whose common name is money cowry. The shells are attractive, but while the animal is alert, it extends a fleshy mantle which hides the shell from view. Cowries eat algae, but only the smallest specimens seem to fare well in the aquarium. I recommend that you avoid the larger, pear-size specimens. They tend to starve from lack of sufficient food.

Many snails are predatory and are poor choices for the marine aquarium. Baby queen conches are sometimes available, but they get much too large for the aquarium. Murex snails, though attractive, are also predatory. Cone shells are best avoided, too—many species have a venomous bite that is capable of killing a human being.

Octopuses

The octopus is arguably the most intelligent invertebrate. Everyone finds them interesting, and indeed, they readily interact with humans, touching and seeming to play with us.

Unfortunately, the octopus is extremely delicate. The survival rate in captivity is extremely low. I would say less than 10 percent of collected specimens ever arrive alive upon delivery to the dealer. And most of those will be dead within the week. Do you really want to support that kind of carnage by buying an octopus?

Even if you can keep it alive, the octopus has a short life span. Species collected for the aquarium live only about a year in the wild. Further, they die after breeding. This may account for the low survival rate in captivity, since the individuals that have already bred are the easiest ones to find and collect.

Please do not buy octopuses. Ever. Besides being delicate, they are escape artists extraordinaire and are highly predatory. It's hard to believe, but that soft-bodied creature can capture a crab and crack through its shell like an m&m candy. Likewise, avoid the related squids and cuttlefishes.

Something's Fishy

The deadly blue-ring octopus *(Hapalochlaena lunulata)* is occasionally seen in the trade. One bite from this inch-long creature can kill a human in minutes. Never tempt fate by trying to keep one of these.

Like the octopus, the chambered nautilus is a cephalopod, but with a shell. Here, one munches on a crayfish. Only advanced hobbyists should attempt to keep this animal.

Worms

Marine worms come in a wide array of forms, colors, and sizes. There are segmented and unsegmented worms, worms with frilly external gills or leglike tufts, threadlike worms, and flatworms. There are even species that grow to several feet long. A few species of marine worms are large and interesting enough to add to your marine aquarium.

Featherduster Worms

Featherduster worms (family *Sabellidae*) are probably the most popular worms introduced to the marine aquarium. Several species are available, but the large Hawaiian featherduster worms are the most sought after. Their bodies can be larger than a man's finger, but the body of featherduster worms is not normally seen. It resides inside a leathery tube built of mucous and debris, which is attached to a rock crevice.

Fish and Tips

In some instances, featherduster worms will lose their heads. That is, the feathery gill fronds will be ejected from the body. The fronds do grow back, so don't discard a featherduster worm that has lost its fronds unless you are sure the worm itself is also dead.

Only the protruding featherlike gills of the worm are normally seen, as they sift food from the water. When the worm is startled, the fronds are withdrawn into the worm's tube at a speed that can only be described as instantaneous. New introductions will withdraw their fronds often, but as the worm grows accustomed to its surroundings, it will become less fearful.

Featherduster worms are poor choices for fish-only tanks, due to the predatory nature of many fish, but the worms will prosper in seahorse tanks, semi-reefs, or reef tanks.

Christmas Tree Worms

Christmas tree worms *(Spirobranchus giganteus)* are members of the family *Serpulidae*. These worms (also called fanworms) are quite similar to featherduster worms. The main difference is that they secrete a hard calcareous tube and have double sets of gill fronds.

These worms live as colonies embedded in porites coral heads. In fact, you are more likely to see them labeled and sold as worm rock. They should only be kept in a reef tank that is capable of maintaining live stony corals.

Bright red, yellow, or blue specimens are easily obtained. One species builds a white calcareous tube the size of a cigar and sells as individual specimens under the name koko worm *(Protula magnifica)*.

A colony of multicolored Christmas tree worms inhabits this porites coral head.

Hitchhikers

Most worms introduced to your aquarium will be small, harmless scavengers that barely attract notice. They will be hitchhikers that sneak into your tank, hiding in holes in the live-rock.

➤ **Medusa worms** *(Thelepus spp., Amphitrite spp.,* and others), also called spaghetti worms, are useful scavengers. These small worms may have a body only an inch or two long. They live within holes in the rock. You may never know they are there, but in the evening they extend a multitude of threadlike tentacles, each several inches long, that reach out to scavenge for debris. The bits of food are drawn back into the burrow for supper. The animal gets its name from the mythical being that had snakes for hair. Do not confuse this with the echinoderm of the genus *Synapta*, which is also sold as a Medusa worm.

➤ **Bristleworms** are also hitchhikers on live rock. There are many species. Most have pink bodies resembling the familiar earthworm, but with rows of bristled tufts down the side that may resemble legs. The tufts are commonly white, pink, or red. Sometimes, the whole worm looks bristled. Bristleworms are usually harmless scavengers. As long as the worms are small and the populations low, you have little need to worry about them. However, bristleworms have been reported to damage live corals—probably when they are having trouble finding other suitable foods. Large specimens (I have seen them over a foot long) may be dangerous to other small creatures in your tank and should be removed.

Sponges and Sea Squirts

These days, most household cleaning sponges are artificial. Years ago, though, the sponges that people used to clean house were the actual porous skeletons of sea creatures, and natural sponges are still sometimes harvested and sold for this purpose. But hey, we're not here to talk about dead sponge skeletons.

Live sponges are interesting animals. Actually, they are colonies of animals. They group together to build a structure that is filled with pores and channels. Inside, the individual animals use tiny beating hairs (called *flagella*) to pump seawater through the sponge colony. The water stream brings microscopic food to the sponge and also flushes out waste. Sponges are natural filters.

Encrusting sponges are common bonuses found on pieces of live-rock. When you buy a sponge, look to see if the porelike mouths are open. This denotes an animal that is pumping water through itself and is probably healthy.

Sponges come in many forms and colors. Some are branch- or finger-shape, others are round, and there are even sponges shaped like a vase. You can find sponges in almost any color of the rainbow, with red, orange, yellow, and blue sponges being the most prized.

Sponges can make colorful and interesting additions to the reef tank. Wedge a sponge between a couple of rocks and it will eventually grab hold and grow.

Sponges are delicate creatures, though. They require high water quality and sufficient current to keep them free of pore-clogging sediment. Most sponges do best in areas where there is good current but little light. A sponge that has algae growing on it is not a healthy sponge. Try increasing the current to help the sponge rinse away detritus and algae attached to the outside. Consider moving the sponge under a ledge to reduce the amount of direct light it receives.

Some popular varieties include the Indo-Pacific blue sponge *(Haliclona spp.)* and the Caribbean red ball sponge and red finger sponge.

When you first introduce it, I recommend turning and tapping your new sponge underwater a few times to try to knock loose any air bubbles that were inadvertently trapped. Trapped air bubbles will kill a sponge by blocking the passage of water through it. If you buy a sponge that was exposed to air, parts or all of the sponge may die. You can sometimes salvage a damaged sponge by using a knife to cut away the damaged parts—underwater, of course.

Sea squirts are similar to sponges. They are usually found in small colonies, but they each resemble a small, untied water balloon. Like sponges, they pump water through their bodies to filter out microscopic food particles. When disturbed, sea squirts contract quickly, expelling a jet of water— hence the name. Some sea squirts have heavy leathery texture, while others are more like delicate membranes.

Fish and Tips

You can use a turkey baster to feed your sponges and other filter feeders. Your dealer will offer liquid invertebrate foods, or you can use finely powdered baby fish foods or even clam juice. Mix them with aquarium water to make a suspension, then temporarily turn off filters to reduce current and slowly squirt a small quantity of the suspension around the sponge. Don't overdo it. You can clog and kill the sponge.

Stinging Animals

Back when I studied biology, this group of invertebrates was called the coelenterates (pronounced *sih-LEN-ter-ets*), meaning *hollow bodied*. They were previously known as zoophyta, meaning *animal plants*. Nowadays, though, they are known as the cnidarians—the *stinging animals*. (Ignore the first *c* and pronounce it *nih-DARE-ee-enz*.) However, the most descriptive term that I've heard for this class of animals comes from the translation of some early German reef aquarium texts, where this group of invertebrates was called the *flower animals*. How appropriate.

Before I mention some of the most popular cnidarians, let me remind you that this group encompasses some of the most delicate species kept in the aquarium—and that includes both freshwater and saltwater aquaria. Most cnidarians require intense lighting, exceptional water quality, strong current, and (in the case of stony corals) calcium supplementation to survive. Unless specifically noted otherwise, you should only attempt to keep the following species in a reef aquarium.

Sea Anemones

Most hobbyists buy their first anemone *(uh-NEM-uh-nee)* to act as host to colorful marine clownfish. The flowerlike anemone is beautiful in its own right, as is the clownfish, but the two together make an exciting ballet. The clownfish lives happily among the tentacles of the sea anemone—tentacles that would sting and kill most fish.

Fish and Tips

Sea anemones are easily damaged, and tears in the flesh are often fatal. Your dealer should take extra care in removing any animal that has attached itself to the substrate, as should you. Gently prodding around the base and gradually working a fingernail underneath will eventually pry the animal loose.

Sea anemones are unusual animals. Their stinging tentacles are used to catch small prey and draw it toward the central mouth. Many species are also photosynthetic (like plants, they convert light to energy), requiring intense lighting to prosper. The Indo-Pacific species associated with clownfish are like this.

Sea anemones attach themselves to the substrate with a pedal base. Despite having this single "foot," they can be quite mobile and will commonly move around the tank until they find a suitable spot. Generally, anemones like to position themselves where the light and current are strong and where there is a protective alcove (such as a cave in a rock) for their base.

Offer regular feedings to your sea anemones. Small bits of assorted seafoods, jelly-bean-size or smaller, can be offered. Bits of krill, shrimp, scallops, or clams are good choices. I recommend against offering feeder goldfish or other freshwater fish as food.

➤ **Pink-tip anemone** *(Condylactis gigantea)*. This anemone is the most inexpensive and readily available. Color varies from cream to tan or pink, with pink tips on the tentacles. It hails from the Caribbean. It is beautiful and hardy enough to survive in a semi-reef aquarium. Regular feedings should be offered. The pink-tip anemone is not a species associated with clownfish. They don't even come from the same hemisphere. Clownfish have occasionally been known to accept it, but you shouldn't count on that happening. Buy a proper Indo-Pacific species for clownfish.

➤ **Long-tentacle anemone** *(Macrodactyla doreensis)*. Here is an Indo-Pacific anemone that is readily available and is accepted by most clownfish. The base is usually reddish or pink, with rows of warts. White lines radiate out from the mouth. Tentacles may be cream, tan, or pink, usually with purple tips.

Something's Fishy

Be vary careful handling sea anemones. Human susceptibility to their stings varies widely, depending on the species of anemone, the person involved, and the location of the sting.

➤ **Bubble-tip anemone** *(Entacmea quadricolor)*. Also sold as the rose anemone, bulb anemone, or maroon anemone, this species is characterized by the bulbous tips of the tentacles. The base is usually pink or maroon, and the tentacles are usually shades of translucent green. This is the only species associated with the maroon clownfish in the wild and is often the only species they will accept in captivity. Other clownfish take to it readily, as well.

Assorted pink-tip anemones cluster around a live-rock.

➤ **Colored carpet anemone** *(Stichodactyla gigantea)*. This Indo-Pacific species is especially prized. Undulating folds in the oral disk and bright colors make it stand out. I have seen specimens in green, yellow, pink, purple, and even blue. The colors are natural. Some specimens exhibit twitching tentacles.

➤ **Saddle carpet anemone** *(Stichodactyla haddoni)*. This creature has large green anemone, often with radiating white stripes. The tentacles are small and stubby. Be especially careful handling this species, as the nematocysts (stinging cells) grab tightly to human skin and can give a severe sting. When you pull away, many nematocysts (resembling bee stingers) will be left stuck to your skin and must be scraped away. I've noticed no ill effects from having the thick skin on my palm stung, but an employee who touched a forearm to a specimen developed a large chemical burn that took weeks to heal.

Something's Fishy

Occasionally, bright yellow sea anemones are offered for sale. These have been dyed with food coloring and should not be purchased. The color interferes with the animal's ability to photosynthesize and will likely lead to death. Even if the animal survives, the yellow color will disappear.

Mushroom Anemones

Hardy and colorful, mushroom anemones are easily cultivated and are popular additions to the reef tank and semi-reef. Most have flat oral disks about the size of a silver dollar. Colors include reds, greens, blues, and browns. Some are solid colored, while others have stripes radiating from the center or even spots. One variety, with its brown body and smudged mint-green surface, reminds me of iced molasses cookies.

Mushroom anemones are largely photosynthetic but may benefit from small feedings. However, such feedings are not necessary. The following species are all Indo-Pacific:

These mushroom anemones are brick red.

> ➤ **Smooth mushroom anemones,** of the genus *Discosoma,* are my favorites. The flesh is either smooth or may be slightly pimpled. Patches of these animals resemble patches of pansies.

> ➤ **Hairy mushroom anemones,** of the genus *Rhodactis,* have feathery tentacles on the skin. Although they are photosynthetic, they accept feedings more readily than the smooth mushroom anemones.

> ➤ **Elephant ears** *(Amplexidiscus fenestrafer)* are mushroom anemones capable of growing to 18 inches across. They are considerably less colorful than the others, tending to be dull gray or green. The large size and predatory nature are the attractions. Yes, these mushroom anemones are fully capable of catching and eating fish. When a fish hovers above, the edges of the anemone slowly curl up and draw around the fish, sealing it within. The mouth then opens and ingests the fish.

Soft Corals

Many species of corals can be kept in the reef aquarium. They are generally classified in two categories: soft corals and stony corals. Soft corals do not build skeletons. They tend to be hardier and easier to propagate, and some species are capable of moving slowly about the aquarium. Unless otherwise specified, the following species are Indo-Pacific:

Something's Fishy

Tube anemones *(Cerianthus spp.)* are not true anemones. They live in mud or substrate and build a leathery tube. Rows of tentacles trap prey. Tube anemones are attractive and hardy, but they are notorious for catching and eating fish at night. Because of this, it is probably best to avoid them.

➤ **Leather corals** get their name from their rubbery texture and typical brown coloration. Several genera of animals, including *Lobophytum, Sarcophyton, Alcyonium,* and *Sinularia,* are sold as leather corals. Forms vary from fingery to umbrellalike to leafy. Most are shades of brown, but green and dull yellow specimens will be found in the aquarium trade, too. Most leather corals have short, tiny polyps on the surface of their meaty bodies, but the polyps of some are on slender, elongated stalks which ripple in the current. With strong light, leathers grow quickly. Large specimens can be pruned with a razor blade, and the trimmings can be anchored to become new colonies. Place your leathers where the water current is not strong.

➤ **Star polyps** *(Pachyclavularia spp.)* are among the hardiest of the soft corals. They grow as colonies that encrust rock and, when established, will even grow onto the aquarium glass and become a living background. The fine, daisy-like polyps are about a half-inch in length and form a carpet of brown or green. Put them where the light and current are strong.

➤ **Yellow polyps** *(Parazoanthus gracilis)* are a pleasant departure from the common browns and greens of many corals. The 1-inch polyps resemble miniature sea anemones in bright yellow. Although found in colonies, yellow polyps are individuals that do not share a communal body, the way many other corals do. They are photosynthetic, but I find that they do best when offered occasional feedings.

➤ **Button polyps** *(Zoanthus spp.)* grow in tight colonies, with short, sunflowerlike disks. The most common colors are green or brown, but specimens with blue or orange centers are also seen. The **sea mats** *(Palythoa spp.)* are similar but share an encrusting base. Place these animals where they can get good light but are out of swift water current. Indo-Pacific and Caribbean varieties are available.

Properly kept, colonies of green button polyps will spread over the rocks in your reef tank.

➤ **Colt coral** *(Alcyonium spp.).* Excellent choices for the beginner, colt corals are hardy, fast growers. Place them where they can receive strong light and current. Growing from a central stalk, colt corals grow into large, flowing trees. When they get too large, simply take a razor blade and prune the extra branches. Anchor them in place and they'll grow into new colonies. Typical colors are brown or cream. By the way, it is a mystery where the name *colt* originated. If anyone knows, drop me an e-mail (the address is on the inside back cover of this book) and satisfy my curiosity. I wonder if large colonies flowing in the current don't look a bit like a horse's mane flowing in the wind.

When colonies of colt coral grow this large, you can slice off branches with a razor blade and anchor them elsewhere. They will grow into new colonies!

➤ **Waving hands** *(Xenia spp.)* are especially interesting soft corals. Light-colored, flowery polyps grow from a central stalk. The interesting thing is that the polyps pulse. They resemble tiny hands opening and closing rhythmically. Xenia polyps reproduce quickly, but I've seen fields of colonies melt within a day, too. Many hobbyists recommend the use of one of the commercial iodine supplements for these and other corals.

Soft corals to avoid: The carnation or cauliflower corals *(Dendronephthya spp.)* are often seen in dealers' tanks but should not be purchased. They are nearly impossible to keep alive in captivity. The carnation corals are not photosynthetic. They will readily accept feedings of baby brine shrimp, prawn eggs, and so forth, but the latest information indicates that they are phytoplankton feeders. That is, they filter microscopic algae from the water column. These animals are found in caves and overhangs, where the current is strong and the light is weak.

Stony Corals

The stony corals, also called hard corals, build a skeleton of calcium carbonate. The skeletons of dead corals are what many people picture when they think of corals, but when corals are alive the underlying skeleton is hidden by the jellylike polyps of the coral colony. As the colony expands outward, it builds new layers of calcium carbonate upon the old. This is how reefs are formed in the ocean. Stony corals can rapidly deplete calcium levels in the process of building their skeletons. Calcium supplementation is, therefore, a requirement in the reef tank.

Most stony corals are photosynthetic, and feeding is unnecessary. Still, occasionally offering of bits of seafoods can increase growth.

All the following species are Indo-Pacific in origin. It is illegal to collect stony corals in the Caribbean, with the exception of those that develop on aquacultured live-rock. Typical colors are shades of green or brown.

➤ **Frog spawn coral** *(Euphyllia divisa).* Sometimes called grape coral, this stony coral gets its name from the fact that its polyps resemble a mass of frog eggs. Other species of Euphyllia are sold as hammer or anchor corals. When positioning this coral, beware. They can extend special sweeper tentacles, which are several inches long—usually at night. Sweeper tentacles are capable of stinging and killing many other species of coral and are the animal's way of assuring itself a clear territory for growth. Yes, even immobile corals can be aggressive to their neighbors.

➤ **Elegant coral** *(Catalaphyllia elegans)* builds an undulating skeleton that is similar to that of frog spawn coral. The living tissue, however, is quite different in appearance. Elegant corals have meaty bodies, edged with tentacles. Central mouths punctuate the tissue. Elegant corals are very hardy and accept feedings readily. They also extend sweeper tentacles.

195

A large colony of frog spawn coral.

➤ **Acropora coral** (*Acropora spp.*) is not easy to say—I've heard it pronounced both *ak-roh-POR-uh* and *uh-KROP-er-uh*. Corals from this group—often sold as table, bird's nest, staghorn, or elkhorn coral—are probably the fastest growers of the stony corals. With proper care, including adequate calcium supplementation, acropora corals can grow several inches per year. Typical forms resemble bushes with thorny branches. However, the species and direction of current will affect the shape of these corals as they grow. In addition to the typical greens and browns, acropora corals are especially prized for the occasional pink, purple, blue, and yellow specimens.

Acropora corals are the easiest stony corals to propagate.

➤ **Flowerpot coral** *(Goniopora spp.)*. When closed, the flowerpot coral colony is rather spherical, but when the polyps extend, it resembles a pot full of green or brown flowers. Most hobbyists report poor success with these species, so beginners should avoid them. I have seen some thrive and grow for years, though. In my opinion, strong current and the use of wave-making devices to randomize that current are requirements for success with the flowerpot corals.

➤ **Bubble corals** *(Plerogyra spp.)* are named for the large, bladderlike sacs that they display instead of polyps. Though largely photosynthetic, they also have feeding tentacles that can be extended, particularly at night. Coloration is tan, pearl, or light green.

➤ **Open brain coral** *(Trachyphyllia geoffroyi)*. Also called meat corals, the open brain corals are colorful and hardy. The green open brain is green overall, with brown striations. The red open brain is green in the center with a large reddish outer ring.

Note the large, meaty polyp of the open brain coral.

➤ **Plate corals** *(Fungia spp.)*. Shaped like plates or Chinese coolie hats, these stony corals have an unusual characteristic—they are mobile. They live on the substrate and "walk" around, regularly piling themselves against the edge of the reef. The animals are covered with small tentacles that maneuver food to the mouth and sweep away sediment that has settled on top. The similar **long-tentacled plate corals** *(Heliofungia spp.)* have longer, thicker tentacles. Fully opened, they resemble sea anemones more than corals. A similar group, the **tongue corals** *(Herpolitha spp.)*, gets its name from an elongated body shape.

A brain coral clearly shows the reach of its stinging sweeper tentacles. Many corals can exude these tentacles, stinging nearby neighbors to keep them at bay.

➤ **Sun polyps** *(Tubastraea spp.)* may be the most beautiful of the stony corals. Colonies are bright orange with large yellow polyps. (Black colonies are also available but seem to be less hardy.) However, sun polyps should be avoided by all but the most dedicated hobbyists. They are not photosynthetic, as are all the other species I've described so far, and absolutely must be fed. In the wild, they live in caves and overhangs, catching tiny shrimp and other organisms that wash through in the current. Strong current and shady locations suit this coral best. They will accept live foods, but frozen seafoods work equally well. Squeeze a little bit of the juice into the water to encourage the sun polyps to extend their feeding polyps. A few minutes later, you can tuck bits of food directly into the polyps.

Fish and Tips

Gorgonians and some stony corals should be anchored firmly in place with marine epoxy. Most dealers stock a variety sold as puttylike sticks. The core and outer layers of the stick are different components that you knead together to activate. Then use the putty to attach the gorgonian in place. Once it hardens, the animal will grow tissue over the putty, hiding it from view. You can even attach animals to the back glass using this method.

Sea Plumes and Sea Fans

The gorgonians, also known as sea fans and sea plumes, develop in many forms. Some resemble candelabras or feathers. Others build a fan-shape lattice. Gorgonians share traits of both soft and stony corals. Colorful living tissue surrounds a horny skeleton.

Gorgonians like strong water current, particularly strong alternating current. Use of wave-making devices is highly recommended for the sea plumes and should be considered a requirement for the sea fans. Most species seen in the aquarium trade are Caribbean.

➤ **Sea plumes.** These animals, also called sea rods, do best in strong current. Stick to photosynthetic species, including the purple and brown varieties, for best results. Attractive red and yellow sea plumes are also available, but they are not photosynthetic and will require feedings of live baby brine shrimp, frozen prawn eggs, or other foods.

This photosynthetic sea plume will be happier when it is permanently attached to a rock.

➤ **Sea fans.** Strong current is a requirement for these organisms, and it should be alternating in direction. Water movement helps the animal slough off algae and debris. Sea fans are more delicate than sea plumes and are best left to the advanced hobbyist.

Even the Rocks Are Alive

So far, I've only talked about the larger fancy invertebrates that act as focal points in your aquarium. However, you will find many more species of tiny invertebrates that arrive as hitchhikers on your live-rock. Keep your eyes peeled for tiny shrimp, copepods, fanworms, snails, clams, and more. Just for fun, use a flashlight to look into your tank at night. You will be amazed at how many tiny planktonic creatures are in there that you didn't know about.

Fish and Tips

Sea plumes can be easily propagated. As the animals grow, you can take cuttings. Wedge the cuttings tightly into a hole in a rock, and they will take hold and grow.

Over time, you will see changes occur, too. Some species will seem to disappear, while others blossom. Every time you look, you are likely to see something that you didn't notice before. Have fun!

This well-established reef has been colonized by many types of animals.

The Least You Need to Know

➤ Most invertebrates are poor choices for the fish–only aquarium. Keep them in a reef tank instead.

➤ Learn about the animals before you buy them.

➤ Avoid species with high failure rates in captivity.

➤ Corals and sea anemones need strong light and water current.

Chapter 14

On the Road with Your Fish and Invertebrates

In This Chapter

➤ How fish and invertebrates get to your local shop

➤ How livestock is packaged for the trip home with you

➤ How to acclimate your fish and critters

➤ How to transport your animals

Before I tell you how to take your fish and plants home without killing them, you might be curious about how the livestock gets to your dealer's shop in the first place. Over the years, I have occasionally had customers ask if we raised all the fish ourselves. I guess they think we've got a jillion tanks and ponds in the back room, reserved strictly for breeding. I have even had customers ask where we go to catch all these fish.

Legal Aliens

Well, it may surprise you, but it is unlikely that your dealer breeds any of his own fish. He just doesn't have the time or the space. Besides, nearly all saltwater fish are wild-caught. We don't yet have the technology to successfully breed and rear most species.

Your saltwater aquarium inhabitants are hand-collected from reefs in the wild. Caribbean and Hawaiian collectors ship their catch directly to wholesalers or retailers. Species collected from farther afield travel a more circuitous route. For example, in the Philippines, it starts with local divers who collect the fishes. They store the fish in net traps or large tubs, or even in individual plastic bags, until a jobber comes around to buy their catch. The jobber sells the catch to exporters in Manila. From there, the fish and invertebrates are shipped to foreign distributors, wholesalers, or retailers.

A Fish in a Bag in a Box

There is a standard way to ship live saltwater fish. First, each fish is put into a separate plastic bag, filled approximately one-third full of water. The remainder of the bag is filled with pure oxygen. The added oxygen allows the fish to be shipped in a smaller space, saving shipping costs. It also allows the fish to remain confined longer without suffocating. Each bag is then sealed and double-bagged, often with a layer of newspaper in between to keep sharp spines from poking through.

Next, the individually bagged fish are placed inside a large outer bag and sealed inside a large Styrofoam box. The Styrofoam box insulates against sudden temperature changes. Sometimes, a small chemical heat or ice pack is added to regulate temperature during the trip. The Styrofoam also helps keep leaky bags from leaking on other cargo. It would be nice if fish bags never leaked, but sometimes it just happens.

Dan oxygenates a bag of fish and packs it in Styrofoam for shipment.

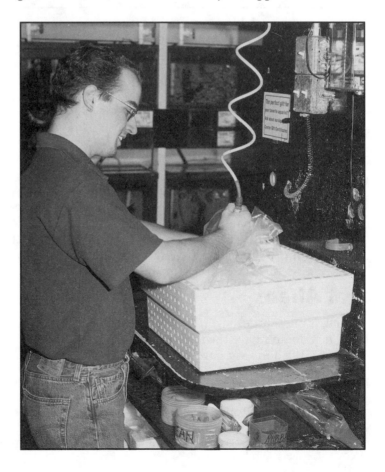

Next, the Styrofoam box is placed inside a cardboard box. The cardboard box provides another layer of insulation and protection, and contains all the shipping information needed for the package to find its way to the proper destination.

Depending on destination, these fish may be in transit a few hours or a couple of days. So it may be some time before the fish see light and fresh water again. Fish are amazingly hardy, though, and most will survive the trip. Still, it can be quite rough on them. Imagine bouncing around in the dark in a bag of stale water for up to two days, and you can see why the fish may be stressed upon arrival. Now, imagine being a wild-caught fish that has to make similar trips up to five times before arriving home at your tank.

So much for how the fish get to your local shop. Now let's talk about how you get them home from there.

Wrapping Up Your Fish

When you purchase your fish, your dealer will net them out and place them inside a plastic bag approximately one-third full with water from the aquarium. The remaining two-thirds is to hold the necessary air. Your dealer will either tie off the bag or seal it with a rubber band. The bag should be sufficiently inflated to hold its shape. Fish can get trapped in the corners and squashed in an underinflated bag.

Fish are placed directly into the plastic bags, but live corals are often wrapped in an additional plastic bag before being placed inside the bag of water. Live-rock may be wrapped in plastic or newspaper, or not at all. Live rock is usually shipped without water. Don't worry—it comes all the way from the Caribbean or the Indo-Pacific that way and gets here in fine shape. The short trip to your house is no big deal. Besides, live-rocks are very rough and tend to poke through the bags, making all the water leak out.

Most dealers simply trap enough air in the bag to oxygenate it for the trip home, but some dealers go the extra measure and inflate the bag with pure oxygen. This increases the amount of time that fish are safe in the bag. However, it really isn't necessary to use pure oxygen, unless you plan to leave the animal in the plastic bag for more than a few hours.

Sometimes, customers ask if they can have extra water because they have a long trip. Believe it or not, that is probably a bad idea. It is better to have more air than water. You see, the water only keeps the fish wet. It is the air within the bag that keeps the bag oxygenated. So the more air, the better. There is a lot more oxygen in air than in water. However, if your trip home is going to last more than a couple of hours, you may want to ask the dealer to use the next size larger bag. This will give you both more water and more air.

Clyde shows a fish bagged up for the trip home.

Fish Tales

Did you know that damselfish come all the way from Asia (often a two-day trip) packed one fish per tiny bag? If they can safely make that long trip in 2 ounces of water, your dealer's packaging for the short trip home will be quite roomy by comparison.

Fish with spiny fins, or invertebrates with spines, should be double bagged. Your dealer will first bag the specimen in a single plastic bag, which will then be inserted upside-down into a second plastic bag. The double layers of plastic make it more punctureproof, and putting one bag upside-down within the other rounds off corners, making it more difficult for the fish to lodge and poke through.

Most saltwater specimens are bagged individually. However, if you buy a small group of the same species—say, three damsels—it is common to put them together in the same bag. You may want to ask if your dealer has a central filtration system. If so, the same water is recycled through all the tanks, and it is OK to bag fish from different aquariums in the same bag. However, if each tank is a separate environment, your dealer should not combine fish from different aquariums in the same plastic bag.

The water quality in each tank could be quite different. Why put the fish through the added shock of water mixing when you are going to have to do it again when you get home and introduce them to your tank?

The procedure for packaging macroalgae is similar, but generally they go into the plastic bags without water. Also, plain air is used to inflate the bag, not pure oxygen. Customers often worry that the plants won't survive the trip when packaged this way. Some ask for water to be added to the bag. The truth is that the plants will be fine without water. In fact, they arrive wrapped only in wet newspaper when your dealer gets them, and they have been in transit for much longer. Also, adding water is sometimes counterproductive. If the water sloshes a lot on the way home, it may bend and break up the plants.

When you ring up at the cash register, your plastic bags of fish and invertebrates will be packaged in typical grocery bags for the trip home. In cooler weather, double-folding the top of the grocery bag will help it retain heat.

The Invertebrate 500

No need to enter your fish in the Invertebrate 500 road race to get them home. Your fish can handle the trip just fine. The main precaution you need to take is to protect the fish and invertebrates from temperature extremes. If you are comfortable, the fish are probably comfortable, too.

In hot weather, be very careful about setting the fish anywhere where they might cook. Think of a sealed plastic bag as being much like a closed-up car. If the sun hits it directly, it will get very hot, very fast. So do not set your fish on the dashboard or leave them in the trunk. Try not to set them on a seat that is getting direct sunlight. Placing the fish on the floor in the shade is a better choice. Also, don't put the fish too near an air-conditioning duct, or they will get chilled.

Yes, a sealed plastic bag is very much like a closed-up car. A closed-up car is very much like a closed-up car, too. So don't leave bags of fish and plants in an unattended vehicle. If you have to make a stop somewhere, take the fish in with you.

The grocery bag should provide ample protection from the cold for the short trip home in cold weather—particularly if you turn on the car's heater. Be careful, though, not to set the fish too close to the heating ducts, or they may cook. Again, if you have other stops, take the fish inside rather than leaving them in an unattended car.

Try not to jostle the fish too much during the trip home. That doesn't mean that you have to drive

Fish and Tips

If the weather is especially hot or cold, you may want to take the added precaution of bringing along a Styrofoam container or empty Coleman cooler. This provides extra insulation for the fish on your trip home. Some dealers sell Styrofoam fish boxes.

Fish School

The fancy word for adjusting to changes in level of salt in the water is **osmoregulate**.

5 miles per hour and have the kids try to balance the bag on the way. If you've ever seen fish in a stream or in the ocean, you know they can take quite a bit of jostling without a problem. In fact, a little bit of jostling is helpful because it agitates and oxygenates the water in the bag.

Acclimating New Arrivals

Ideally, all new specimens should be quarantined for two weeks before being introduced to your tank. This helps prevent the introduction of disease and is especially important in reef tanks. The medicines used for treating many saltwater fish diseases are lethal to invertebrates. See Chapter 22 on disease and stress to learn how to set up a simple quarantine tank. If you are setting up a fish-only aquarium, your main tank can act as a quarantine tank this one time when you are bringing home your first fish.

I know that you will be quite anxious to get your new fish into the tank, but you cannot just dump them right in. The temperature and water quality in the bag may be quite different from that in your aquarium. So you must acclimate the fish. Whether you choose to use a quarantine tank or to put fish directly into your show tank, there are several popular methods for acclimating fish to their new home.

The Float and Dump Method

First off, you need to equalize the temperature in the fish bag with the temperature that is in your tank, to prevent the fish from suffering temperature shock. To do this, float the unopened plastic fish bag on top of the water in your tank for 20 minutes. This will allow the temperatures to equalize. There is no need to float longer than this. Floating longer serves no purpose, as the temperature should already be equalized. In fact, since there is a limited amount of oxygen in the fish bag, floating longer could be detrimental.

After the bag has floated for 20 minutes, open it and dump the contents into the aquarium. It's quick. It's easy. But there is more risk of shock to your fish and transmission of disease—because your fish will be going from one type of water to another with no adjustment, and if the dealer's water is carrying parasites, adding this water to your aquarium is a good way to spread them.

I generally do not recommend this method.

The Float and Net Method

The float and net method is a little better. Again, float the unopened fish bag, but instead of dumping the bag into the tank, gently net the fish out of the bag and place them in the tank. It will still be an instantaneous change from one type of water to another, but there will be a bit less chance of introducing disease into your tank. Discard the dealer's water.

Float new arrivals, bag and all, for 20 minutes. It will equalize temperature and prevent shock.

The Float and Mix Method

Even better is the float and mix method. While the fish bag is floating, open it up and pour a bit of water from your tank into the bag every few minutes. This will provide a more gradual change in water quality for your fish. After 20 minutes, you can either dump the contents into the tank, or better, gently net the fish from the bag, place the fish in the tank, and discard the water in the bag.

The Drip Method

Best of all is the drip method, which is just a more methodical version of the float and mix method. The difference is, instead of making staged additions of water to the fish bag, you place the fish in a container on the floor and use a piece of air line with a valve on it to siphon water from the tank at a slow drip into the container on the floor. This makes the smoothest transition in water quality for the fish. Let a gallon or so of aquarium water drip in to mix with the dealer's water. Then net the fish and place it in the aquarium. Throw away the water in the container. If you use the drip method, don't walk away and forget it, or you will be wading through a puddle when you get back.

Acclimating Invertebrates

Live-rocks are usually added directly to the aquarium, without mixing water or floating them to adjust temperature. Any of the preceding methods can be used for corals and invertebrates, although the echinoderms (starfish, urchins, and their cousins) do not easily adjust to changes in salinity. So I recommend using the float and mix method or the drip method with them.

Fish and Tips

Turn off your tank light while floating new arrivals. Reduced light has a calming effect on both the fish in the bag and the fish in the tank.

Monitoring New Inhabitants

When you release your first batch of fish into the tank, your natural inclination will be to sit there a while to watch what they do. After all, watching the fish is the whole point of keeping an aquarium, isn't it?

Taking time to watch is a good thing. You can keep your eyes open for problems. However, don't expect to get the full picture right away. Plopped into unfamiliar territory, the new arrivals are not likely to be themselves. Some will explore, seeking a territory to claim. Others will hide until they feel safe from attack.

If you are going to encounter problems with new tankmates, they will probably occur at night when you are not watching. Initial aggression levels tend to be low as new residents scope out each other and their surroundings. Keep your eye open for serious fights, but the occasional jockeying for territory is normal. Take corrective action (see Chapter 23 on dealing with aggression) only if damage occurs.

Something's Fishy

Do not feed new arrivals until they have been in the tank for a few hours or more. You may even want to wait a full day. New fish are under stress and are unlikely to eat, so most of the food will be wasted. You will just end up polluting the tank. Be patient.

Fish and Tips

When introducing fish to an existing tank, it may help to feed the resident fish first. Fish with full stomachs are less likely to be aggressive toward new tankmates.

The New Guy in Town

When adding fish to an existing tank, things may get rougher. Established residents have their territories already staked out. The new arrival must fight its way into a territory. So keep an especially close eye when adding to an existing tank.

When adding fish to a new tank, it can be helpful to rearrange all the decorations first. Moving the rocks and driftwood around, for example, will force existing inhabitants to find new territories, too. That way, the new guy won't be at such a disadvantage.

Don't let that scare you too much, though. There is no need to remove a fish at the first bite. Some sparring is normal. Whenever possible, allow the fish to work out their differences. Just don't let it progress to the point where someone gets seriously wounded . . . or seriously killed.

Keep an extra watch out for disease the first week. Fish are under the most stress when introduced to a new tank, and of course, new fish may bring disease with them. So take time to notice changes, and follow the advice in Chapter 22 on stress and disease if you need to.

Have Bucket, Will Travel

A time may come when you need to move your aquarium or transport your fish. Maybe you want to move your aquarium to a different room, or you bought a new house and need to take the aquarium with you. Or maybe one of your favorite fish has grown too large for its existing aquarium and your dealer is willing to accept it in trade. With a little planning, the chore shouldn't be too difficult.

Moving Your Tank

Sometimes, moving an aquarium to a new location is no big deal and can be easily done without help. Other times, it can be a major production requiring several helpers. A few factors come into play:

➤ Size of the tank

➤ Distance of the move

➤ Stairs

Something's Fishy

The most important rule in moving aquariums is to never move an aquarium that is full. Most tanks are too heavy for that, anyway, but even smaller tanks will twist and break more easily when full.

Smaller tanks are easiest to manage. In most cases, the simplest method is to drain the tank until the water just covers the fish. Then pick the whole thing up and transfer it. Refill the tank at the destination. Fish and invertebrates remain in place, although you may temporarily need to remove rocks or decorations that might fall and crush the fish.

Draining a tank until it just covers the fish may work with bigger tanks, too, but I don't recommend it. Big tanks are heavy enough as it is. Some large aquariums may require six guys to carry them when empty. Also, bigger tanks often contain bigger fish, which means more water would be required to keep the fish covered. That is not good. You need the water to be very shallow if you plan to move the tank with fish and decor intact. Otherwise, the weight of the water could twist and crack the tank.

When moving a tank, don't forget to consider how many staircases you will encounter along the way—especially if you try moving the tank with decorations or fish in it. Will you be able to carry the tank up the stairs without tilting it? Tilting a tank with water in it is a very good way to break the seams of a tank, by shifting all the stress to one end or corner. Worse, if you are already struggling to handle the weight, what do you think will happen when you tilt the tank and the water sloshes to one end—putting all the weight on one person? Disaster!

Fish and Tips

Use a gravel vacuum to drain the water from your tank for moving. That way, the tank will be clean and fresh when you refill it at the new destination.

If you move an aquarium that is too large for one person to carry easily, it is probably best to empty it completely and carry it that way. If necessary, use a hand truck or appliance cart to move the tank up the stairs. (Stand the empty tank on its end on the hand truck.) You can rent hand trucks and appliance carts at any U-Haul.

Haul Your Bass

If your trip is going to be longer, or if you are moving large fish, it is best to pack and transfer the fish separately from the aquarium. You can either package the fish in plastic bags—like your dealer does—or put them in your fish bucket for transfer. Be sure to put a lid on the bucket or line it with a garbage bag that you can tie off. For really large fish, you might use a clean garbage can.

For cross-country or other moves that will take more than a day, things get more complicated. You may need to add pure oxygen to the fish bags to keep the fish safe for the trip, or you may need to bag the fish much more sparsely. Some dealers will package your fish for shipment, using Styrofoam boxes and bags inflated with pure oxygen, for a small fee. Shipping via air freight may be necessary, as well.

If you'd rather not move your fish across country, considering selling them via a classified newspaper ad, trading them for supplies with your dealer, or even donating them to a school. That way, you can move the aquarium and restock it at your convenience once you reach your destination.

The Least You Need to Know

➤ Protect fish and invertebrates from temperature extremes on the way home. Don't leave fish unattended in the car, or place them too close to heating or cooling ducts.

➤ Quarantine new arrivals whenever possible. This helps prevent the introduction of disease to your tank.

➤ Float new arrivals for 20 minutes to equalize temperature. That is, float the fish bag with the fish in it on the surface of your tank.

➤ It is best not to add the dealer's water to your tank. It may harbor disease.

➤ Monitor new arrivals. Watch for aggression and shock.

Part 4
The Tank Is Running; Now What?

*The lyrics of an old song say, "All I need is the air that I breathe and to love you."
Well, if you want your fish to love you, it's not the air you have to worry about so
much—it's the water. Healthy water is the basis for a healthy aquarium and healthy
fish. In fact, the air your fish breathe is in the water!*

*Part 4 largely deals with water in the aquarium. You will start by learning how to
cycle your new tank. That chapter (Chapter 15) may be the most important one for you
to read. Don't skip it! Next, you will get a brief lesson in water chemistry. This chapter
is a bit more technical than others in this book, but don't let that scare you. I've put
things in simple terms. You don't need to be a chemist to understand it. The last
chapter on water deals with how and why it is important to change it regularly.*

*Aquariums are very low-maintenance, but once you get your tank up and running, you
can't just ignore it. There are a few chores necessary to keep your equipment working
and to keep your animals alive. I'll talk about these, and you'll also learn how to feed
your fish properly, and how to keep your tank clean and looking nice.*

*Finally, for those of you who are dying to keep coral, I'll explain how reefkeeping
works.*

Chapter 15

Cycling Your New Aquarium

In This Chapter

➤ Why bacteria aren't always bad

➤ The nitrogen cycle in detail

➤ The fastest, safest ways to cycle a new tank

➤ What to do if there is a problem

Please read this chapter *very* carefully. It could make the difference between life and death for your first batch of fish. The environment that you set up in an aquarium is always a fragile thing, but it is especially fragile in a new tank. This is because your aquarium must achieve a balance between the waste excreted by your fish and the helpful waste-reducing bacteria that live in the tank. Earlier in the book, I mentioned that you cannot add a full load of fish to your new tank all at once. You are about to learn why that is, and how cycling or breaking in a new tank can prevent problems.

Good-Guy Bacteria

The first thing you need to understand is that every healthy, established aquarium is heavily populated by helpful bacteria. These "good-guy" bacteria are essential to the proper functioning of your aquarium. They break down ammonia and other fish waste. Without them, fish waste quickly builds up to levels that are lethal to your fish. Eventually, all the solid surfaces in your aquarium—including the glass sides, gravel, decorations, and debris—will be coated with jillions of helpful bacteria.

Unfortunately, those helpful bacteria are not present in sufficient quantity in a new aquarium. The bacteria won't develop a big enough population until after you have added your first batch of fish. That is because the fish produce the ammonia that is the food for the bacteria. Without ammonia to feed them, the bacteria can't multiply.

Without bacteria to break down the toxic ammonia, your fish risk poisoning themselves with their own waste. That is why a new tank is more fragile than an older, established aquarium. Until you add fish, the bacteria won't develop, but until the bacteria develop, the fish continue to excrete toxic ammonia that won't all be broken down. There is a time lag between the introduction of waste-producing fish and the development of full colonies of waste-reducing bacteria. Since ammonia and other levels will increase during this period, it is a very dangerous time.

Fish School

The term **cycling** derives from the nitrogen cycle, which is what is happening chemically during this process. I will tell you more about that in detail a bit later in the chapter.

However, over a period of weeks, your tank will develop plenty of helpful bacteria. The time lag between the introduction of fish and the final catch-up of waste-neutralizing bacteria is called the break-in period. We also say that we are cycling a new tank as we progress through this period.

The key point to remember here is that, as weird as it may seem, your fish are at much more risk in a brand new, sparkling clean tank than in an old dirty one. That is because there are sufficient helpful bacteria in the established tank. Now, don't take this to mean that you shouldn't keep a clean tank. On the contrary, performing the routine maintenance that keeps your tank clean is very important. Clean tanks are good, but sterile tanks are bad.

It Depends on the Bioload

How long does it take to cycle a new tank? Well, every aquarium is different. There are many factors that influence how long it will take to break in a new tank, but it will probably come down to two things:

1. How big is the initial bioload of the tank?
2. Did you do anything to seed the filter bed with helpful bacteria?

Wastes must be removed or neutralized to keep a system healthy. The fish and invertebrates comprise the majority of the bioload in your aquarium. Animals eat and excrete waste. Obviously, the more fish and invertebrates you put into your tank, the more waste will be produced, and that will result in a higher bioload.

Algae counts as bioload, too. However, we don't really concern ourselves with the bioload of algae—unless it dies and decays. In fact, algae acts to remove nutrients from the water and may actually increase the carrying capacity of your tank.

While you may use the number of fish to judge how large a bioload your system has, when it comes right down to it the fish really aren't the problem. You are the problem. Now, don't get all defensive. Stop and think for a moment. The fish can't excrete waste unless they first eat something. Right? And who is it that puts the food into the tank? That's right, you do. So when we get right down to it, you ultimately determine the bioload in your tank by how much you feed. Always remember that you are not just feeding the fish— you are feeding the tank.

Fish School

The **bioload** of your tank refers to waste-producing animals and plants. The size and number of specimens introduced into your aquarium will determine its bioload.

Speeding the Process

Your aquarium cannot safely hold a full load of fish until it has cycled. Since you now know that cycling a tank is the process of developing enough helpful bacteria to handle the bioload of that aquarium, you have probably already figured out that there are ways to speed the process by introducing some extra bacteria to get the cycle moving. Let's talk about how to do this.

The easiest, cheapest, and most effective way to speed the process is to seed your aquarium with some gravel from an established tank. Established tanks are fully colonized by helpful bacteria, which have attached to the substrate and other surfaces. Mixing old cycled gravel in with your new gravel will give your system a head start in developing all the good-guy bacteria it needs.

Where do you get some seeded gravel to add to your tank? If you have another saltwater aquarium up and running, you can take some from there. If not, perhaps a friend will give you some gravel from their tank. Ask your dealer if he will provide some precycled gravel from his tanks. Some dealers will give you a free handful or two, and others will sell you some. I wish that all dealers would make cycled gravel available to their customers. Dealers, are you listening?

An excellent way to speed the cycling of your tank is to add plenty of cured live-rock. The live-rock will be loaded with helpful bacteria. In fact, if you add enough, you may start out with a fully cycled aquarium.

Adding used filter media from an existing aquarium is another way to speed up the cycle.

Fish and Tips

If your dealer doesn't normally sell used gravel out of his tanks, offer to buy a new bag of gravel and trade it for some used gravel. This is good for both of you, because you get some gravel with bacteria to seed your tank, and he gets to freshen up the appearance of his tanks by trading some possibly worn looking gravel for some newer stuff.

Filter media will be coated with lots of helpful bacteria. So swapping some media from an established filter into your new filter can be a big help.

Many dealers will recommend products that claim to contain helpful bacteria in a dormant state. Adding these products to your tank is supposed to speed up the cycle. I can't recommend these products, though. When I've tried them, I've seen little or no difference in how long it takes an aquarium to cycle. While many of these products will, indeed, break down ammonia, they don't actually seed your tank with the right kind of bacteria—the kind that will establish themselves permanently to keep ammonia from building up again. Additionally, there is the question of shelf life. My recommendation is to save your money and skip these products.

Safe Cycling

Patience is the most important quality needed for cycling a new aquarium. Rush this process, and you risk killing all your fish and invertebrates.

The most common way to cycle a new aquarium is to do so by adding the livestock in small increments. Add too many animals at once, and they could poison themselves with their own ammonia. To prevent that, introduce only a few specimens at a time. This gives the system time to develop enough helpful bacteria to handle the lower, less toxic amount of waste (produced by fewer animals) before adding more livestock.

Again, the most important thing is to avoid the temptation to add too many fish at once. You will remember from Chapter 11 that an established aquarium can usually hold 1 inch of fish per 2 gallons of water. When cycling a new tank, though, don't exceed 1 inch of fish per 10 gallons of water. If you start with fewer fish and feed only lightly, less ammonia will be produced. This will provide some ammonia to grow the helpful bacteria without letting ammonia levels get so high that they poison the fish. Later, you will be able to add more fish.

Fish and Tips

Many dealers offer a water testing service that is either free or inexpensive. Feel free to make use of this service, but I still recommend that you buy your own test kits. Even if you use your own kits, your dealer can help you interpret the results of the tests.

You are probably wondering how long this process will take. Well, each tank is different. The only way to know for sure is to monitor the rise and fall of ammonia and nitrite levels with water test kits. I'll discuss them in more detail in a bit. For now, a general rule is that it will take two to three weeks to cycle most tanks with the first batch of fish. However, I have seen some tanks take over a month to cycle.

After your tank has gone through the first cycle, you may add more fish. Again, add only a few and then monitor your ammonia and nitrite levels to see when it is safe to add more fish (up to the maximum 1 inch per 2 gallons, as described in Chapter 11). Adding fish in stages is a safe and easy way to cycle a tank, and chances are good that you won't lose a single fish during the process. But if you rush things and put too many fish in at once, you risk losing them all.

Cycling without the Fish

Ammonium chloride can be used to cycle a new aquarium, and it is totally safe when used as directed, but it requires even more patience. Instead of adding a few fish to add the ammonia that gets the cycle started, you add the ammonia directly. That means you'll have *no fish at all* while the tank is cycling. Most aquarium stores will sell products that contain ammonium chloride for seeding new tanks. Follow the recommended dosage and procedures on the package.

After adding the ammonium chloride, you monitor ammonia and nitrite levels in the aquarium. By monitoring those levels, you will be able to tell when the tank has cycled. At that point, you do a major water change and then add your fish. The advantage of this method is that you can add all your fish at once, because your tank will be fully cycled and ready for them. The disadvantage is that you will not be able to add a single fish until the process is complete. The ammonia levels would quickly kill them. So be prepared to look at your aquarium for two to three weeks without the fish.

Something's Fishy

Never use the ammonium chloride method to cycle a tank while the fish are in it. It will kill them!

Finally, let me say that it is not uncommon to lose fish during the cycling of a new tank. So if it happens to you, don't feel too bad, because it happens to many people. However, if you follow the guidelines that I've presented, you have a very good chance of having every fish survive the process. If things go wrong, don't be afraid to seek help.

The Nitrogen Cycle in Detail

I am going to get a bit more technical in this section. I am going to delve more deeply into the chemistry of cycling a tank. Don't let this scare you off! You should be able to maneuver through this section, even if you didn't breeze through high school chemistry. *It is important that you read this part*, even if you don't memorize all the details. When you emerge from the other side, you should have a better understanding of how the cycling process works and, therefore, a better understanding of why you don't want to rush it and what happens if you try to bend the rules.

Ammonia Is Excreted

Unless you have an existing problem with your tapwater, there will be no ammonia or nitrite in the water when you first set up your tank—but not for long. Once you add animals to the aquarium, ammonia will begin to build up.

Now, I don't think I have to tell you how toxic ammonia can be. Just as we produce ammonia in our urine, fish produce ammonia (NH_3), too. However, they excrete it largely through their gills and only to a lesser extent in their urine. No matter; the result is the same, and that is that ammonia ends up in the water. Ammonia also enters the water when heterotrophic bacteria break down uneaten food, dead organisms, feces, and other garbage in the tank. These bacteria are different from the nitrifying bacteria, which are the good-guy bacteria.

Fish School

Aerobic bacteria use and require oxygen. **Anaerobic** bacteria do not. **Heterotrophic** bacteria cannot synthesize their own food and must eat organic matter.

Ammonia Is Converted to Nitrite

It's time to meet the good guys. Nitrosomonas are the helpful aerobic bacteria that break down ammonia. They convert the ammonia into nitrite (NO_2^-)—which is still toxic to your fish, although not as toxic as ammonia. In a new tank, the ammonia levels will typically rise for about seven days after you introduce the first batch of fish. By this time, the helpful nitrosomonas bacteria will usually have grown enough in population to break down the ammonia faster than it is produced. So a week after introducing fish, you usually will see ammonia levels drop back to zero.

Nitrite Is Converted to Nitrate

Now, remember that the ammonia is being converted to nitrite. So as the helpful bacteria get things under control and the ammonia levels drop, you will see a simultaneous increase in the nitrite levels of your tank. Nitrite levels will tend to rise for roughly another seven days; then they, too, will drop.

By this time, another group of helpful bacteria, the nitrobacter, will have developed a big enough population that they will be oxidizing the nitrite faster than it is produced. The result is that nitrite levels will drop back to zero as nitrate (NO_3^-) levels increase.

Nitrate End Product

Fortunately, nitrate is generally considered harmless to fish, except in very high levels. Your regular partial water changes will keep nitrate from building up to toxic levels. Additionally, algae may remove some nitrates from the water for use as a nutrient. In most cases, the process pretty much stops here. However, if you have live-rock in your tank, helpful anaerobic bacteria deep within the rocks can break down the nitrates to nitrogen gas (N_2). The nitrogen gas then escapes into the atmosphere.

Monitoring

Once you've seen the ammonia level rise and fall back to zero, and then see the nitrite level rise and fall back to zero, your tank will be cycled. It should be safe to add the rest of your fish. Be aware that because you have increased the bioload in your tank, you may see some temporary spikes in those ammonia and nitrite levels. The helpful bacteria need time to increase their population to adjust to the added load.

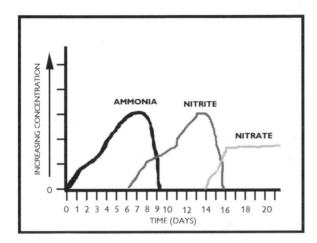

This graph shows ammonia, nitrite, and nitrate levels during the cycling of a typical aquarium. Your results may vary.

Disclaimer

The information I just gave you on the nitrogen cycle represents the way this subject has been taught for decades. However, I would like add a few notes:

1. My friend, Tim Hovanec, of Marineland Aquarium Products in Simi Valley, California, has done experiments recently that seem to show that nitrospira bacteria, not nitrobacter, are probably responsible for breaking down nitrite in the aquarium. Is this going to change the way you cycle your tank? No.

2. There are serious questions about whether nitrite is toxic to saltwater fish (if you're really interested in this, it's discussed in detail in *Captive Seawater Fishes* by Spotte and Stephen, John Wiley & Sons, 1992, pp. 62, 609–610). Salt has been used for years to reduce the toxicity of nitrites to fish in freshwater aquariums. Still, toxic or not, monitoring nitrite levels is necessary to determine when you have sufficient biological filtration.

Fish and Tips

The normal full load for a community tank is 1 inch of fish per 2 gallons. However, when cycling a new tank, don't put in more than 1 inch of fish per 10 gallons.

The Timetable

Every aquarium is different, so the timetable for cycling your tank will be different, too. The numbers I'm going to use in the list that follows are typical for tanks that I set up, but your results may vary. Let me stress that you should *use the timetable I'm giving you only as a guideline*. You must do your own ammonia and nitrite tests to determine what stage your tank is in the cycle and to determine when it is safe to add more fish. Do not ignore your test results because you are expecting something else to be true. If you are careful, you probably will see the following:

➤ No ammonia or nitrite until after you introduce fish. The clock doesn't start ticking until you add the fish.

➤ Once fish are added, ammonia will climb for approximately seven days. Then it will fall back to zero over a day or two.

➤ As ammonia falls, nitrite will climb for approximately the next seven days. Then it, too, will fall back to undetectable levels.

➤ As nitrite falls, nitrate will increase. Note, however, that I normally consider it a waste of time to test nitrate levels unless you are having problems and no other cause can be found.

The Nitrogen Cycle.

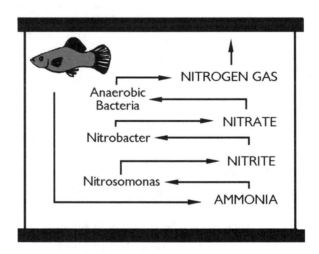

Again, I want to emphasize that you must not rush the process. Let me illustrate what can go wrong by relaying something I see happen all the time. A customer stops by the local fish store on his day off and buys his first batch of fish. Sometimes he already knows not to start out with too many fish. Sometimes he doesn't. If he doesn't, I hope the salesperson will discover that and instruct the customer not to buy too many fish at once.

Whether or not he buys too many fish, the customer then goes merrily home to introduce his fishy treasures into his tank. A week goes by and it's the customer's day off again. He is excited. So far, everything is working well in his tank. He hasn't lost any fish. Surely it would be safe and fun to go buy some more fish. Wouldn't it?

Do you remember what is going on in a typical new tank seven days after it has been set up? That's right. The ammonia is peaking at its highest, most dangerous level. Adding more fish would be a very big mistake, because it will increase the bioload and drive the ammonia levels even higher.

Unfortunately, our customer isn't thinking straight. He only sees that he has been successful so far. So off he goes to buy more fish. He adds them to his tank, the ammonia level climbs even higher, and then the fish all begin dying off. Even his favorite angelfish takes a trip to fishy heaven.

Corrective Action

It is wise to run your water tests for ammonia and nitrite every day until the cycle is complete. Levels can rise fast in a new aquarium, and you should be aware of them. After the tank cycles, you can test your water every week or two.

What should you do if you find that ammonia or nitrite levels are elevated? The answer that is usually best may surprise you: Do nothing. That's right, nothing—but only if you aren't experiencing any problems with your fish. If they all appear healthy, if none are dying, leave well enough alone. As the tank continues to cycle, Mother Nature will fix those ammonia and nitrite problems all by herself.

On the other hand, if you are losing fish or if the fish appear stressed, corrective action may be necessary.

Moaning About Ammonia

What can you do if your ammonia level is high and the fish are having problems? Here are some possible choices that you can mix or match:

➤ **Add one of those dormant bacteria products** to break down the ammonia quickly. Note that some may cloud the water temporarily.

➤ **Change some water.** Partial water changes will remove some ammonia.

➤ **Add Amquel.** This product neutralizes the toxicity of ammonia. There are also some lesser-quality copies of it on the market. Make sure you follow the directions, and be sure you test the water with a compatible salicilate-based ammonia kit.

Do not waste your money on ammonia-removing chips (zeolites or clinoptilolites) for your saltwater aquarium. Ammo-chips do not work in saltwater. In fact, saltwater is used to recharge them by making them release collected ammonia.

Fish School

New tank syndrome is a term often used to describe the high ammonia and nitrite levels seen in new, uncycled aquariums.

Fish Tales

It is common myth that dissolved ammonia makes the water look cloudy. While ammonia may be present, it is not ammonia that is making your water look cloudy. If there were enough ammonia in your tank to make the water cloudy, your fish would be long dead.

When Nitrite Is Not Right

What if the nitrite level is high and the fish are dying or looking stressed?

➤ **Do a partial water change.** This will dilute the nitrite.

➤ **Try one of the dormant bacteria products.** Some claim to reduce nitrites as well as ammonia, although my experience shows otherwise.

When Nitrate Is Left

Nitrates are generally considered to be harmless in the marine fish-only aquarium—at least, in the levels typically seen. Reef hobbyists sometimes want to lower nitrate levels to help starve undesirable algae that can choke out live corals. Consider these methods:

➤ Partial water changes to dilute nitrates are usually the preferred method. In some regions, tapwater may be naturally high in nitrates, though, so extra water changes may be ineffective.

➤ Nitrate-absorbing compounds are commercially available and may be helpful.

➤ Add live-rock. Anaerobic bacteria deep within the rock are capable of reducing nitrate to nitrogen gas, which escapes into the atmosphere.

The Least You Need to Know

➤ Helpful bacteria break down toxic ammonia and nitrite in your tank.

➤ Don't put more than 1 inch of fish per 10 gallons into a tank that you are cycling.

➤ Most new tanks take two to three weeks to cycle.

➤ You cannot tell the condition of your water by eye. You must run ammonia and nitrite tests to determine when your tank has safely cycled.

Chapter 16

A Chemistry Lesson

In This Chapter

➤ How much salt is too much?

➤ Acid vs. alkaline

➤ General hardness vs. carbonate hardness

➤ The scoop on oxygen and carbon dioxide

Many things are necessary for the happiness of your fish—compatible tankmates, proper diet, comfortable temperature, and so forth. But for fishkeeping success, nothing is more important than the quality of the water. Your fish breathe it, they drink it, they soak in it, they rest in it, and they breed in it. A clear understanding of water quality and how it affects the sea life in your tank is key to your success as an aquarium hobbyist.

In this chapter I am going to help you learn the basics of water chemistry. Some topics will be a bit technical, but don't worry. Even though the geek in me likes technical topics, I'm no chemist. So I promise to keep things as light as possible and to stick to layperson's terms. If you haven't already, be sure to read Chapter 15 on cycling a new aquarium. It is a water chemistry chapter, too, but with a different focus.

Better Living Through Chemistry

As we progress through this chapter, two things will become clear to you:

1. There are many interactions between the chemical processes in your aquarium.

2. Your dealer offers a whole pharmacy of chemicals and snake oils you can use to futz with your water chemistry.

Your dealer is likely to have a plethora of concoctions on his shelves, many claiming to work various miracles in your aquarium and all claiming to be necessities. Some are important, some are not. For example, avoid adding vitamin potions directly to your aquarium water. They are more likely to feed the algae than your fish. (Chapter 18 on feeding your fish will explain how to safely add vitamins to your fishes' diet.)

Always be sure you understand what you are doing before adding chemicals. Changing one parameter usually results in changes to another. It's the old "for every action, there is an equal and opposite reaction" rule. I recommend that you seek out some texts that explain the chemical reactions in more detail. The more you know, the safer you should be.

Something's Fishy

Be careful when using chemicals to alter water quality. Fixing one parameter can make another worse. Be sure you understand what you are doing before adding chemicals. Stop to consider if a partial water change is a better remedy.

However, just as too little knowledge can be a dangerous thing, so can too much. Reef hobbyists, particularly, seem to fall prey to what I call "tweaking syndrome." They can become so preoccupied with tweaking individual chemical parameters to "perfection" that they end up ruining their tanks!

Anyway, as you read further, be sure to watch for ways that changing one parameter can affect another, and especially remember that partial water changes are usually the best cure for poor water quality. Just because your dealer has a product on the shelf doesn't mean that it works or that you need it.

Salinity

Your saltwater tank wouldn't be much of a saltwater tank without salt, would it? So let's talk about salt. Sea salt is a mixture of dozens of elements—some major, some in trace amounts. The most important thing about using your sea salt is to be sure you use the proper amount. How can you determine how much to use?

Simple. Use a hydrometer. (That's hydrometer, not hygrometer. A hygrometer measures relative humidity in the air.) Your hydrometer is a device that measures the density, or specific gravity of your water—abbreviated SG. The more salt you dissolve in the water, the higher its specific gravity. Typical specific gravity of seawater is 1.023, which means it is 1.023 times as dense as pure water. A range of 1.020 to 1.025 is acceptable. In Chapter 9, I explained how to choose a hydrometer for your tank.

Salinity can also be measured in other ways, although these methods are rarely used in the aquarium hobby. One way is with an electronic salinity monitor. Some shops stock them. A probe that conducts electricity is immersed permanently in the aquarium, and a digital readout gives salinity in parts per thousand (ppt) or as a percentage, with 35 percent being the norm. The other method uses a refractometer, which is a device that measures salinity by measuring the way disolved salts bend light in a prism.

The process of using a hydrometer to read specific gravity is quite simple, but understanding the reading may be a bit more complicated. You see, the reading is affected by temperature and atmospheric pressure. Many hydrometers are calibrated to be used at sea level at a temperature of 60°F! You are not likely to be duplicating either of those conditions in your tank, so you may need to use a conversion chart to get your true reading.

Fish and Tips

Try to buy a hydrometer that is calibrated for use at typical room or aquarium temperature. You will need a conversion chart to use standard lab-grade hydrometers.

Check the instructions that come with your hydrometer. If it is not calibrated for use at room temperature, take your reading and then look at the conversion table that comes with the instructions. Find your reading in the column on the left, and trace over to the column beneath the listing for your current water temperature to find the true reading.

Pondering pH

pH (always spelled with a lowercase *p* and a capital *H*) is the measurement of how acid or alkaline your water is. The term *pH* comes from the French *pouvoir hydrogène*, which means *hydrogen power*. It is a measurement of hydrogen ions. We measure pH on a scale from zero to 14, with a pH of seven being neutral. A pH of less than 7 is acid, and a pH above 7 is alkaline (sometimes called basic). The lower the pH, the more acid. The higher the pH, the more alkaline.

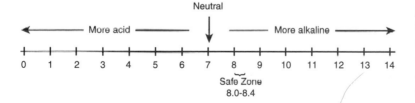

pH is measured on a scale of 0 to 14, with 7 being neutral. Low pH is acid. High pH is alkaline. A pH of 8.3 is ideal for seawater.

The pH scale is logarithmic, which means each numerical change in pH actually represents a tenfold change. That is, a pH of 7 is 10 times more alkaline than a pH of 6. Likewise, a pH of 6 is 100 times more acid than a pH of 8. Don't concern yourself too much with learning that detail. The main thing to remember is that a 1-point change in pH is a pretty big change, and a 2-point change is a huge change! It is dangerous to change the pH of your aquarium too rapidly—either up or down.

Why should you care about pH? Because the toxicity of ammonia excreted by the animals is greatly affected by the pH of your aquarium. Ammonia (NH_3) is much more toxic in alkaline water than in acid water (where it ionizes into the less toxic ammonium, NH_4^+). Seawater is naturally alkaline, so ammonia is always dangerous stuff in the marine aquarium.

The ocean is the most stable environment in the world. Aside from temperature differences, seawater in one part of the world is not much different from seawater everywhere else. Most experts set the pH of seawater at 8.3, and this is the number that you should strive for in your aquarium. However, anywhere from, say, 8.0 to 8.4 is acceptable. Most fish, no matter where they come from, can tolerate a pH in that range. Your invertebrates may be less tolerant, though.

Assessing Acidity

How do you know what your pH is? Simple—you test it. There are many pH test kits on the market that are cheap and easy to use. Be sure you buy a pH kit designed for saltwater, or it may not give readings in the proper range. Each kit works a bit differently, but the basic procedure is to fill a vial with water from the aquarium, add a chemical reagent, and then compare the resulting color to a color chart to get your numerical reading. The most accurate saltwater pH kits use powdered reagents.

Fish and Tips

Follow your test kit's directions carefully. Some kits require you to view through the side of the vial to determine the color, and some require that you view down through the top of the vial. Improper viewing will distort the reading.

My pH Has pHallen and It Can't Get Up

Commercial sea salts will normally mix to provide an ideal pH of 8.3. This is good! But not for long. Many things affect the pH of your aquarium water, and you will find that the pH in your tank will fall over time.

Why does the pH tend to drop? The main answer is biological activity. You will remember that bacteria convert ammonia to nitrite, and nitrite to nitrate. Well, a byproduct of that process is the formation of acids, and these acids will cause the pH to fall. Fortunately, your sea salt mix contains buffers. Buffers are chemicals that resist the changes in pH by neutralizing these acids. These buffers will help keep your pH from falling, but the process depletes them. So the buffers in your salt mix don't prevent the pH from falling—they only slow it. Depending on the bioload of your tank, this could happen within days, or it could take weeks.

What else affects pH? When carbon dioxide is dissolved in water, it forms carbonic acid. So if your aeration is insufficient to drive off the carbon dioxide that your animals excrete, the carbon dioxide can build up and cause the pH to fall slightly.

Photosynthesis also affects pH. Plants use carbon dioxide when they photosynthesize. That means that during the day they will pull carbon dioxide from the water, and less carbonic acid will form. So your aquarium's pH will rise slightly during the day. At night plants respire, and the pH will fall a bit as the dissolved carbon dioxide levels rise again.

Fish School

A **buffer** is a combination of an acid or base with a salt that, when in solution, tends to stabilize the pH of the solution.

Altering pH

In most cases, you should not need to alter your pH. Sea salt mixes tend to set it at a desirable level, and regular partial water changes will help keep the pH from falling. However, there may be times when you need to intervene—particularly if you were bad and over-crowded your tank. A higher bioload means more waste, which means more acids produced, which means more rapid depletion of the buffers in your seawater, and that means your pH will fall faster.

Bumping the pH Up

It is usually fairly easy to increase the pH. Here are some ways to do it:

➤ **Change some water.** This is usually the best choice. When your pH is low, it is probably a sign that you are not changing enough water. Remember that pH tends to drop over time, due to biological activity in the tank. Partial water changes are usually the best way to bring the pH back up. Water changes work by replacing lost trace elements and buffers, and by removing dissolved organics. Buffers in the sea salt will then take care of the pH.

➤ **Add a buffer.** Many brands of powdered commercial seawater buffers can be found at your local aquarium shop. These chemicals will increase your pH, as well as your alkalinity or carbonate hardness. Buffers can be quite useful, but be careful with them. Add buffers in moderation. Buffers can make your pH perfect, but that can lull you into a false sense of security. You may be replacing the buffers that were lost from your system, but you are not removing the waste products that removed them. Only water changes can do that! Adding a buffer is a bit like spraying perfume on a dirty litter box. It may smell fresh, but it's still dirty.

Fish and Tips

Don't waste your money on liquid pH-adjusting chemicals. They are too weak for use in saltwater. Buy a proper powdered buffer.

Fish and Tips

When adding chemicals to alter the pH, always start out with less than you think you'll need. If you overdose, you can't remove the stuff without changing water. It may be helpful to put some aquarium water in a bucket, add some adjusting chemical to it, and then test to see how much it changes. You can then prorate to dose the whole tank.

➤ **Kalkwasser topoffs.** Kalkwasser is the German word for chalkwater or limewater (lime as in limestone, not the citrus fruit). Basically, kalkwasser adds concentrated solutions of calcium hydroxide ($Ca(OH)_2$, if you must know) or calcium oxide (CaO) to replace aquarium water that has evaporated. The solution raises both calcium levels and alkalinity, and therefore, general hardness and pH.

➤ **Calcareous substrate.** The crushed coral gravel in your aquarium will help keep the pH from falling. But adding extra isn't likely to do you any good. I only mention calcareous substrate here in case you didn't use any when you set up the tank!

Knocking the pH Down

Lowering the pH in a marine aquarium is much more difficult and is rarely necessary. Frankly, the only reason I can imagine you might need to lower your pH is if you overdosed some chemicals while trying to raise it. In that instance, changing some water to dilute the pollution is probably the best route. If the pH is only a little high and the animals look good, it would probably be best to just leave things alone. The pH will fall on its own, probably overnight.

Attention to General Hardness

I'm sure that you have heard the terms *soft water* and *hard water*. When I talk about water hardness, usually called general hardness (abbreviated GH), I am referring to the measurement of certain dissolved minerals—particularly calcium and magnesium.

If you live in an area where the local bedrock is limestone, you probably will have hard, alkaline tapwater. If you live where the base rock is granite, you probably will have soft, acid tapwater. Although hard water is usually alkaline and soft water is usually acid, hardness and pH are not the same thing. People often confuse the two. Nevertheless, the hardness of your tapwater is relatively unimportant, because your sea salt mix will set the level of general hardness in your aquarium.

Marine aquarists don't usually measure the hardness of their water. Reef aquarists, on the other hand, pay special attention to the calcium levels in their aquariums. Dissolved calcium is a major constituent of the general hardness reading. More about calcium shortly.

If you decide to test your GH, there are kits available. Often, general hardness and carbonate hardness kits (described later in this chapter) are packaged and sold together.

Typically, you run the test by filling a vial with water and then slowly adding one drop of reagent at a time, shaking the vial between each drop. You count off the number of drops required to produce a particular color change. The number of drops determines the reading. Most kits are designed so that each drop represents 1 degree of hardness (abbreviated dH) or 1 ppm (parts per million).

Alkalinity

Do you remember that I said hard water is usually alkaline and soft water is usually acid, but that pH and hardness are different? It gets even more confusing! There is more than one kind of hardness. The other type is *carbonate hardness*, measured on the German scale of KH (Germans spell *carbonate* with a *k*). In the saltwater hobby, carbonate hardness is more often called *alkalinity*, which doesn't refer to an alkaline pH!

Fish and Tips

When it comes to alkalinity, 3.5 to 4.0 meq/l is ideal for marine aquariums, particularly reef tanks.

Acid-neutralizing capacity would be a better, less confusing term, but it is rarely used. Alkalinity is a measurement of ions that act as buffers and stabilize the pH in your aquarium. These ions neutralize the acids that are produced by biological filtration, as I discussed earlier. The more ions present (usually carbonates and bicarbonates), the more stable the pH in your tank.

Even though the alkalinity of your aquarium is not measuring alkaline pH, its level does affect the pH. Raising alkalinity raises and stabilizes pH. This is one of those complex interactions I talked about earlier.

Alkalinity or carbonate hardness kits vary by brand, but all work on the same principle. You add reagent drops to a water sample, one at a time, and count how many drops it takes to make the sample change color. Then you compare the required number of drops to a chart to obtain your result. Depending on the test kit you use, your alkalinity may be stated in the German scale of degrees (dKH or KH), or the metric milliequivalents per liter (meq/l). Here's a conversion chart.

Alkalinity Equivalents

dKH	meq/l
8.4	3.0
9.8	3.5
11.2	4.0
12.6	4.5

Adjusting Alkalinity

There are a couple of ways you can change your aquarium's alkalinity. Most are the same methods I described earlier in the chapter to change pH, so you may want to review that material for more details.

➤ **Partial water change.** Regular partial water changes tend to raise and stabilize your alkalinity. Usually this is the best choice. However, if this isn't enough, try one of the following methods.

➤ **Add a buffer.** Commercial seawater buffers will increase your alkalinity and, indirectly, your pH.

➤ **Kalkwasser topoffs.** Kalkwasser raises alkalinity and calcium levels and, indirectly, pH and general hardness.

➤ **Calcareous substrate.** The crushed coral gravel in your aquarium affects alkalinity. In a complicated chemical process, carbon dioxide excreted by the animals dissolves the calcium carbonate substrate, which can increase the general hardness and alkalinity. In reality, however, it is not enough to increase alkalinity.

➤ **Reducing alkalinity.** I can't foresee a need for this. A need to raise alkalinity is much more typical. Nevertheless, special reverse-osmosis or deionized waters can be used for topoff or make-up water to reduce the natural buffers in your tapwater, slightly reducing alkalinity.

Something's Fishy

Follow the instructions of your calcium test kit carefully. Many kits give readings not in ppm calcium ion (Ca^{++}), but as ppm calcium carbonate ($CaCO_3$). If your kit gives readings in ppm $CaCO_3$, multiply by 0.4 to get ppm Ca^{++}. Otherwise, you will think you have 1,000 ppm calcium when you really have 400!

Calcium

If you keep a fish-only marine aquarium, you probably don't need to concern yourself with calcium levels in your aquarium. Your sea salt should provide enough calcium, and regular partial water changes will replenish any that is lost.

The reef aquarist, however, should have a big interest in calcium levels. Stony corals, clams, and other invertebrates remove calcium from the water to build skeletons and shells. Sufficient calcium levels in the aquarium water are necessary to keep them alive and growing. So if you keep a reef tank, be sure to purchase a proper calcium test kit and use it.

Maintain levels of 400 to 450 ppm calcium ion (Ca^{++}). Additionally, consider buying a brand of sea salt with extra calcium included, designed especially for reef tanks.

Adjusting Calcium Levels

This is another parameter you should have no need to lower. In fact, if you think you need to lower it, you may be misreading your calcium test results. It's much more likely that you'll need to replace depleted calcium. Here are some methods to raise calcium levels:

➤ **Use kalkwasser as your topoff water.** Kalkwasser is a $Ca(OH)_2$ solution, and it will increase both calcium levels and alkalinity.

➤ **Use other calcium supplements.** The most common brands use calcium chloride to boost calcium levels. Calcium chloride will raise your calcium levels quickly—much more quickly than kalkwasser—but the reactions that occur will lower your alkalinity. So you will probably need to follow up the next day with the addition of a buffer.

Something's Fishy

Warm water holds less oxygen than cool water. Saltwater holds less oxygen than freshwater. Be careful not to let your aquarium overheat, and top off evaporation regularly.

Dissolved Oxygen

Oxygen is essential to all animals, including your fish and invertebrates. Fish take their oxygen directly from the water, via the gills. Invertebrates use many methods to obtain oxygen, including absorbing it through the gills or other tissues. You must be sure that there is enough dissolved oxygen in the water to sustain the animals.

You can buy test kits to measure the level of dissolved oxygen in your aquarium. But if you provide adequate water circulation, aeration should be sufficient and these test kits are probably unnecessary. However, if you see your tank occupants gasping, a dissolved oxygen kit can help you determine if the problem is due to lack of oxygen or due to disease or a contaminant.

I'll bet many of you are thinking that photosynthesis plays a big role in the oxygenation of your aquarium. You learned in biology class about how plants take in carbon dioxide that the animals have excreted and, through photosynthesis, release oxygen. Indeed, that happens in the aquarium, too, but unless your aquarium has no aeration or filtration to circulate the water, photosynthesis has little effect on the tank.

While it is true that algae can convert carbon dioxide to oxygen, they only do it when the light is strong enough for them to photosynthesize. At

Something's Fishy

Proper circulation is critical to the marine aquarium. Without it, oxygen levels can dip to lethal levels. Seawater contains only 7 to 8 ppm of oxygen. That is 1/30,000 the amount found in the air above your aquarium! You can see that there is little margin for error.

night, algae respire. That is, they use oxygen—just like animals. So in an algae-laden tank with no circulation, the dissolved oxygen levels could dip drastically at night. Besides, even an algae-laden aquarium doesn't contain enough algae to oxygenate the water through photosynthesis.

The real exchange of carbon dioxide for oxygen takes place at the surface of your water. It is the circulation of the water that aerates your tank. Circulation takes the carbon-dioxide-laden water from down below and carries it to the surface, where the carbon dioxide can escape and new oxygen can be absorbed. Without circulation, your tank becomes stagnant and has trouble making this gas exchange.

Fish and Tips

Many people mistakenly think that the bubbles from the aerators add oxygen. It is easy to see why they think so. However, experiments have shown that the bubbles add practically no oxygen to the water. Rather, their job is to circulate the water past the top surface, where carbon dioxide can be exchanged for oxygen.

Carbon Dioxide

Your fish and invertebrates excrete carbon dioxide (CO_2). This compound is probably the one that has the most extensive effects in your aquarium, because it interacts with water quality in so many ways. Obviously, if the carbon dioxide level is too high or the oxygen level too low, your fish will suffocate. Also, carbon dioxide is a source of nutrition for plants.

But carbon dioxide's role in the aquarium goes much further than that. Dissolved carbon dioxide is the key ingredient in the *carbonate system* of your aquarium. The carbonate system is a complex interaction of carbon dioxide that affects both the general hardness (including calcium levels) and the carbonate hardness (alkalinity) of your aquarium.

Let me say that this relationship is so complicated and dynamic that even I have trouble understanding it. So I'll just list a few key points that you may find interesting.

For starters, let's look at carbon dioxide and its relationship with pH. Yes, here's another one of those interrelations that I mentioned earlier:

➤ In acid water, dissolved carbon dioxide exists mainly as free carbon dioxide (CO_2).

➤ In neutral or slightly alkaline water, dissolved carbon dioxide is mostly found in the form of bicarbonate (HCO_3^-).

➤ In highly alkaline water, dissolved CO_2 exists largely in the form of carbonate (CO_3^-).

Looking at this list, you can see that the pH of your aquarium water affects the forms that carbon dioxide takes. Likewise, the form it takes affects the alkalinity. Remember that carbonates and bicarbonates increase alkalinity.

Now let's look at the relationship of carbon dioxide to calcium, another important element—particularly for reef tanks, where many corals and invertebrates use calcium carbonate to build their skeletons and shells:

➤ Carbon dioxide forms carbonates and bicarbonates in solution. Corals and invertebrates form their exoskeletons more easily when there are high levels of carbonate hardness.

➤ Carbonates can combine with free calcium to fall out of solution as calcium carbonate, lowering both general and carbonate hardness. This robs the water of materials needed for shell building.

➤ Carbon dioxide can dissolve calcium carbonate by lowering pH.

As you can see, carbon dioxide can both raise and lower calcium levels and alkalinity. There is a delicate balance. Carbon dioxide is busy stuff! There are test kits available, if you are curious about your tank's CO_2 level.

Phosphates

Phosphorus is necessary for life, and is found in all living things, and the things they eat. The primary way phosphates get introduced into the aquarium is via food. If you have a fish-only marine aquarium, you probably do not need to be concerned about phosphate levels in the tank. Phosphates, however, are a food source for algae, which can choke out live corals. So reef hobbyists often monitor phosphate levels in the aquarium.

Limiting phosphates can help control unwanted algae growth. Here are some methods of doing so:

➤ Kalkwasser additions can cause phosphates to precipitate out of solution, much the way that sugar settles to the bottom of a cup of coffee.

➤ Protein skimmers can remove phosphates. The phosphates adsorb onto the tiny air bubbles and are released into the atmosphere.

➤ Phosphate-adsorbing compounds are available at your local aquarium shop. Place them in a filter compartment.

Hydrogen Sulfide

Once you start your filter systems, you should never turn them off except to do maintenance. The helpful bacteria in your tank need oxygen to do their job. They are aerobic bacteria. If you turn off the filters, especially with undergravel filters, the water won't circulate enough to get the oxygen where it needs to be. Then the good-guy bacteria die off. In their place, anaerobic bacteria develop. They break down waste, too, but they do it in a manner that produces toxic hydrogen sulfide gas as a byproduct. Hydrogen sulfide is the gas that makes rotten eggs smell. If you smell it in your tank, something may be wrong with your filters.

The Least You Need to Know

➤ Use your hydrometer to maintain an ideal salinity of 1.023 SG.

➤ A pH level of 8.3 is ideal.

➤ Ammonia is more toxic in alkaline water. Seawater is alkaline!

➤ It is circulation, not bubbles, that oxygenates your water.

➤ Reef hobbyists should measure calcium levels.

Chapter 17

Be Partial to Water Changes

In This Chapter

➤ The importance of water changes

➤ How to use a gravel vacuum

➤ Conditioning tapwater

➤ Dealing with evaporation

Let me be blunt. Your fish are swimming in their own toilet. It is your job to flush it for them once in a while! Regular partial water changes are extremely important to your fish. They are so important that they get a whole chapter of their very own, separate from the chapter that discusses other routine chores.

Partial water changes have two main purposes:

1. Remove dissolved wastes. (If you use a gravel vacuum to perform this chore, you also will remove solid waste.)

2. Replace depleted trace elements.

Partial water changes have other incidental benefits. Your fish will show better colors. Your animals will grow faster. They will be more resistant to disease. If you want your fish to breed or your invertebrates to multiply, you will have better success.

Time for a Change

Water quality degrades as waste accumulates in your tank. If it wasn't for your filter, water quality would degrade even faster. But filters can do only so much. How fast the water quality degrades will depend on many factors, including the number of fish in the tank, their size, how much food you feed them, what type of filter system you have, and how often you clean it. How often you change water is also a major factor.

To keep your water quality acceptable, I recommend that you change 20 percent of the aquarium water every two weeks. That is enough to keep the typical aquarium in healthy condition. However, be sure to consider the bioload in your tank. If you are keeping large fish or if your tank is crowded, you may need to change more water, more often, to keep the water in good condition.

Fish and Tips

Evaporation doesn't count! Your partial water changes should be made in addition to replacing any water that has evaporated.

Be a Quick-Change Artist

Many hobbyists put off changing their water because they think it is too much work. It shouldn't be. If you know the right way to make a partial water change, you can do it quickly. Of course, like anything else, practice makes perfect. So you may not be able to achieve maximum speed on your first try. Here is a quick summary to speed you along.

Suck Muck? Yuck!

Let me introduce you to the aquarist's best friend: the gravel vacuum. This inexpensive muck-sucking device makes it very easy to clean gravel and change water. Some would even say that a gravel vacuum is fun to use. (I wouldn't say that, but some would.)

A simple device, the gravel vacuum consists of a large-diameter tube attached to the end of a siphon hose. You use it to siphon water from your tank. While siphoning, you poke the large tube into the gravel. The flow of water through the large tube is fast enough to tumble the gravel and to rinse out the detritus, but not fast enough to siphon out the gravel, too.

With a little practice, you will soon be able to use your gravel vacuum to clean the entire gravel bed during each partial water change. If you can't cover the entire bottom while siphoning the allotted amount of water, don't worry. Just take up where you left off at the next

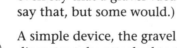

Fish and Tips

For tanks up to 29 gallons, you should be able to do a 20 percent water change in around 10 minutes or so (not including time to let salt dissolve). That's quick! Bigger tanks will take a little longer.

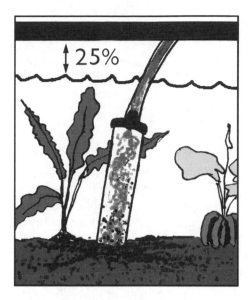

A gravel vacuum makes life easy.

water change. Work around the rocks, corals, and other decorations. It is not necessary to get 100 percent coverage of the bottom. If you want, you can move large rocks every few months to vacuum underneath. Or, if you like, change a bit more water than the usual 20 percent.

Starting a Siphon

Gravel vacuums work by siphoning water. That is, simple gravity causes water to run down through a hose to a lower level. There are no motors or moving parts. The hose acts a bit like the spout on a watering can.

There are several easy ways to start a gravel vacuum. I use the quickest way. I place the large tube in the tank. I use my mouth to give a quick draw on the hose end of the device, and then quickly flick that end of the hose down into a bucket before water comes out. If you do it right, you can start the siphon without ever getting a drop of fish water in your mouth.

Other methods of starting a siphon involve filling the hose with water by scooping with the large end or by submerging the whole thing in your aquarium. Once the hose is full of water, put your thumb over the small end to keep the water from flowing out. Then, being certain to keep the vacuum end of the device underwater in your

Fish and Tips

Don't waste money buying a siphon hose. Buy a gravel vacuum instead. A regular siphon hose removes only the old, waste-laden water, but the gravel vacuum also removes solid waste from the gravel bed. You will never have to move your fish or tear down the tank to clean the gravel.

aquarium, lower the small end of the hose outside the tank, point it into a bucket, and then remove your thumb to let the water flow.

I suppose I should mention that some brands of siphon hoses have a built-in squeeze bulb that can be used to start them easily, but I don't recommend them. Bits of debris, such as plant leaves, will quickly lodge in the valve inside the squeeze bulb. Keeping such a device in working order is a major pain.

Cleaning the Gravel

Once you have the siphon started and water is flowing into the bucket, simply poke the large tube deep into your gravel, and lift. When you lift, the water flow will rinse up through the gravel in the tube, washing away any detritus. The gravel, being heavier, will tumble back down into the tank. Continue the poke-and-lift method until you've removed the amount of water intended for replacement.

Something's Fishy

Be careful not to suck up any fish while vacuuming. Usually, the fish are smart enough to stay away, but not always. Plus, they sometimes rush over, thinking that the particles of tumbling gravel are bits of food. If a fish does enter the vacuum tube, place your thumb over the output hose to stop the flow until the fish swims back out.

The smaller your particles of gravel, the higher they will rise inside the tube of the gravel vacuum. If they start getting too close to the hose—close enough to where they might siphon out—place your thumb over the end of the hose to reduce or pause the flow. With a little practice, you can master the technique of lightly pinching or releasing the end of the hose to increase or decrease flow.

Once you finish, discard the bucket of dirty water that you collected. You may be surprised at how much crud you pull out of a tank! Another great thing about gravel vacuums is that they remove all that crud without stirring up things in the tank.

Kick the Bucket

Personally, I don't mind lugging buckets of water. I figure that the exercise never hurts, and besides, I have the strength of 10 men (10 really wimpy men). Carrying buckets is also the quickest way to get the job done. Still, if you would rather not carry buckets of water—maybe you are afraid you will slop water on the floor, or maybe the bucket is too heavy for you (a full 5-gallon bucket weighs 40 to 50 pounds)—there is another way.

Consider buying a clean-and-fill unit. Often, these are called *pythons* because the Python No-Spill is the most popular brand. In any case, the clean-and-fill style of gravel vacuum is just like a drain-and-fill kit for a waterbed, with a gravel vacuum on one end instead of a hose fitting. They come in various lengths, ranging from 25 to 100 feet.

The Python No-Spill clean-and-fill system attaches to your sink to both drain and fill your tank. (courtesy Python products)

A clean-and-fill unit consists of a gravel vacuum with an extra-long hose and a special valve unit that fits on any faucet. Water powers the device. To drain water from your tank, you attach the valve to your faucet and turn on the water. The water pressure from the tap forms a suction inside the valve that draws water through the gravel vacuum hose. Since pressure from the tap is powering the gravel vacuum (instead of gravity), a clean-and-fill device makes it possible to siphon uphill. The device will still function, even if the sink is higher than the aquarium.

A disadvantage of the clean-and-fill unit is that several gallons of tapwater will be wasted for each gallon drawn from your tank. If you live in an area where there is water rationing, this device may be a poor choice. Also, if you have low water pressure in your pipes, the device will function much more slowly.

Clean-and-fill devices not only drain your tank, but also refill it. First, you make sure that water of the correct temperature is flowing through the sink connector. Then you turn a switch, and it directs

Fish and Tips

If you buy a clean–and–fill gravel cleaning device, consider buying an optional brass faucet adapter. The metal threads of your faucet will soon wear away the threads on the soft plastic connector that comes with the unit.

Something's Fishy

When refilling a tank via a clean-and-fill system or any other hose, always make sure to keep the water jet above water. You want to agitate the new water as it enters the tank—both to aerate it and to prevent gas saturation problems.

tapwater through the gravel vacuum hose back into your aquarium. There is no need for buckets to drain or fill the aquarium. All water pumps directly to or from your sink. That is, it would if you had a freshwater tank.

These devices do a nice job, and many people swear by them. However, they don't get me very excited because I'm too impatient. It takes time to drag out the hose and attach the valve to the faucet to get the thing running. Afterward, you need time to drain water from the hose and time to roll up the hose and put it away. Remember, too, that you can't pump water directly from the sink to the aquarium anyway, because you need to mix it with sea salt. So the refill feature is of limited use.

Mixing It Up

Before you can refill your aquarium, you need to premix the seawater. The easiest way to do this is to set up a large bucket or plastic garbage can, fill it with enough water, dechlorinate the water (I'll discuss that in a minute), and begin adding sea salt. Always start by adding less salt than you think you'll need. Dissolve it completely before adding more salt—in steps—until you reach the desired salinity. Check regularly with your hydrometer to monitor your progress.

Something's Fishy

Do not use metal buckets for mixing saltwater! Saltwater is corrosive, and dissolved metals can poison your fish. Besides, the buckets will rust.

You may want to put a powerhead or other small pump into the container to keep the water circulating. This will help dissolve the salts faster. Plus, you can use the powerhead to pump the newly mixed seawater into your aquarium.

In with the New

Make sure all the salt in the newly mixed seawater is fully dissolved and the water is at the right salinity and within 2°F (1°C) of the aquarium water, so that there will be no temperature shock to the fish.

You can use whatever method is necessary to transfer the new seawater from the mixing container to the aquarium, but the easiest and least messy way is to attach a hose to a powerhead or other water pump, and then use the pump to transfer the new seawater to the aquarium. If you mix the seawater in a bucket, you may be able to carefully pour it into the aquarium without a pump. Place a coffee saucer on the bottom of the aquarium to keep the poured water from stirring up the gravel.

Conditioning Tapwater

Water that comes straight from the tap may be safe for humans to drink, but that does not mean it is safe for fish. Before adding sea salt to your tapwater to make seawater, you should treat the tapwater with a water conditioner.

As I talk about this topic, remember that we don't all live in the same place. (Thank goodness! My apartment is too crowded already.) Your local tapwater may be very different from mine. It is, therefore, impossible for me to give a simple tapwater conditioning recipe that will work for everyone. You should ask your local aquarium dealer, and maybe even your local water department, if there is anything special you need to know about your tapwater.

However, almost all of you will need nothing more than a good dechlorinator.

Something's Fishy

Never add sea salt directly to your aquarium! Always premix it in a separate container. Until the salt is completely dissolved, complex chemical reactions are occurring. These reactions are caustic and dangerous to aquatic life!

Removing Chlorine and Chloramine

If you don't draw your water from your own well, you probably get it from a municipality, and chlorine has probably been added to kill microscopic organisms. It does its job well, but if you have ever been swimming in a chlorinated swimming pool, you know that chlorine is rough on mucous membranes, such as the eyes and nose. It does the same thing to fish, but they have an added disadvantage. Their gills are exposed to the chlorinated water, and chlorine damages gills.

So you need to remove chlorine from the tapwater before you can mix in your sea salt. The easiest way to do this is to buy and use one of the many commercial tapwater conditioners. Your dealer will carry many brands, all inexpensive. To remove chlorine, you dose the product according to directions—usually in drops per gallon or teaspoons per 10 gallons. It's quick and easy.

In some areas, the local water supplies have high levels of dissolved organics. Chlorine can combine with these to form carcinogenic substances (trihalomethanes). To prevent that, some municipal water supplies add both chlorine and ammonia to the water. These two combine into new compounds called chloramines. Chloramines also disinfect water, but they don't combine with organics.

Your dechlorinating water conditioner will neutralize both chlorine and chloramines. However, when chloramines are neutralized, the ammonia is released. And we know how dangerous ammonia is to fish. If you have a well-established tank, it probably will not be a big deal. Your biological filtration will quickly neutralize the ammonia. In a new, uncycled tank, though, the ammonia could be especially deadly.

Ask your dealer if your local tapwater contains chloramines. If it does, you would be best to dechlorinate with a product that will neutralize the ammonia, too, such as Amquel.

Removing Heavy Metals

Some water conditioners also remove heavy metals such as zinc, lead, and copper from your tapwater. Is that feature important? Probably not, but it may well depend on where you live and what is in your local water.

Everything Must Go!

Do you live in an area where the tapwater is loaded with undesirable dissolved compounds such as nitrates, phosphates, and copper? Are you a reef hobbyist? Are you just plain picky? If so, you may want to go the extra mile to run your tapwater through a reverse-osmosis unit or deionization unit before mixing up your saltwater. These devices remove most impurities, including chlorine, and leave only the purest water to mix with your sea salt. Most hobbyists will find this unnecessary, but you may be one of the exceptions.

Liquid Bandage

Many water conditioners include compounds that provide a "liquid bandage" for your fish. Fish that have been in a fight or have been recently netted may have had some of their protective slime rubbed off. This slime is the fish's first defense against disease-causing organisms. Some water conditioners will provide a temporary slime for your fish that will protect it until it regenerates its own body slime.

Gas Saturation

Water can absorb more gases when it is under pressure in your tap. Have you ever drawn a glass of water and noticed that it was cloudy for a minute? Jillions of tiny bubbles eventually float to the top and the water clears. When you fill your aquarium the first time, you may find a layer of bubbles coating the glass after a few minutes. These bubbles are the result of gas saturation.

Here's the problem: If you place fish into water that is still supersaturated with gases, it is very rough on the fish. These gases may be absorbed into the bloodstream and condense out of solution there. Bubbles build up in the bloodstream and may kill the fish. The same thing happens to scuba divers that surface too quickly. Deep underwater, divers are under more pressure—so more gases are absorbed into their bloodstreams. If they surface too fast, those extra gases condense into bubbles in their bloodstream, and the divers contract a highly painful and often fatal condition called the bends.

To prevent gas saturation problems, all you have to do is aerate your water. This is easily done by agitating your tapwater as you draw it. As you draw tapwater into your bucket or plastic trash can, set the stream so that a real turmoil results. This will drive off excess gases. If you use a hose to fill your tank, put your finger over the end to make the spray jet out hard and then spray it against your hand instead of spraying directly into the tank. This will agitate the water quite well and drive out the extra gases.

Vanishing into Thin Air

Evaporation is a continuous process that occurs when water molecules escape into the air. Molecules are always in motion, bumping into one another. Sometimes they obtain enough energy to bounce free.

Evaporation occurs in every aquarium. How fast it happens will depend on several factors, including the humidity of the air in the room, water temperature, whether the tank is covered or open, and how much circulation occurs at the water surface. Evaporation can be a good thing or a bad thing.

In most cases, it is probably a bad thing. As evaporation occurs, only the water leaves. The dissolved wastes and minerals remain behind. In the case of marine aquarium, the direct affect is that salinity will increase. Remember, the water leaves but the salt stays. So the same amount of salt becomes concentrated in less water. Too much evaporation can raise salinity enough to kill your fish.

Since only the water leaves, you should top off your tank with dechlorinated tapwater only—not with more seawater. Do not add more salt!

OK, put on your thinking cap because it is time for a quick quiz. Remembering that I recommend a 20 percent partial water change every two weeks, what if your tank evaporates by 20 percent within that period? Is it OK to just top it off with conditioned tapwater? (I'm humming the Final Jeopardy theme while you think about it.)

The answer is both yes and no. Yes, it is OK to top off with tapwater to replace the evaporation, but no, it is not OK to stop there. You still have to make your 20 percent water change because you have removed nothing. You have only added. Make regular partial water changes in addition to topping off evaporation!

Fish and Tips

Reef hobbyists should encourage evaporation in their aquariums. It will allow for increased additions of kalkwasser to provide necessary calcium for growth of live corals.

The Least You Need to Know

➤ Partial water changes remove dissolved waste and replenish trace elements.

➤ Change at least 20 percent of your saltwater every two weeks for best results.

➤ Use a gravel vacuum to remove debris from gravel while making partial water changes.

➤ Consider local conditions before deciding how to condition your tapwater.

➤ Almost everyone needs a dechlorinator.

➤ Always premix your saltwater, and be sure that the salts are completely dissolved before adding the water to your aquarium.

➤ Do regular partial water changes in addition to topping off for evaporation.

Chapter 18

Fish Food

In This Chapter

➤ Find a balanced diet for your fish

➤ How much is enough?

➤ Discover delicious dinners and tasty snacks

➤ How to hatch your own live baby brine shrimp

➤ Vacation foods and electronic fish feeders

One of the most fun things about keeping an aquarium is feeding the animals. Whether offering brine shrimp to all or hand feeding a pet spiny lobster, it is a time when you can truly interact with the inhabitants of your tank. Your fish will soon learn that their meals come from you, and they will flock to the front of the tank whenever you come near. Yes, your fish will learn to recognize you.

If several different people regularly feed the fish, they may learn to come rushing forward to greet any human that is nearby. However, if you are their only caterer, you may be the only one who can approach the tank and receive that excited response. You will feel loved. Awwww!

It is not just the attention of the fish you will enjoy at feeding time. You also will get a major kick out of watching the show they put on. Bold damselfish will noisily snap food from the surface. The comically shy jawfish will pop from its burrow to grab a tasty morsel before quickly retreating into the burrow again. Watching two gobies play tug-of-war with a tasty blackworm is also quite entertaining. Ever been squirted by an excited triggerfish? It could happen.

You can interact with your fish at mealtime. Here, Tina hand-feeds a sailfin tang.

Fishin' for Nutrition

Proper nutrition is a cornerstone of successful fishkeeping. You can do everything else right, but if you don't offer the proper types of food, and in sufficient quantities, your fish will not survive for long.

Feeding saltwater fish is quite a bit different from feeding freshwater fish. Do not expect your saltwater fish to subsist on flake foods alone. Indeed, many species will not even touch them. Be prepared to offer the various frozen seafoods available for aquarium fish, and some species will require live foods.

Something's Fishy

Find out what diet is required by the species that you want to buy *before* you purchase it. A good dealer will alert you if you choose a species with specialized dietary requirements, but you can't count on that happening.

This is a good place to bore you with dull talk about proteins and carbohydrates and fats. Lucky you, I'm not going to do that. Just like humans, fish need all these types of nutrients in the proper quantities and proportions to stay healthy. Just like human foods, most fish food packages will list percentages of crude protein, crude fat, crude fiber, and moisture—but such lists are of little or no use. Listing minimums and maximums allows for quite a variance, and besides, "crude" protein is not the same as "digestible" protein, anyway.

The Spice of Life

Customers often ask me what is the single best food for their fish. I always give them the same answer: variety. There is no single food that is perfect for all fish all the time. Carnivorous species prefer more animal matter in their diet. Herbivores prefer plant-based foods. Offering a variety of foods is absolutely the only way to go. It lets individual species pick the foods that best suit them, and it gives everyone a chance at a more stimulating diet.

I always offer my fish a good selection of foods. I usually keep a half-dozen or so different frozen foods in the freezer. Some freeze-dried krill, marine flakes, and other dried foods are on hand, too. And I bring home the occasional live food treat. Every meal is something different for the fish at my house. It should be the same at yours.

Only one person should be in charge of feeding your aquarium. Or perhaps make one person responsible for breakfast every day, and someone else responsible for dinner every day. The reason for this is that you are not just feeding the fish—you are feeding the tank. The more food that goes into the tank, the more polluted it will become. When many people have responsibility for feeding the fish, things tend to go wrong. When everyone thinks the other guy is feeding, the poor fish may not get fed enough, or perhaps not at all. Alternatively, everyone who walks by the tank may throw in some food—resulting in feedings that are doubled, tripled, or worse.

Share and Share Alike

A nice sentiment, but don't expect your fish to share it. It is not in their nature. In the ocean, and in the aquarium, it's every fish for himself. It is up to you to be sure that each individual gets its share of food.

Fish and Tips

The quantity and types of fats in marine and freshwater animals are quite different. Avoid feeding freshwater fish to your marine fish. For example, feeding goldfish to lionfish over the long term results in liver damage to the lionfish. Instead, offer frozen silversides, krill, and other marine animals.

Fish and Tips

Designate yourself to be the sole person responsible for feeding. It will prevent too many cooks from polluting the aquarium with excessive feedings. Besides, your fish will come to recognize you. Guess who the fish will be happiest to see come near their tank?

Particularly, it is up to you to be sure that each fish gets its share of the right foods. For example, toss some algae flakes onto the surface of the water and your tangs will gorge themselves happily. The food will never reach the bottom of the tank, and even if it did, it would be of no interest to the shy, bottom-dwelling jawfish. The jawfish is a carnivore, not an algae eater. Offer the right foods for the species you keep, and use these tips to be sure they get their share:

➤ **Distraction.** If you have a fish that is a shy, unaggressive feeder and is not getting its share of food, try offering food to everyone else at the opposite side of the aquarium. While the rest are distracted, you may be able to sneak some food to the shy, hungry animal.

➤ **Delivery.** Many species are reclusive or territorial. They don't move far from home. You must make sure enough food reaches them. A turkey baster works great for squirting some live brine shrimp or other foods near a jawfish's burrow. A feeding stick can be used to place a shrimp or crayfish within reach of an eel.

Fish and Tips

A feeding stick is a simple plastic rod with a slightly sharpened end (usually bent at an angle so that it can reach under ledges). Impale a shrimp or other bit of food lightly on the end and then use the stick to place the food in the desired location. By wiggling the stick to make the food appear live, you can teach predatory species, such as lionfish, to accept frozen foods.

➤ **Satiation.** Sometimes, it seems impossible to get food to everyone (or anyone) in the tank because there is one fish that is such a major chowhound. The goatfish is such a fish. I swear that they have ESP. No matter where you put the food, they will be there before it hits the water, waiting with open mouths. They are ravenous feeders and will stuff themselves like a Thanksgiving turkey. With fish such as this, you may have no choice but to fill them up before you can expect anyone else to get a bite of food.

➤ **Timing.** Finally, don't forget that many species are nocturnal. They are not geared to eat during the day and may not be tempted by any foods offered while the lights are on. If you keep such species, offer a little food after the lights are out for the night.

Don't Stuff Them to the Gills

How often should you feed your fish? That depends on the species. Usually, twice a day is best. I like to feed my fish when I get up in the morning and again in the evening when I come home from work. Work out a feeding schedule that fits your own schedule, and don't worry too much if you have to alter it occasionally. You won't hear the fish complain. (If you do, I'll send you the number of a good psychiatrist.)

If you miss the occasional feeding, don't try to make it up by feeding twice as much at the next meal. A fish's stomach can hold only so much food at once. Extra food is going to go uneaten and pollute the tank.

Anyway, feeding twice a day works well with most species. But there are exceptions. Predatory fish commonly eat larger single meals that will last them the whole day, or even several days. Other fish—anthias, for example—like to nibble all day long. So it doesn't hurt to toss them an extra morsel or two throughout the day. Your sea anemones and live corals may enjoy two or three small feedings per week, in addition to the nutrients they obtain through photosynthesis.

Learning how much food to feed can be difficult. People often say to offer just a pinch of food, but how much is a pinch? Your pinch may be quite a bit different from mine. It may consist of just a couple of flakes or a couple of hundred flakes. Here are guidelines to help you learn how much food to offer.

One old rule of feeding suggests that you think of a fish's stomach as being about the size of its eye. If you base the amount of food you offer on the size of the fish's eye, you won't overdo it. Most fish will be able to eat more than this, but more is not necessary, and it can be excessive.

Rule 1: A fish's stomach is about the size of its eye.

My favorite rule of feeding is based on a time limit. Offer only what the fish can eat in 3 minutes. If there is any food left over at the end of that time, you have probably overfed.

Even better, offer what they will eat in 30 seconds to a minute. Of course, there are some exceptions. For example, if you clip a leaf of seaweed or romaine lettuce to a rock, it may take the fish more than a few minutes to consume it. In fact, there is an advantage to letting them nibble at it throughout the day. Or, if you offer live brine shrimp, all of them may not be found and caught right away. It is OK to allow the fish more time to hunt them down.

Using these rules, or a combination of them, should give you a very good estimate of how much to feed. Until you learn just how much that typically would be, be sure to err on the side of underfeeding. That is, offer a small quantity of

Fish and Tips

When you buy your first batch of fish, ask your dealer to show you how much to feed. Don't settle for him giving you a general a rule or saying "a pinch." Ask him to spread some food in his hand to show you how much is right.

Rule 2: There should be no food left after 3 minutes, or you have overfed.

Fish and Tips

You are probably aware that you can kill your fish by overfeeding, but overeating is unlikely to kill them. It is the pollution resulting from excess food that causes problems. Remember that you are not just feeding the fish, you are also feeding the tank.

food, and if the fish snap it up quickly, offer a little more. You can do that until you get a better idea of how much is safe to offer all at once. It is very important not to overfeed, especially in a new tank.

Munch, Munch, What's for Lunch?

Good dealers carry a veritable smorgasbord for your fish. Dry prepared foods are always readily available and most convenient, but dry foods alone are insufficient for most marine species. Your fish will do best if you offer lots of live and frozen foods. Let's look at some common choices in aquatic foods that are often stocked by dealers.

Flaky Choices

Most hobbyists start out with at least one variety of flake food. Flake foods contain an amalgamation of ingredients that are mixed into a porridge and then cooked and dried into thin sheets. These sheets are broken into bits and packaged. No doubt you are familiar with this type of food. Be sure you get a flake food designed for marine fish, as the fatty-acid balance of freshwater foods is wrong for saltwater fish.

But fish do not live by flakes alone. Only the hardiest species will survive solely on flakes, and many species won't touch them at all.

Sheets of dried marine algae are a great new addition to the types of dried foods available. The sheets are available in green, red, or brown varieties, and fish go nuts for this stuff. You can break the sheets down and feed them like flakes or clip larger pieces inside the tank for the fish to nibble.

Cold Facts About Freeze-Dried Foods

Freeze-dried foods are another type of prepared dry food. They share the convenience of dry foods and the nutrition of live or frozen foods. Unlike most dry foods—which are a mix of ingredients, including items fish would never eat in the wild (such as rice, wheat, eggs, and yeast)—freeze-dried foods are actual preserved aquatic animals eaten by fish in the wild. Once these foods soak up some water, they are very much like offering freshly killed foods. However, your fish probably will gobble them down before they get a chance to soak.

Your dealer may offer an assortment of freeze-dried foods. Of the varieties available, only various types of freeze-dried shrimp, such as krill, plankton, and brine shrimp, are properly balanced for marine fish. Freeze-dried freshwater foods, such as mosquito larvae, daphnia (a tiny crustacean), and bloodworms (sometimes labeled as red mosquito larvae or red grubs) may also be offered sparingly. Freeze-dried tubifex worms are a good choice, too.

The Lowdown on Foods for Bottom Feeders

Your dealer also offers foods in pellet or tablet form. Pellets may either sink or float, but tablet foods are especially for bottom dwellers. They sink straight to the bottom, where scavengers can get at them.

Spirulina algae tablets are a popular choice. Pellets and tablets are more popular with the freshwater crowd, but there is nothing wrong with offering them to marine fish, too.

A Pleaser from the Freezer

Frozen foods are the next best thing to live foods. Cross your fingers that your dealer will stock a large supply of frozen fish foods. Many dealers have glass-fronted display freezers (similar to those found in grocery stores) filled with yummy frozen foods for your fish. Unfortunately, smaller stores stock little in the way of frozen foods, often hiding them back in the store's lunchroom freezer—available only by request. If you

Fish and Tips

When feeding flakes, pellets, or other dry foods to your fish, do not sprinkle the food directly from the can into your tank. Instead, sprinkle first into the palm of your hand and then sprinkle that into the tank. That way, if you accidentally sprinkle too much, you can put some back, rather than having excess food enter and pollute your tank.

Fish and Tips

Ask if your dealer carries *feeding rings*. These are floating plastic rings about 2 inches in diameter. When you sprinkle food inside them, they keep the food from drifting all over the tank and getting lost. You can monitor the quantity of food better, and there is less chance for waste. You also can try making one from a loop of air line tubing.

Fish and Tips

Freeze-dried tubifex worms come in cubes. A fun way to offer them is to reach into the tank and press the cube against the glass, squeezing the air bubbles out. The cube will stick to the glass, and you will then have a front-row seat to watch all the fish nibbling at it. Fish aren't very smart, so the first time you do this, they probably won't all come rushing up to eat. But after that, watch out!

don't see frozen foods on display, *ask*. You may want to give the cold shoulder to a dealer who doesn't offer frozen foods.

Most stores carry frozen brine shrimp, which is the old standby. When I was a kid, it was the only frozen fish food you could find.

These days, the choices are much better. Frozen krill, plankton, squid, clam, scallop, silversides, prawn eggs, sea urchin, kelp, and more may be available. There are also many frozen prepared foods, which include an amalgamation of ingredients. Many of these specifically target carnivores or herbivores. Some even contain marine sponges, necessary for many marine angelfish and other species. There are many freshwater frozen foods, too, but it is better to stick to the marine ones.

You will find frozen foods packaged as *flat-packs* or *cube-packs*. Flat-packs are Zip-Lok bags with a block of food frozen inside. To feed these foods, you can either break off a chunk and toss it in the tank, or squeeze some out the edge of the plastic wrapper and swirl it in the tank until a sufficient quantity melts free. Of course, if you toss in a chunk, you can still swirl it around to get bits to melt free, to keep the more voracious feeders from hogging it.

Cube-packs offer even more convenience. They come in clear plastic flip-top or foil-covered trays that resemble miniature ice cube trays. The cost is slightly higher than flat-packs, but cubes are much simpler to use. You simply push on the back of the container to pop out the number of cubes that you need (much like popping cold medicine out of one of those foil packs) and then pop the cubes into the tank. The fish do the rest.

Now Appearing Live

Live foods are the best of all. Live foods not only offer the most natural, freshest ingredients, but they also entertain you and your fish. If you want to see your fish have a good time at mealtime, offer live foods. Your fish will go nuts for them. Live foods are also ideal for tempting picky eaters.

Unfortunately, most dealers carry little in the way of live foods. Many stores just don't have enough room for them. After all, vats or refrigerator space are necessary to store these foods. Also, many stores don't have easy access to them. If the store's distributor doesn't stock live foods and the store doesn't need quantities large enough to justify buying them direct, you will be out of luck.

Anyway, here are some live foods you may be lucky enough to find at your local shop. Some will be relished by almost all fish, while others will only be useful for feeding large carnivorous fish. So take note.

➤ **Brine shrimp** *(Artemia spp.)*. This animal is not one that your fish would encounter in the wild, but they will love it nonetheless. Brine shrimp live in salt marshes—where the water is too salty for most fish. In fact, brine shrimp live in areas where the water may dry up, and they have evolved a unique way to survive this. Their dehydrated eggs can last for many years, hatching when the rains return. I have read accounts of thousand-year-old sediments that still held viable eggs!

You can buy brine shrimp or brine shrimp eggs to hatch as food for your baby fish. Don't feed the eggs directly, though. The shells are not digestible.

Brine shrimp are sold by the portion. The typical 1-teaspoon portion may contain several hundred of them. If you don't crowd them too much, you can keep brine shrimp at room temperature until they are fed to the fish. You also can refrigerate them. Refrigerated brine shrimp will stop moving but will regain activity when rewarmed.

Pour the shrimp through a net before offering them to your fish to strain out the water. Some hobbyists give them a quick freshwater rinse, too.

➤ **Blackworms** *(Limnodrilus spp.)*. These are an excellent food for most small to medium fish. Blackworms are 1 to 2 inches long and as big around as a pencil lead. In the wild, they live in freshwater mud, poking their heads out to filter bacteria and debris as food. The blackworms sold in stores are farm-raised. Fish absolutely love them, and they are especially good for tempting picky eaters. Live blackworms typically sell by the portion, which may contain several hundred worms.

Keep live blackworms in the refrigerator, and change their water every day or two. You may want to purchase a device called a worm keeper that consists of a tray with a fine mesh bottom. This tray nests into an outer tray. You fill the lower tray with water, and when it is time to change water, you lift the top tray. The water will sift through the mesh, leaving just the worms, and then you change the water in the bottom tray. Easy! If you buy small portions, you can store them in the container in which they are sold.

Fish and Tips

Blackworms are freshwater animals. Saltwater kills them quickly. Feed only what your fish will eat immediately. Simply toss them into the tank or use a turkey baster to squirt them to an appropriate spot.

Live foods add action, suspense, and drama to your tank.

➤ **Tubifex worms** (pronounced *TOO-bih-fex*). These are very similar to blackworms but are not seen as often. They have a more reddish color, and when disturbed, clump into mats so tight that you will have a bit of trouble tearing them apart. Care and feeding is the same as with blackworms.

➤ **Ghost shrimp.** A variety of freshwater grass shrimp that grows to 1½ inches in length, the ghost shrimp is completely transparent except for the internal organs. The heart can be seen beating inside, and you can always tell what the ghost shrimp last ate, because his stomach will be that color. I like to feed assorted colored flakes to the ghost shrimp at the store and then laugh at all the pink and green and brown spots I later see swimming around. Ghost shrimp are readily accepted by seahorses and other predatory fish.

➤ **Feeder guppies.** The common guppy was one of the first aquarium fish. Large-tailed fancy varieties of this fish are now kept as pets, and the original short-finned form has been relegated to inexpensive food-fish status. Guppies are small enough to be accepted by most popular saltwater fish. Believe it or not, guppies can survive just fine in saltwater, too. So uneaten specimens will live until they're eaten.

➤ **Rosy red minnow.** Rosy reds are a bit bigger than guppies and smaller than goldfish. So if you need a midsize feeder fish, this is it. They are also popular as pond fish because of their delicate pink color and peaceful nature. This freshwater fish will not survive long in saltwater. Offer only what will be eaten quickly.

➤ **Goldfish.** Yep, this is the cheapest version of the fish that commonly sells as a pet or is won in carnivals. Believe it or not, about 99.5 percent of all goldfish raised are sold as food for other fish. Most dealers offer several feeder goldfish for a dollar. Goldfish are freshwater fish. As such, they do not survive long in saltwater. Remember also that freshwater fish have the wrong fatty-acid balance for proper nutrition for saltwater fish. So they should not make up a major part of the diet.

➤ **Earthworms.** Various sizes and species of earthworms are sold as bait and fish food. They will be relished as a treat by fish large enough to eat them. Earthworms also can be diced into bits for smaller fish.

➤ **Crayfish.** Many larger fish will readily eat these. Some moray eels are particularly fond of them.

Vitamins and Supplements

I'm not big on recommending vitamin supplements for aquariums. I prefer to feed a varied diet of healthy foods. However, there are many vitamin preparations on the market and they can be useful if you use them to presoak foods. That way, the vitamins find their way directly into the fish.

Some vitamin brands recommend dosing the stuff directly into the water. This is of little or no use to your fish. Those vitamins end up feeding the algae in the aquarium instead. If you want more and healthier algae, then hey, I say go for it. Your fish might actually eat a bit of that algae and get a little something from those vitamins.

One nutritional supplement I highly recommend is a product called Selcon. Selcon is a solution of essential fatty acids, which are often lacking in prepared foods. Presoak other foods in it for best results. You can also feed it to live brine shrimp before offering them to your fish.

Something's Fishy

If you use fish as food for other fish, be aware that there is a risk of introducing disease, unless you first quarantine the feeder fish. Additionally, feeder fish are food, and you should treat them as such. That is, you should introduce only one meal's worth to your tank at a time, to prevent overcrowding. Keep the rest in a separate holding tank until needed.

Hatching Baby Brine Shrimp

I've already talked about adult brine shrimp as nutritious food for your fish. You can also hatch your own baby brine shrimp. Baby brine shrimp, which are really the larval form called nauplii (pronounced *NAW-plee-eye*), make wonderful food for small fish and filter-feeding invertebrates.

What You Need

Your dealer probably sells everything you need to hatch your own baby brine shrimp. You need:

➤ **Brine shrimp eggs.** Brine shrimp live in salty lakes and marshes that may dry out seasonally. Because of this, they can tolerate broad ranges of salt, but more important, their eggs have evolved to survive through dry spells. You can buy cans of dry brine shrimp eggs at your local aquarium dealer.

Fish and Tips

Even if a fish doesn't eat algae, part of its natural diet is probably fish or other creatures that do. So before offering goldfish or other feeder fish as food to large carnivorous fish, consider serving algae flakes or other assorted foods to the feeder fish. That way, the stomachs of the feeders will be packed with added nutrition from foods that the large carnivores might not normally eat directly.

➤ **Salt.** Sea salt is best, but even table salt should do. One cup of salt makes around 2 gallons of seawater.

➤ **Hatching container.** Your dealer may offer several styles, but the most popular is the hatching cone. This is a clear vinyl cone-shaped bag that hangs on a hook. You put the salt, water, and eggs inside and drop in an airstone to keep things circulating.

➤ **Air pump and airstone.** These items keep the water circulating in your hatchery so that it stays oxygenated and so that the eggs don't settle to the bottom and form a lump.

➤ **Brine shrimp net.** A special extra-fine net for sifting out the baby shrimp.

➤ **Air line.** A 3- to 6-foot piece of air line will be needed to siphon out the hatched shrimp.

Setting It Up

Use salt and your hydrometer to mix a hatching solution with a specific gravity of 1.023 or a bit higher. Fill your shrimp hatchery with the solution, and drop in an airstone to circulate the water.

Hang the hatching container in your hatchery, and add some shrimp eggs. It is best to hatch only what you think you can feed in a day or two. There should be directions on the can to give you an idea of how many eggs to add.

Fish and Tips

Shrimp will hatch faster in warmer water. Around 80°F is best. Hatch may occur in 24 to 48 hours, depending on temperature, salinity, species of brine shrimp, and viability of your batch of eggs.

After 24 hours, remove the airstone and check your hatch. If the shrimp have hatched, give them a few minutes to settle. The empty dark brown eggshells should float to the top, and the shrimp will sink toward the bottom. Of course, if the shrimp haven't hatched, allow more time.

Harvesting the Shrimp

Brine shrimp are attracted to light, so putting a small night light at the bottom will draw them there more quickly. The shrimp are very tiny, transparent orange specks. Once the baby brine shrimp collect at the bottom, you can use a piece of air line to siphon them through a brine-shrimp net or handkerchief. As much as possible,

avoid collecting eggshells. The eggshells are indi-
gestible and, if eaten by your fish, can clog their
intestines. Give the shrimp a quick rinse under
freshwater and then feed them to your fish.

If you hatched more than you need, you may want
to leave some in the hatchery, or put some of the
water aside in a jar with an airstone and toss them
in there. Baby brine shrimp will eat powdered
egglayer food, or you can buy special Artemia Food.
A little brewer's yeast works, too.

You may want to go ahead and discard the water and
empty eggshells in your hatchery and set up a new
batch. Or you may want to return the airstone and
run things a bit longer to see if more shrimp hatch.

Something's Fishy

Never feed more than one meal's
worth of food at a time. You cannot
throw extra food into your tank
when you go on vacation. The food
that is not immediately eaten will
pollute the tank and kill the fish.

What to Do on Your Summer Vacation

One great thing about fish is that you can leave them unattended and without food for
short periods of time. If you are going to be gone for a weekend, don't worry about
them. They will be fine.

Of course, if you have someone you trust—someone who knows how much to feed
fish and how to watch for problems and take corrective action—you may want to use a
fishsitter while you are away. Fish can go for days without food, but predators will start
looking upon their tankmates as snacks if they get hungry enough.

Electronic fish feeders are another option. These
are devices that clip on top the aquarium and,
based on timer settings, dispense meals of dry
foods to your fish. Some models are fully pro-
grammable, while others are preset to automatically feed twice a day. Electronic fish feeders may
seem a bit expensive, but remember that you
don't have to use them only when you are on
vacation. You can use them to feed dry foods to
your fish 365 days a year, and supplement with
live and frozen foods at will. Of course, electronic
fish feeders are of no use for feeding fish that
require live or frozen foods.

The various "weekend foods" or "vacation foods"
sold in shops are worthless. First, they are more
chemicals than food, and the chemicals dissolve too

Fish and Tips

When using electronic fish feeders,
make sure the flakes or pellets are
small enough to fit through the
dispenser opening, or it will clog.
Also, do not pack food too tightly
into the storage hopper or it can
become compacted and will not be
released.

slowly in saltwater. Second, the little bit of food inside is really only going to be available to fish that are willing to feed off the bottom. Finally, there is a real question about how long the food stays fresh once it hits the tank and gets wet. I often wonder if vacation food isn't rotten after the first day.

The Least You Need to Know

➤ Most saltwater fish will not survive on flakes alone. Frozen and live foods are better.

➤ For best results, offer your fish a variety of foods.

➤ Three minutes after feeding, if any food remains in the tank, you have overfed.

➤ Your fish will put on an extra show if you offer live and frozen foods.

➤ You can hatch live baby brine shrimp to feed small fish and filter-feeding invertebrates.

➤ Going away for a weekend? Don't worry about the fish. Going on vacation? Consider buying an electronic fish feeder or hiring a fishsitter.

Chapter 19

Your Routine Chores

In This Chapter

➤ Your daily and weekly duties

➤ Stuff you have to do every month

➤ A maintenance checklist

➤ How to clean and maintain your filter

Chapters 17 and 18 paid special attention to the two most important duties of maintaining your aquarium— changing the water and feeding the fish. This chapter will cover the rest of the things you need to do to keep your aquarium in tip-top condition. I will help you set priorities by dividing chores into daily, weekly, and monthly duties. Of course, these are just guidelines. Don't be afraid to tweak the schedules a little to fit your needs. Use your common sense.

Daily Duties

➤ **Turn on the aquarium light.** You can buy an inexpensive electric timer to take care of this automatically. The timer will also turn off the light at the time you program.

➤ **Check the fish.** Take a quick look to see if there are any symptoms of disease. When you first turn on the lights, many fish will still be sleepy. So a fish that is lethargic first thing in the morning may not be having any problems. If you see such a fish, give it some time to wake up and then check again.

Something's Fishy

Dead fish should be removed immediately, so that they don't spread disease or pollute the tank.

➤ **Look for dead fish.** Fish usually die at night, so it is best to check first thing in the morning. Look carefully. Scan the surface and the bottom for bodies. Look for corpses lodged in the decorations. Consider taking a head count to see if anyone is missing. Fish can jump out, so a missing specimen may be dried up on the carpet. Don't expect to find dead fish often. It should be a rare thing. In fact, it should be such a rare thing that you will soon quit looking for dead fish altogether. I never look for them in my tank anymore, but hey, you should do as I say, not as I do!

➤ **Feed the fish twice daily.** In most cases, I recommend feeding once in the morning and once in the evening, but tailor feedings to the species you keep. Some should be fed more often and some less. Don't forget to close the lid afterward, so the fish don't jump out. If you forget to close it, you will spend more time dealing with the previous item.

➤ **Check for leaks.** If you are a paranoid person, this checklist item is for you. Leaks are rare and will be obvious. If you ask me, hunting for leaks is not so important. But if you see a sign of one, check it out.

➤ **Run water tests.** I recommend testing the water in your new tank daily for the first couple of weeks. After that, you can move it to the weekly checklist. Once you are satisfied that parameters are remaining stable between water changes, you can move the water tests to the biweekly checklist. Check pH, ammonia, nitrite, and salinity.

➤ **Monitor evaporation.** Replace evaporated water as needed. Evaporation increases salinity! It can also cause pumps to run dry and burn out. If you have a trickle filter, remember that evaporation will lower the water level in the sump, not in the tank.

Fish and Tips

If you have to spend more than 10 minutes a week to maintain your aquarium, you are probably doing something wrong or fiddling with it too much.

➤ **Check the equipment.** Is the temperature of the tank right? Are all filters running? Are bubblers bubbling? If you installed a trickle filter, pay special attention to the siphon tube on the overflow box. If bubbles get inside the siphon tube, flow will be restricted or stop altogether. Make sure no animals have climbed in the intake tubes and clogged them.

➤ **Protein skimmers need special attention.** Some brands need daily calibration to function optimally. All brands should be checked daily. Empty collection cups as necessary. If sludge is building up on the inside of the riser tube, wipe it off with a paper towel or take the collection cup to the sink for cleaning. Protein skimmers function best when the riser tube is clean.

➤ **Turn off the light.** Fish need to sleep at the end of the day, just as you do. And since they have no eyelids, they'll really appreciate it when you turn out the light.

Weekly Work List

There really aren't any required weekly duties. However, there are some things that it wouldn't hurt to check—either to play it safe or just to keep the tank in peak condition.

➤ **Loosen sediment on live-rocks.** Sediment tends to collect in all the nooks and crannies of live-rocks, where they may choke out desirable animals or induce growth of undesirable algae. Use a turkey baster or powerhead to blast the sediment loose, so that your filter can pick it up.

➤ **Check filters.** Most filters will not need to be cleaned weekly, but it depends on the type of filter you have and the bioload in the tank. So it's a good idea to give the filter a quick look each week. If it seems too dirty, or if it is clogged enough to restrict flow, clean it. If you have a protein skimmer that uses wooden airstones, check the airstones to see if they need to be replaced.

➤ **Clean strainers.** Bits of plant leaves and other debris can clog the intake strainers of many filters. Be sure your strainers are clear.

➤ **Run water tests.** Check your salinity at least once a week. Evaporation increases salinity! After your tank has finished cycling, test the water weekly for a few weeks. Once you are satisfied that the parameters are stable between water changes, you can move the water tests to the biweekly checklist. If a water change is due this week, run the test before the change to establish a baseline.

➤ **Clean the glass.** Take a quick look to see if algae is building up on the inside glass. If so, take a scrubber pad and wipe it away. You may want to give the inside glass a quick wipe, whether it appears to need it or not.

Check the outside glass to see if there are water spots that need to be wiped away. If so, a paper towel moistened with plain water is usually best. It is OK to use window-cleaning solutions on the outside glass, but be very careful not to get any in the tank. Ammonia kills fish!

Fish and Tips

When cleaning glass, don't forget to check the underside of your canopy glass. Algae can grow there and block the light.

Fish and Tips

Water changes are extremely important, but time passes quickly and it may be hard to remember when you did the last one. Set up a system where you plan your water changes on your days off that are closest to the 1st and the 15th of the month. That way, it's easy to remember.

Biweekly Business

Perform these chores in addition to your weekly duties.

➤ **Use a gravel vacuum to make a 20 percent water change.** Regular partial water changes are so important that I gave this maintenance item an entire chapter of discussion! If you haven't already done so, go back and read Chapter 17. Don't skip water changes. Use a gravel vacuum to remove solid waste from the gravel bed, while removing the old water. Mix the new seawater in a separate container—not in the aquarium. Don't forget to dechlorinate the tapwater before mixing up your seawater, and make sure the new water is the same temperature as the old before adding it to your aquarium.

➤ **Clean filters.** A biweekly cleaning schedule works best for most filters. If your filter gets too dirty faster than that, you may be overfeeding or have an overcrowded tank. Or you may have an undersize filter. Some filters will go longer than two weeks before they need cleaning. Canister filters can normally go a month or more.

Monthly Missions

Here are some additional duties to perform once per month.

➤ **Check airstones.** If you have any air-operated filters or devices, check the airstones at least once a month. Is the output sufficient, or have the airstones partially clogged? Clogged airstones wear out the diaphragm in an air pump much more quickly. Airstones can be clogged by algae, a buildup of calcium carbonate, and even cigarette smoke. Incidentally, if there are smokers in the house, your air pump is blowing smoke-laden air through your aquarium 24 hours a day.

Fish and Tips

If you have a protein skimmer that uses wooden airstones, be sure to replace them at least monthly. Their life span is limited. Replace them more often if air flow slows.

➤ **Clean your filter's impeller.** Motorized filters use impellers to drive the water. Slime can build up on the impeller, and hairs or other debris can tangle around the axle, reducing efficiency. Follow the manufacturer's instructions for your brand. It is common for customers at my store to bring in filters that have stopped working. Nine times out of 10, I clean the crud out of the impeller and the filter starts right up—leaving the customer a little embarrassed. People clean the filter media but don't clean the impeller. So while the filter is turned off for cleaning, slime on the moving parts makes them stick together and the filter can't restart. Consider cleaning the impeller every time you clean the filter.

➤ **Clean the glass canopy or full-hood.** Splashing water tends to keep the underside of your light unit a bit wet. Algae will thrive there. Use an algae scrubber pad to wipe it away. A razor blade may be necessary in tough cases.

➤ **Perform any necessary pruning.** This chore is not likely to apply to the fish-only aquarium, but if you have a lagoon tank you may need to trim and remove some of the fast-growing leafy macroalgae. Reef hobbyists may need to prune soft corals that have overgrown. Indeed, some stony corals may require occasional pruning.

➤ **Clean decorations.** If you have a fish-only setup, you may want to remove ornaments or artificial corals for cleaning. A simple scrub brush and plain water should remove most algae and grime.

Quarterly Chores

Add these jobs to your monthly checklist in March, June, September, and December.

➤ **Replace light bulbs.** Fluorescent bulbs and metal halide bulbs may burn for years, but they will lose much of their intensity within the first six months. Bulbs should be replaced at least yearly, whether they are still burning or not.

➤ **Check the air filter on your air pump.** Many brands of air pumps have small felt air filters on the underside. Check to see if the filter is clogging with dust. If so, you may be able to wash and reuse it, but it is probably better to buy a replacement.

➤ **Clean filter tubes.** A thin layer of algae growing inside the lift tubes of your undergravel filter or the intake tube of your power filter can be left there. It is harmless. However, you should watch for thicker growth. Many small marine animals, including tubeworms, sponges, and tunicates, love to grow inside your aquarium's plumbing. The strong currents there make them happy. Enough life can grow there to clog the tubes! Special brushes are available for cleaning filter tubes and hoses.

Reef aquarists need to watch for an additional problem in their plumbing. Additions of

Fish and Tips

Fluorescent bulbs should be replaced yearly. Consider replacing them on a rotating basis. For example, if you have four bulbs over your tank, replace one every three months. It is easier on your budget, and it maintains a more stable level of light.

Fish School

Cavitation is the formation of gas bubbles in a liquid, caused when an impeller forms a partial vacuum. Gas falls out of solution in the low-pressure zone, forming bubbles.

kalkwasser and other calcium solutions are essential for the growth of stony corals, but the corals don't make use of all the calcium. Some precipitates as calcium carbonate—often along the inside walls of the plumbing of trickle filters. If you restrict the input of your water-return pump, you can cause cavitation, which increases this problem. Necessary flow reductions should always be done on the output side of the water-return pump.

➤ **Give a thorough exterior cleaning.** Most people dust off their aquarium when they dust the other furniture in the room, and that is sufficient most times. However, splashing water can cause dirt and dust to stick, and evaporating water may leave mineral deposits—the dreaded *salt creep!* Give your tank's top a more thorough cleaning, as necessary. You can use an old toothbrush to get into nooks and crannies. The toothbrush also works well for scrubbing deposits that have accumulated around the tank frame.

Filter Maintenance

Your filter cleans the tank. You clean the filter. Filters don't remove waste from the system, they only separate it. It is your job to remove the waste. Usually, you do so by replacing filter media, but sometimes you rinse and reuse the media. Here are some common types of filters and typical methods for cleaning them.

Undergravel Filters

Undergravel filters are the easiest and least expensive to maintain. The gravel functions as the filter medium, and you clean it with a gravel vacuum when you make your partial water changes. Since you have to siphon water to make your partial water change anyway, using a gravel vacuum is no extra work at all. There is no filter medium to change. However, don't forget to replace your airstones as needed.

Fish and Tips

A little vinegar can help remove mineral deposits from your equipment. The acetic acid in the vinegar will dissolve some of the minerals. Don't get vinegar in your aquarium, though!

Use the gravel vacuum to clean around the rocks and decorations, removing as much debris from the gravel as possible. If you draw out the allotted amount of water before you clean the whole bottom, don't worry about it. Just take up where you left off at the next water change.

Outside Power Filters

There are many brands of outside power filters, but all have magnetic impellers. Don't forget to remove the

Routine Maintenance Checklist

Daily Duties

- ❏ Turn on the aquarium light.
- ❏ Check the fish.
- ❏ Look for dead fish.
- ❏ Feed the fish morning and evening.
- ❏ Check for leaks.
- ❏ Run water tests daily until the tank cycles.
- ❏ Monitor evaporation.
- ❏ Check the equipment.
- ❏ Check the calibration on your protein skimmer.
- ❏ Turn off the aquarium light.

Weekly Work List

- ❏ Loosen sediment on live-rocks.
- ❏ Check filters.
- ❏ Clean strainers.
- ❏ Run water tests weekly until the tank is stable.
- ❏ Clean inside and outside glass.

Biweekly Business

- ❏ Use a gravel vacuum to make a 20 percent water change.
- ❏ Clean filters.

Monthly Missions

- ❏ Check airstones.
- ❏ Clean your filter's impeller.
- ❏ Clean the glass canopy or full-hood.
- ❏ Perform any necessary pruning.
- ❏ Clean decorations in the fish-only tank.

Quarterly Chores

- ❏ Replace light bulbs that are due for a change.
- ❏ Check the air filter on the air pump.
- ❏ Clean filter tubes.
- ❏ Give a thorough exterior cleaning.

Fish and Tips

Some brands of undergravel filters come with replaceable cartridges of activated carbon that fit on top of the lift tubes. It is really better not to use them; they restrict water flow. Use a small outside power filter to provide chemical filtration instead.

Fish and Tips

Most outside power filters use unique proprietary filter cartridges. When you go shopping for filter media, be sure you know what brand and model filter you have, or you may buy the wrong media.

impeller occasionally and use a small filter brush to clean inside the impeller well. If slime builds up in there, the filter can stop. Be careful not to get sand in the well. You also may need to use a filter brush to clean inside intake tubes and strainers.

Most outside power filters use special filter media that won't fit other filters. However, there are two basic categories of outside power filters. One group uses replaceable, slide-in filter cartridges. The other has reusable sponge filter media.

There are many brands of filter cartridges, and they come in many sizes. The basic design is a flat polyester filter cartridge, about the size of a slice of bread. Some brands have activated carbon inside. Other brands use a method that applies a coating of activated carbon directly onto the polyester fibers. The best cartridges of this type are refillable, allowing you to add extra activated carbon inside.

Cartridge filters are designed to be easy to clean. You slide out the dirty filter cartridge and pop in a new clean one. It doesn't get much easier than that. Still, there is a disadvantage to that ease of use. When you throw away your filter media, you also throw away the helpful bacteria that colonized the media. So you temporarily reduce the biological filtration capacity of your tank.

There are a couple of things you can do to help, though. Larger outside power filters may have two cartridges instead of one. If so, it is better to change them on a rotating basis, instead of replacing both cartridges at once. That way, you retain the helpful bacteria on one cartridge while the other recolonizes. If you use the refillable cartridges, you may want to replace the outer polyester medium one time and the activated carbon the next. Rotating the two types of media retains helpful bacteria. It's a bit of a pain to do, though, and definitely not as easy as tossing out one cartridge and popping in another.

One very popular brand of outside power filter uses a separate filter sponge and a bag of activated carbon. When the sponge gets dirty, you rinse it and reuse it . . . forever. Rinse the sponge with water that is close to aquarium temperature, so that you don't kill the helpful bacteria living on the sponge. You want to rinse out the debris, not sterilize the sponge.

Fish Tales

Activated carbon works in an unusual way. The manufacturing process forms millions of microscopic capillaries in each grain of carbon, greatly increasing the surface area of each particle. The exposed carbon on this surface bonds with organic matter, collecting it. The process is called *adsorption*.

The bags of activated carbon should be replaced at least monthly. Activated carbon can adsorb only so much waste and then it is no good. Worse, if you don't change your activated carbon often enough and your pH drops, substances may be released back into your water.

You can buy premeasured bags of activated carbon to fit your model of filter, or you can buy net filter bags and bulk activated carbon and bag your own. If you buy bulk carbon, get the good stuff. The price will usually reflect the quality. Good activated carbon will have a dull luster and relatively rough finish. Avoid the cheap glassy black filter carbons. They are nothing more than crushed coal and are close to worthless. There are some excellent brands of activated carbon that come in pellet form. I highly recommend those.

Canister Filters

There are several brands of canister filters. Follow the manufacturer's instructions for advice on how to take them apart and for recommendations on getting the best performance. When cleaning filter

Fish School

During **adsorption,** substances are taken up by binding to the surface of a solid. During **absorption,** substances are taken up by soaking into internal recesses, as with a sponge.

media, you also should take time to clean the impeller assembly and make sure intake and output valves are not clogged with debris. Here are brief directions for various styles of canister filters:

➤ **Filter compartments.** My favorite canister filters have separate plastic compartments inside. One uses ceramic noodle filter media, another holds activated carbon, and a third holds a filter sponge. At cleaning time, the ceramic noodles and sponge get rinsed and reused forever. The activated carbon should be replaced at each filter change.

➤ **Open design.** At least one brand of canister filter has a single large compartment for filter media. You can use several types of media, all of which have unpronounceable German names. Follow the manufacturer's recommendations for best results.

➤ **Filter sleeves.** Some brands have a central core, around which you wrap a replaceable filter sleeve. One type of sleeve is soft polyester, another resembles a pleated oil filter. The type that looks like an oil filter will filter finer particles. Both types should be replaced when dirty.

Trickle Filters

Trickle filters are also easy to maintain. Most use a prefilter sponge in the overflow box. Rinse it as needed. Some brands have a polyester filter pad at the entry to the sump, which should be cleaned or replaced, too. Of course, if you have bags of activated carbon in the sump, they should be replaced at least monthly.

If your filter uses bio-balls, give them a quick rinse if they start to accumulate crud. This should rarely be necessary, though—perhaps once or twice a year. If your filter uses the DLS filter medium, you probably should unroll it and rinse it out every month or so.

Fluidized Bed Filters

Since these filters provide biological filtration only and are not intended to collect dirt, there is little maintenance involved. The most common chore will be to make sure that the intake on the powerhead is clean. Bits of debris can clog it and reduce flow. Over time, some sand will disappear from the filter and should be replaced.

Protein Skimmers

There are many styles of protein skimmers, so follow your manufacturer's recommendations for best results. Here are some general guidelines:

➤ **Check the calibration daily to optimize performance.** It is common to have to tweak the settings, because various things affect performance, including the level of dissolved organics in the water, the age of any airstones, clogged pump intakes, and water levels in the tank or sump.

➤ **Clean and empty the collection cup as needed.** If you plumbed your protein skimmer's collection cup to drain into a milk jug or other container, empty it regularly.

➤ **Replace wooden airstones at least monthly,** or when air flow slows. (Of course, this applies to air-driven models only.) Clogged airstones produce fewer bubbles, which reduces efficiency. Old wooden airstones develop large holes, which produce large, useless bubbles. Tiny bubbles collect waste much better.

➤ **Check the Venturi port for clogs.** Use a paper clip to clear buildup as necessary. (This one applies to Venturi models only.) A clogged Venturi port will reduce the number of scum-collecting bubbles.

Other Filters

➤ **Sponge filters** are often used in quarantine tanks. Rinse them with water that is close to aquarium temperature. The sponge should last a long, long time. If you see the sponge starting to collapse or notice reduced output, it is a sign that the sponge needs cleaning. Depending on the bioload in your tank, you may need to do it weekly, biweekly, or monthly.

➤ **Powerheads**, though not really filters, are used to drive filters or just to provide extra circulation. Keep an eye on them to be sure the intake strainers don't become clogged. Sometimes, you will need to take apart the powerhead to remove crud that gets inside.

The Least You Need to Know

➤ Feed the fish twice daily, and check for dead fish.

➤ Check the calibration of protein skimmers daily.

➤ Use a gravel vacuum to change 20 percent of the water every other week.

➤ Replace fluorescent bulbs at least one a year.

➤ Clean filters as needed, but replace the activated carbon monthly.

➤ Clean the inside and outside aquarium glass as needed.

Chapter 20

Reef Madness

In This Chapter

➤ What a reef tank needs to survive

➤ How much light is enough?

➤ Why live-rock is so important

➤ There are several styles of reefkeeping

➤ Dealing with common reef pests

The reef tank can be the most spectacular and interesting style of aquarium. It is the most natural, too. There are no artificial decorations or ornaments in this microcosm. Nor is there a need for them. When even the rocks are alive, and the reef is composed of a garden of colorful and flowery creatures, nothing manufactured by humans can exceed its beauty. Add the world's most beautiful fish on top of that, and you create a natural spectacle that is engaging, enthralling, engrossing.

Every time you look at your reef, you will see something new—a snail that seems to have come from nowhere, a colony of mysid shrimp hiding beneath a stone, tiny featherduster worms reaching for the current, an unfamiliar crab, or a new encrustation of colorful sponges or coralline algae. The reef is a dynamic place. Species flourish, flounder, relocate, or disappear. Your reef tank is never exactly the same today as it will be tomorrow.

Caveat Aquarist

You know, I almost didn't include this chapter in my book. Reef tanks should not be attempted by beginners—at least, not unless they are first willing to do a lot more research. Reef tanks are the most sophisticated of aquaria, and a full understanding of them is beyond the scope of this book. Before any hobbyist attempts to install a reef aquarium in their home, they should buy and read some of the texts in my recommended reading list, included as Appendix C of this book. I especially recommend the two-volume set *The Reef Aquarium,* by Delbeek and Sprung.

However, to leave a discussion of such a tempting style of aquarium out of this book would almost be a sin. After all, keeping a reef aquarium is the closest thing to keeping a piece of the ocean itself. A reef tank is something you can aspire to after you get some practice with other, simpler styles of aquaria. So please consider this chapter to be an introduction to reefkeeping. What I'll do here is tell you how reef requirements are different from the saltwater aquarium care I've discussed throughout the book.

Reef Requirements

In many ways, the same basic rules apply to both a reef tank and a fish-only marine aquarium:

➤ Mix compatible species.

➤ Provide a proper diet in the right quantity.

➤ Perform regular partial water changes to maintain water quality.

➤ Don't overcrowd the fish.

➤ Don't overfeed.

➤ Don't fall in.

But the reef aquarium is more demanding. Since its centerpiece is delicate live coral, you must take extra steps to be certain their needs will be met. Here are some fundamental requirements of the reef aquarium:

➤ **Intense lighting.** A fish-only aquarium requires enough light for you to see the fish. Reef tanks, however, require much more intense lighting. Without strong light, photosynthetic corals and anemones will die.

➤ **Strong protein skimming.** Water quality is even more important in the reef aquarium than it is in a fish-only tank. Not only are many of the organisms more delicate than fish, but many are also susceptible to being choked by the growth of undesirable algae—growth encouraged by the combination of intense lighting and nutrients. A protein skimmer removes many nutrients that would help algae flourish.

➤ **Calcium supplementation.** Live stony corals deplete calcium from the water in the process of building their calcium carbonate exoskeletons. Kalkwasser or other commercial additives are available to replenish calcium levels.

➤ **Live-rock forms the structure of the reef.** Helpful bacteria within the rock can provide all the biological filtration the system needs. Even more important are the microfauna that hitchhike into your tank via the rock. These tiny animals provide food, interest, and even decoration in the reef aquarium. They contribute to the microcosm.

➤ **Water motion.** This is the final essential element. It brings food to filter feeders, and it washes away waste.

Fish School

You remember **photosynthesis** from high school biology, right? It's the process by which plants—and corals—use the energy in light to synthesize carbohydrates.

Fish and Tips

Prescribed filters for reef aquariums include trickle filters and protein skimmers. Do not use undergravel filters, since once the live rocks are positioned on top, maintenance will be impossible.

A Matter of Light or Death

Most live corals kept in the home aquarium are photosynthetic. That means they use light to synthesize their nutrients. Actually, it is more correct to say that they have a symbiotic relationship with photosynthetic dinoflagellates that live within their tissues (or, it would be more correct to say that if you could say it at all!). These 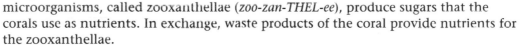 microorganisms, called zooxanthellae (*zoo-zan-THEL-ee*), produce sugars that the corals use as nutrients. In exchange, waste products of the coral provide nutrients for the zooxanthellae.

Live corals require special lighting for this photosynthesis to occur. Unfortunately, the typical single strip light or fluorescent full-hood does not provide nearly enough light for proper photosynthesis. And without the proper light, your corals will die.

When it comes to lighting, there are three things you must provide for maximum benefit to the corals:

➤ Proper spectral color

➤ Sufficient duration

➤ Effective intensity

Spectral Color

While almost any light bulb, if it's bright enough, will permit photosynthesis, some bulbs are much better at it than others. And some encourage the growth of undesirable algae. So which light is best?

Full-spectrum light is the best for a reef tank. Full-spectrum bulbs contain the complete range of colors of the visible spectrum, and a bit of the invisible spectrum, too. Full-spectrum bulbs will give off light that appears white but may have accents in particular parts of the spectrum.

Zooxanthellae make particular use of near-ultraviolet wavelengths, so many full-spectrum bulbs have extra peaks in those parts of the spectrum. Bulbs of differing spectra can also be mixed to achieve desired results. Supplementary near-UV bulbs, known as *actinic* or *Phillips O3* bulbs, are also sold by your dealer (I discussed these in Chapter 7). Actinic bulbs are mixed with other bulbs, such as *daylight* bulbs, to achieve an effect that is white enough to be pleasing to the eye but has extra blue wavelengths for the live corals.

Common Bulb Combinations

2 daylight fluorescent for every 1 actinic fluorescent

1 daylight fluorescent for every 2 50-50 fluorescent

1 5,500°K metal halide for every 1 or 2 actinic fluorescent

Duration

Twelve hours of light a day works quite well. I usually run mine a bit longer—around 14 hours. Note, however, that you cannot take a bulb of insufficient intensity and get enough light by running it longer. Intensity is more important than duration.

Fish and Tips

There is no substitute for sufficient intensity. You cannot take a bulb with poor spectral output and run it longer to get the proper effect. It just won't work. Be bright and buy bright lights.

Intensity: Are You Bright Enough?

So how much light is enough? A good general rule of thumb is to provide 2 to 5 watts of light per gallon. There is a range because some species require more light than others, and because taller tanks require more light than shallow tanks.

Do you recall the *inverse square law* from high school physics class? It states that the intensity of light decreases by the square of the distance. Put simply, if light travels twice as far, it will have one-fourth the intensity. If it travels three times as far, it will have one-ninth the intensity; four times as far, one-sixteenth the intensity;

and so on. So, if your 1-foot-tall tank needs a certain amount of light to grow corals properly, a tank that is 2 feet tall will need four times the light, and a tank that is 3 feet tall will need nine times the light.

Using the 2- to 5-watts-per-gallon rule, you can see that a 29-gallon tank would require 60 to 150 watts of light. Since this size aquarium is not particularly shallow—it's 18 inches tall—using the midrange of that scale is probably the best choice. In other words, 80 to 100 watts of light should be about right.

According to the same rule, a 55-gallon tank would require 110 to 275 watts of light. Since this tank is deeper, you should work off the higher end of the 2- to 5-watts-per-gallon rule. In reality, though, you will have a hard time fitting more than four 40-watt fluorescent bulbs on a tank that size, which leaves you with 160 watts—more toward the low end of the light scale. What should you do? Consider using compact fluorescents or metal halide lighting to achieve the higher wattage ratings.

The table on the next page compares the number of bulbs in a typical fluorescent full-hood with the number recommended to keep live corals properly. You'll see that what you get in a typical full-hood is far less than what you need. You'll also see that some recommended wattages may be slightly under the 2- to 5-watts-per-gallon guideline. That's because power compact fluorescents emit more intensity per watt than other bulbs.

Fish and Tips

Use 2 to 5 watts of light per gallon of water. The lower end of that range will work for shallow tanks and those containing species of soft corals. Use the higher end for deep tanks and tanks containing stony corals.

Fish and Tips

Bulbs lose intensity as they age. While the bulb may continue to glow for three years, it will have lost half its intensity within the first 6 to 12 months. So change your bulbs at least yearly. Changing them on a rotating basis, rather than all at once, is best.

Scum-Sucking Skimmers

A good protein skimmer, also called a foam fractionator, is necessary equipment for your reef tank. Your protein skimmer will optimize your water quality by removing dissolved and suspended organics. Protein skimmers also remove phosphates from the aquarium, reducing the nutrients available for undesirable algae.

Protein skimmers have a major advantage over other means of filtration. Where other filters merely trap waste until you clean the filter or convert it to other substances that remain until you change water, protein skimmers remove waste from the system by bubbling it out into a separate container. Buy the most powerful protein skimmer you can afford. You won't regret it.

See the Light

Tank Size (gals.)	l × w × h (inches)	Typical Full-Hood (# bulbs × watts)	Minimum Lighting Needed for Coral Growth		
			Standard Fluorescents (# bulbs × watts)	Compact Fluorescents (# bulbs × watts)	Halide (# bulbs × watts)
Standard Rectangular Tanks					
29	30 × 12 × 18	1 × 20w	3 × 20w	1 × 55w	1 × 150w
30	36 × 13 × 16	1 × 30w	2 × 30w	1 × 55w	1 × 150w
40	48 × 13 × 16	1 × 40w	2 × 40w	3 × 28w	1 × 150w
44	22 × 22 × 24	2 × 15w	6 × 15w	4 × 28w	1 × 150w
45	36 × 12 × 24	1 × 30w	3 × 30w	2 × 55w	1 × 175w
55	48 × 13 × 20	1 × 40w	3 × 40w	2 × 55w	1 × 175w
58	36 × 18 × 21	1 × 30w	3 × 30w	2 × 55w	1 × 175w
75	48 × 18 × 21	1 × 40w	4 × 40w	2 × 96w	1 × 250w
89	36 × 24 × 24	2 × 30w	6 × 30w	2 × 96w	1 × 250w
90	48 × 18 × 24	1 × 40w	4 × 40w	3 × 96w	1 × 250w
100	72 × 18 × 18	2 × 30w	8 × 30w	4 × 96w	2 × 150w
110	60 × 18 × 24	1 × 40w	6 × 40w	6 × 55w	2 × 150w
120	48 × 24 × 24	2 × 40w	6 × 40w	6 × 55w	2 × 150w
125	72 × 18 × 22	2 × 30w	8 × 30w	4 × 96w	2 × 175w
135	72 × 18 × 24	2 × 30w	8 × 30w	4 × 96w	2 × 175w
150	72 × 18 × 28	2 × 30w	10 × 30w	6 × 96w	2 × 250w
180L	96 × 18 × 24	2 × 40w	10 × 40w	6 × 96w	3 × 175w
180W	72 × 24 × 24	2 × 30w	12 × 30w	6 × 96w	2 × 250w
200	84 × 24 × 24	2 × 30w	14 × 30w	6 × 96w	3 × 175w
220	84 × 24 × 25	2 × 30w	14 × 30w	6 × 96w	3 × 175w
265	84 × 24 × 30	2 × 30w	16 × 30w	8 × 96w	3 × 250w
Hexagons					
27	18 × 18 × 24	1 × 15w	3 × 15w	2 × 28w	1 × 150w
35	23 × 20 × 24	1 × 15w	3 × 15w	2 × 28w	1 × 150w
45	22 × 22 × 24	1 × 15w	4 × 15w	3 × 28w	1 × 150w
60	22 × 22 × 30	1 × 15w	6 × 15w	4 × 28w	1 × 150w
Flatback Hexagons					
26	36 × 12 × 16	1 × 30w	2 × 30w	1 × 55w	1 × 150w
33	36 × 13 × 20	1 × 30w	2 × 30w	1 × 55w	1 × 150w
52	48 × 13 × 20	1 × 40w	3 × 40w	2 × 55w	1 × 175w

Several styles of protein skimmers are available. See Chapter 5 on filter systems for more about how protein skimming works and for advice on choosing between Venturi, countercurrent, and downdraft models. Be sure to install your skimmer according to the manufacturer's directions.

Extra Calcium

If you keep live stony corals, they require calcium to build their skeletons. You must also maintain the proper alkalinity of your aquarium water, or the process will be inhibited. The easiest way to accomplish both is by adding kalkwasser, a solution of calcium hydroxide ($Ca(OH)_2$).

Live stony corals, giant clams, and other organisms that build shells can deplete a system of calcium quite rapidly. I recommend that you encourage evaporation in your reef tank. The more water that evaporates, the more kalkwasser you can add to replenish calcium.

Kalkwasser is highly caustic, with a pH around 12. Remembering that each 1-point change on the pH scale represents a 10-fold change in the water, you can see that kalkwasser is around 10,000 times more basic than seawater. Always add kalkwasser slowly. Set up a drip system. Ideally, kalkwasser should be dripped slowly into a sump, rather than directly into the aquarium.

Kalkwasser is great for maintaining proper calcium and alkalinity levels in the reef aquarium. However, it is not always enough. Calcium hydroxide, which is what it is made of, is not highly soluble and a kalkwasser solution is only capable of adding limited amounts of calcium. It really works best as a maintenance additive. When calcium or alkalinity levels are drastically low, other calcium additives can be used for quicker increases.

Most additives use calcium chloride ($CaCl_2$) as the active ingredient. Calcium chloride will quickly raise your calcium levels, and you can use it to bring the initial calcium level in your aquarium to prescribed levels. Then use kalkwasser to maintain that level.

Fish and Tips

Try to maintain a calcium ion level (Ca^{++}) of 400 to 450 ppm and an alkalinity of 3.5 to 4.0 meq. See Chapter 16 on water chemistry for an explanation of what these numbers mean.

Something's Fishy

Always add kalkwasser to your system slowly. Your dealer should sell an IV drip system, like the type used in hospitals, so that you can slowly administer kalkwasser to your system.

If calcium chloride raises the calcium level faster than kalkwasser, why use kalkwasser at all? Because calcium chloride tends to decrease your alkalinity. So after dosing an aquarium with calcium chloride, you will probably have to follow up the next day with a buffer to bring the alkalinity back to desired levels. The problem with adding buffers is that they can cause some calcium to fall out of solution. So then you need to add more calcium. You see where this is going.

Calcium chloride also raises the amount of chlorides in your system. While a little won't hurt, regular additions could be detrimental to your tank.

Live-Rock

No, I am not talking about a Rolling Stones concert. Live-rocks are porous calcareous rocks, harvested from the ocean, replete with the countless organisms that live upon and within them. Live-rock serves several purposes in your reef tank:

➤ **Forms the reef structure.** Live-rock is the reef in your reef tank. It forms a support structure to hold the corals that you will introduce.

➤ **Provides biological filtration.** Live-rock is fully colonized by the helpful bacteria needed to break down ammonia and nitrites in your tank. Anaerobic bacteria (the kind that doesn't need oxygen) deep within the rock can take the process a step further to remove nitrates.

➤ **Introduces life.** A tank without live-rock would be relatively plain. Aside from the fish and invertebrates that you intentionally introduce, you could expect to see some microalgae develop—and that's about it. Live-rock, however, will introduce an abundance of tiny creatures into your ecosystem. Sponges, algae, shrimp, crabs, worms, and many more interesting life forms will hitchhike into your tank via the rock.

Fish and Tips

Use 1 to 2 pounds of live-rock per gallon in your reef aquarium. Inexpensive, plain base rock can compose the inner layers. Fancier, decorative live-rocks are nice on the outside.

➤ **Provides decoration.** Besides being functional, live-rock is beautiful. The various life forms that encrust the rocks come in every color of the rainbow—literally.

Motion in the Ocean

Water current is extremely important to the proper functioning of a reef tank. You need only look at underwater nature documentaries to see that the ocean is a far-from-stagnant place. Many marine organisms not only tolerate swift water currents, they require it. Here are some reasons why strong water motion is important:

➤ **Brings food.** For the various filter-feeding animals in your aquarium, current is especially important. Without water motion to bring food to them, they will starve. Water motion also brings food to shy species.

➤ **Removes waste from the tank.** Water motion removes waste in many ways. The most obvious way is to rinse debris toward the intake of your filter system, where it can be picked up and removed from the tank.

➤ **Removes waste from animals.** Live corals depend on water motion and the way it makes their bodies sway and undulate in the current to circulate their internal body fluids. It helps them move nutrition throughout their systems, and it helps them excrete waste. Moving water also washes away external parasites and excess body slime.

➤ **Shapes the reef.** Water motion greatly affects the shape and appearance of your reef. Many hobbyists overlook this. For example, a sea anemone likes to anchor its foot where it is protected but where its tentacles receive water current. Place the anemone in a stagnant zone and it will keep wandering off to find a better spot. The shape of live corals is greatly affected by water flow, too. The presence or absence of current will affect the thickness and size of branches and the direction of their orientation. It will also affect the overall shape of the animal as it grows. Sponges may grow into either spherical or fingery masses—all depending on the amount and direction of water current.

A wavemaking device, capable of driving four powerheads.

For best results, the current should not only be strong, but also should be variable. Tides and surge are part of the natural environment. If you've seen those nature documentaries, you know there is no way we can duplicate that type of current in our aquariums. The surge in the ocean is strong enough to smash a diver against the reef. Still, we can try. Using timers and wavemaking devices to vary the direction and flow of supplemental powerheads should be considered essential to the development of a successful reef aquarium.

Substrates for the Reef

As you consider setting up a reef aquarium, you will find that there are many opinions on how to do so. (The next section will list some of the most popular methods.) However, despite the number of methods that have been shown to be successful, they all have common features: intense lighting, ample protein skimming, use of live-rock, and good water motion.

Fish and Tips

It is wise to add animals that help stir and clean the sand bed. Choices include blue-legged hermit crabs, red reef hermit crabs, brittle and serpent stars, and various sea cucumbers. Your dealer may also carry some species of goby noted for their sand-sifting talents.

The one area where you will find the most variety of opinions is in regard to substrate. Should you use it or not? If so, what kind? Even the reef gurus have changed their minds over the years, and it wouldn't surprise me if they changed them again. I remember when substrate was recommended. Then there was a phase when experts were saying you should omit it altogether because it acted as a sediment trap. There was a period where a thin layer was permissible, and there is a method today that uses deep substrate. At one point, gravel was preferred, and the use of sand was frowned upon because it could pack down hard, shutting out all oxygen-breathing creatures. Now, that very same feature is used as a selling point.

Anyway, the current trend seems to be to use a layer of sugar-size calcareous sand about 2 inches deep. Introduce various sand-stirring animals to keep it from compacting and to keep it clean. The fineness of the sand prevents most detritus from falling between the grains, anyway, so it tends to stay pretty clean. Anaerobic bacteria can be active in the lower layers of sand, removing nitrates from your system.

Most hobbyists buy bags of aragonite sand at their local shop, and then top it off with some live-sand to help seed the sand bed with helpful bacteria and tiny critters. Yes, live-sand is just like live-rock, only smaller.

How to Keep a Reef

The reefkeeping hobby is just growing out of its infancy. Here in the United States, it really didn't get a foothold until 1986, when articles on the subject written by Dutch hobbyist George Smit were published in one of the American aquarium magazines. Until that time, it was thought impossible to keep corals alive in captivity for long, and thoughts of propagating them were laughed at. Only a small group of advanced hobbyists in Europe were having any success at it. Their efforts laid the groundwork that has developed into the hobby today.

The hobby of reefkeeping is coming of age. The dedicated work of hobbyists and scientists has made much progress in the last couple of decades. We are now able to grow and propagate many species of corals.

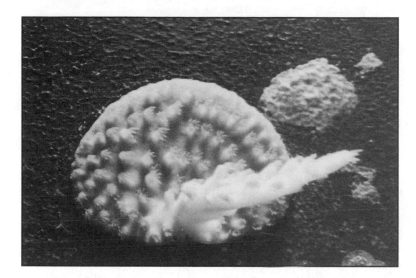

A fragment of acropora coral was Superglued to the back glass, and is now growing into a new colony.

As the hobby evolved, so did the methods used for maintaining a reef tank. As we learn more, we make changes where necessary. Even the proven reefkeeping methods listed in this book may become outdated in a few years. Anyway, here is a brief list of some of the most popular styles of reefkeeping. All of these styles emphasize the use of large quantities of live-rock, ample protein skimming, and intense light.

> ➤ **Dutch method.** This style of reef aquarium was the first to hit the U.S. market. It introduced the trickle filter to us. Emphasis on use of the trickle filter, protein skimming, and lush growths of caulerpa macroalgae are the key features.

> ➤ **Berlin method.** The Berlin method is probably the most popular method used today and is the one I personally prefer. It emphasizes heavy protein skimming and use of ample quantities of live-rock for filtration. Trickle filters are still used, but the media are removed and the device functions solely as a sump, where kalkwasser can be conveniently administered via drip.

> ➤ **Jaubert method.** Developed by Dr. Jean Jaubert at the Monaco Aquarium, this style of reefkeeping is also called the Monaco method. The concept is a bit more complicated. It involves placing a screened filter an inch or two off the bottom of the tank, with no sand beneath. A 2-inch layer of substrate goes on top of the first screen. Do not use aragonite sand for this layer, as it tends to become too packed. A second screen is placed on top of this layer, followed by a second 2-inch layer of substrate—usually live-sand. The principle behind the Jaubert method is that the lower anaerobic layer of sand allows removal of nitrates, while

the upper layer allows removal of ammonia and nitrites. The screen between the two layers keeps digging animals from disturbing the lower layer. This method works, but I don't much like the extra-deep substrate and ugly screens.

Cycling the Reef Aquarium

Like the fish-only aquarium, a reef aquarium needs to be cycled. Usually. It depends on what goes in and how you go about it. First off, any of the methods for cycling a fish-only aquarium will work in a reef aquarium. I devote all of Chapter 15 to cycling aquariums, so I'm not going to repeat that discussion here. Instead, let's talk about some factors that may help you skip or speed the cycling process in your reef aquarium.

Your budget is probably the biggest factor in this equation. Most hobbyists stock their reef aquariums slowly. It is the only way they can afford to do so. Every paycheck adds a bit to the population. Such a tank will cycle at traditional rates, but the process is never completely done until the aquarium is fully stocked, and this may be weeks or months down the road.

The quality of the live-rock is another factor in how fast your tank will cycle. If you purchase pieces that have already cured in your dealer's tanks, you should be able to add them without cycling time. These live-rocks should already have a healthy complement of helpful bacteria, and any die-off of organisms that occurred during shipment from the collection site should have long since rotted away.

Obviously, if you buy live-rock out of your dealer's new shipments, you can expect elevated ammonia levels in your aquarium while the rock cures. If the ammonia levels are elevated, don't expect to safely add animals to the tank until they have dropped.

How would you like to set up your reef aquarium and be able to add fish almost immediately, because the tank is already cycled? With care, it can be done. Here's how.

First, purchase all your live-rock at once. Buy rock that has already cured in the dealer's tank. Adding such rock should introduce more than enough helpful bacteria into your tank to fully cycle it. In theory, you should be able to add a full population of corals, invertebrates, and fish after you've given the rock a day or two to settle in. In practice, it may take a bit longer than that.

Here's how I like to do it. I add all the live-rock at once, being careful to choose cured pieces. After adding the rock, I let the system run for two or three days, monitoring ammonia and nitrite levels. I expect those levels to stay at zero, but there is no guarantee that they will. It is possible to grab a piece of uncured rock by mistake or even to damage organisms on the way home to your own aquarium.

Something's Fishy

Avoid buying your dealer's newest pieces of live-rock. While it may be tempting to get first choice, these pieces will elevate ammonia levels in your aquarium until they are fully cured. Instead, buy pieces that have already cured in the dealer's tank.

However, if I monitor for two days and see no detectable ammonia or nitrite, then I feel perfectly safe adding corals and livestock to the tank. Do not rush this process. Your mileage may vary. If you detect ammonia and nitrite, you should not add more livestock yet. Doing so could crash the whole system by raising those levels even higher.

There are two advantages to quick-cycling the tank this way. First, you get to see a fully operative aquarium right away, instead of having the process take weeks. Second, you may prevent some algae and disease problems. Where there is light and nutrients, algae wants to take hold. However, if there are photosynthetic corals present to use some of those nutrients and lots of live-rocks present to neutralize the nutrients, there will be less nutrients available for algae. Further, the live corals fill and shade parts of the reef—removing habitat that otherwise would provide a good spot for algae to grow.

Finally, filter-feeding organisms present on the live-rocks may filter out some disease organisms as food. Cool, huh? The bottom line is that a fully operational reef is more stable than one that is a work in progress.

Stocking the Reef Aquarium

Rock first. Those two words are most important. The quality of live-rock will relate directly to the health of your other animals. Before buying corals, invertebrates, or fish, buy your rock. Remember that you are setting up a reef aquarium and that it is not a reef aquarium until you install the reef.

Make sure your equipment is functioning (especially the protein skimmer) and that ammonia and nitrite levels are stable at zero before adding fish or invertebrates.

Algae in the Reef

Algae is a natural part of any reef. Still, many consider it to be a scourge of the reef aquarium, and indeed, it can become so. A little algae here and there is nothing to get excited about. It may even be attractive or helpful. It is when algae gets out of control that it becomes a problem, because it can grow on and choke out your precious live corals.

When algae is out of control, don't blame the algae. Blame yourself. Excessive algae growth reflects poor management practices in the aquarium. Since you are the general manager of your tank, that means you. By the way, poor management doesn't necessarily mean you are doing too little for your tank—it may well mean you are doing too much.

I have devoted all of Chapter 21 to algae and its control, so we will skip that discussion here. For now,

Fish and Tips

Consider adding the shyest species or pickiest eaters first. Let them get comfortable with their surroundings before introducing more territorial or aggressive animals.

let me just remind you to be sure that your water quality is good, that you are using the proper type and amount of light, and that you have some herbivores in your tank. I don't know about you, but I'd rather watch a herd of tiny blue-legged hermit crabs eating my algae than try to figure out what tests I need to run or chemicals I need to add.

The Good Stuff

Not all algae are undesirable. Several types of macroalgae are interesting and colorful additions to a reef. Caulerpa, halimeda, and other green varieties are most commonly offered for sale, but you'll occasionally find brown or bright red macroalgae available, too. These make wonderful additions, but be sure you won't be mixing them with species that will eat them.

No reef would be complete without encrusting purple coralline algae. You would never guess that they are algae from their appearance—a hard purple crust that forms on rocks. Sometimes the coralline algae grow into protruding flat plates. Coralline algae should be highly encouraged in your reef. When it coats a rock, there is little chance that undesirable algae will take foothold there, and the bright purple color adds to the interest of your display.

Pests

Microalgae isn't the only pest in the aquarium. There are a few others, too. The most notorious is the tinkering hobbyist. Some people just can't keep their hands off of, or out of, their aquariums. They want to try every techno-gadget that comes out, they want to experiment with every additive, they fiddle with one water-quality parameter, only to mess up another—and then they have fun fiddling with that one, too.

Here are some other common pests of the reef aquarium:

➤ **Crabs.** As your system matures, you will find crabs that you never knew you had. They come in on the live-rock as larvae or juveniles, or they may have been hiding inside or were just so camouflaged that you didn't notice them before. Some crabs are aggressive feeders that, as they grow, will prey on other animals in your tank. If you can't catch a crab for removal, use the trap described later in this section.

➤ **Mantis shrimp.** These creatures live in holes in the live-rock, so it may be some time before you find that you have any of them living in your aquarium. In most cases, they are probably harmless. However, they are capable of killing various invertebrates and small fishes. As the shrimp grows, so does its appetite. Never handle a mantis shrimp with your hand. They have earned the common name of "thumb-splitter" shrimp. The easiest way to remove these guys is to remove the rock with them in it. Suspend the rock in a separate bucket of water, and the shrimp will eventually come out. The rock can then be returned to the aquarium. Traps may be necessary when the rock cannot be easily removed.

➤ **Aiptasia anemones.** Also called glass anemones, these are small, transparent brown sea anemones. Most are under an inch in size. They can multiply readily, feeding on bits of free-floating food. One or two glass anemones is not a problem. Large populations can be troublesome, though, as they can sting giant clams and corals. Control is difficult. Many hobbyists try to squish the anemone, only to find that any bits of its foot that remain will each regenerate into a new anemone. Peppermint shrimp, copperband butterflies, and assorted wrasses are predators of aiptasia, but they are undependable and may bother other desirable invertebrates. The tiny brown sea slug, *Berghia verrucicornis*, is the best bet but is rarely available.

➤ **Pyramidellid snails.** These guys, including *Tathrella iredalei*, are parasites of giant clams. These snails are tiny, less than on eighth of an inch long. During the day, they hide at the base of the clam or in the scutes (folds) of the shell. At night, they cling to the edge of the shell and eat the clam's mantle. Inspect new clams for these parasites and remove them. Many hobbyists keep the six-line wrasse to control these snails.

➤ **Bristleworms.** These are not really pests; they are part of the normal scavenger community in your aquarium. However, they have been known to present occasional problems. Lacking other food, they may attack the flesh of corals and giant clams. Some grow to over a foot long and as big around as your finger. Large specimens such as this may be predatory and should be removed.

It's a Trap!

Your dealer may sell some small traps for capturing crabs, mantis shrimp, or even uncooperative fish. You can build simple traps yourself, too. To catch elusive crabs, take a small plastic cup with a lid, cut a quarter-size hole in the lid, put a bit of food inside, and wedge the cup between some rocks at night. By morning, you may have your crab. The crab crawls in, but the slick sides prevent its exit.

Mantis shrimp are good swimmers and are more crafty. To catch them, take a small plastic box, drill some holes in it, and wrap a rubber band around it. Prop it open with a toothpick with fishing line

Fish and Tips

Some types of succession can be controlled. For example, you may need to prune branches off fast-growing corals to prevent them from stinging neighbors or blocking access to light and current.

attached. Place bait inside, and set the trap outside the shrimp's hiding hole. When the shrimp enters the box, yank the fishing line to dislodge the toothpick. The rubber band will snap the box shut with the shrimp inside. (The holes you drilled allow water to escape, so the closing of the box doesn't blast the shrimp out.)

Succession and Success

Finally, remember that your reef is dynamic. Over time, some corals will prosper and others will die back. One type of algae may disappear, only to be replaced by another, and so on. It is a normal process that biologists call *succession,* and it occurs in every habitat. Species colonize a habitat and then later disappear, as new species move in and take over. So don't expect your reef tank to remain a static display.

The Least You Need to Know

➤ Corals and anemones require intense lighting for photosynthesis.

➤ Protein skimmers provide the highest water quality.

➤ Add kalkwasser to provide calcium for stony corals.

➤ Use 1 to 2 pounds of live-rock per gallon.

➤ Water motion is necessary. Use wavemaking devices for best results.

➤ The Berlin method of reefkeeping is most popular.

➤ Reef aquariums require a lot more research than you'll get from this book.

Part 5
Oceans of Trouble

We all wish that life was easy and perfect, but it's not. Problems can arise. The same is true of your aquarium. Follow the rules and you may never have any problems with your aquarium at all. Your fish and invertebrates could survive for years.

Still, things can go wrong, so in Part 5 I will talk about some common problems and how to deal with them. You will learn how to prevent excessive algae growth, and what to do if you failed. You will learn about some common fish diseases and how to medicate them. Even better, you will learn how to prevent disease by eliminating stress to your fish. Finally, I will talk about what to do when you find that there is a bully in your tank.

Chapter 21

Aww, Gee! Is That Algae?

In This Chapter

➤ Learn what algae is

➤ Discover what causes it

➤ Find out how to control it

Every aquarist has to deal with algae sooner or later. At minimum, you need to wipe it from your glass now and then to keep a clear view of your fish. In most cases, algae growth is minimal and no big deal. But sometimes, algae grows in epidemic proportions and becomes a continuous battle. This chapter tells you what algae is, which types are desirable, how to prevent it from getting out of hand, and what to do if it does.

What's It All About, Algae?

Algae are photosynthetic organisms. When I studied biology, I was taught that they were part of the plant kingdom. Some scientists now classify them separately from the plant kingdom, as part of the kingdom *Protoctista*. Either way, you can think of algae as simple plants. Unlike "higher" plants (higher in the evolutionary sense), they have no vascular systems—tubes and channels that circulate fluids through their structures.

Algae come in multitudes of forms and colors. There are single-celled, free-swimming forms that can make water look like pea soup. There are slimy and hairy forms, and there are leafy forms. You can find algae in shades of brown, green, red, and even blue. The ocean's giant kelp, which grow several hundred feet long, are types of algae. Several hundred feet long? And they say algae isn't a higher plant form? Hmmmpf.

Algae are generally classified into six groups:

➤ Green algae *(Chlorophyta)*

➤ Brown algae *(Phaeophyta)*

➤ Red algae *(Rhodophyta)*

➤ Blue-green algae *(Cyanophyta)*

➤ Diatoms *(Chrysophyta)*

➤ Dinoflagellates *(Pyrrhophyta)*

The green, brown, and red algae take the most familiar forms, developing leafy or stemlike structures. They appear more plantlike. Blue-green algae can form thick, slimy sheets. Single-celled diatoms mostly live in the water column, but may form a thin tint on glass or decorations. Dinoflagellates live in symbiosis within the tissues of corals and anemones.

Algae As Friend and Foe

There are some good things to be said about algae. It absorbs excess nutrients from the water, provides a snack for many fish and invertebrates, converts carbon dioxide into oxygen through photosynthesis, and keeps a tank from looking unnaturally clean and sterile.

The main reasons you don't want algae to get out of control are that it can be ugly, it grows on the glass and obstructs your view of the fish, and it can overgrow live corals and choke them out. Algae can also clog filter systems. Because of these reasons, aquarists tend to think of algae as a pest—but it really isn't. Algae exists in every aquatic system, and even if you start out with a sterile tank, spores in the air will introduce algae to your system. Algae is everywhere, and it's a natural, normal part of an ecosystem.

While it is true that algae can take over a tank and be a problem, I don't think of algae as a pest. Rather, I think of it as a signpost. Algae can tell you a lot about the condition of your tank. Use algae as an indicator. Algae will not grow out of balance unless there is something out of balance in the system that allows, or causes, it to do so. An overabundance of algae may reflect improper lighting, excessive dissolved nutrients, poor maintenance, insufficient water movement, and more.

The Good, the Bad, and the Ugly

Let's talk about the various types of algae that you may encounter in your aquarium. Some are varieties you will want to nurture. Others, you will want to eliminate.

Green Algae *(Chlorophyta)*

The green algae group contains both desirable and undesirable forms. Species of *Caulerpa (kah-LER-puh)* macroalgae are probably the most popular. Various attractive and fast-growing species of this macroalgae are available. Some have feather- or blade-shape leaves. Others look more like clusters of grapes or toadstools. Healthy Caulerpa spreads quickly by extending runners. The Dutch style of reef aquarium relies heavily on Caulerpa to remove organics from the aquarium.

A few popular species of green macroalgae are calcareous, incorporating calcium into their stiff structures. *Halimeda spp.* (*hal-ih-MEE-duh*) have branches shaped like strings of flattened plates, while *Penicillus* (merman's shaving brush), and *Udotea* (mermaid's fan) get their names from their shapes.

These species are desirable and may be purchased at most shops. However, there are many undesirable green algae, including the hair algae that is so dreaded by reef hobbyists. Thick mats of hair algae, such as *Derbesia,* can choke out live corals. Mats of hair algae also act as sediment traps, preventing complete removal of waste from your system. The similar *Bryopsis* tends to grow in isolated tufts.

Another green algae you'll find in the stores is bubble algae (*Valonia spp.*). Some varieties refract light in such a way as to form concentric rings of color—earning them the nickname sailor's eyeballs. Bubble algae forms small transparent balloons on the substrate. Though interesting and attractive, it is best to remove it from your aquarium, as it can grow to epidemic proportions. Twist off the bubbles and discard them. Try not to pop them, as doing so could release spores into the water, resulting in more bubble algae!

Fish and Tips

Generally, macroalgae are desirable and microalgae are undesirable. Macroalgae rarely fare well in the fish-only aquarium, though—most fish view them as tasty salads.

Brown Algae (Phaeophyta)

You won't often find brown algae offered for sale in your local fish store—at least, not by itself. However, the live-rocks sold as plant rock may be heavily populated with various species. One type of brown macroalgae with which you may be familiar is Sargassum weed, and it is occasionally offered for sale. Giant kelp is another brown algae. Brown macroalgae are fine for the aquarium, although herbivores will make quick snacks of them.

Red Algae (Rhodophyta)

A nice clump of red algae can really jazz up your aquarium! The colors are based on the photosynthetic pigments, but they don't always look red to the eye. Sometimes, red algae are more yellow, brown, or pink. The most desirable range from maroon to bright red or magenta. Some dealers sell clumps of red algae attached to small rocks.

Coralline algae are especially important to the reef hobbyist. These algae incorporate calcium carbonate into their structure and are major contributors to formation of the

Something's Fishy

Do not confuse the desirable red macroalgae and coralline algae with the undesirable red slime, which is magenta-colored cyanobacterial slime.

reef. In the aquarium, they are more valued for their bright pink and purple coloration and for the fact that undesirable microalgae are rarely able to colonize areas of rock already colonized by coralline algae.

Blue-Green Algae (Cyanophyta)

The classification of these organisms is a little confusing. Also known as the cyanobacteria, there is some debate over whether these are algae at all. They share features of both algae and bacteria. If that isn't confusing enough, there is more. The blue-green algae may not be blue-green! They form thick, greasy sheets that may be more mustard color or even black. The dreaded red slime is caused by cyanobacteria, which produce an attractive (though undesirable!) magenta film over the glass and decorations.

An easy way to determine if you have blue-green algae (which may be in thick sheets of yellow or magenta) is to reach into the tank and flick water at it with your fingers. Sheets of blue-green algae will normally peel away quite easily when you direct some current toward them. Other algae require rubbing or scrubbing.

Diatoms (Chrysophyta)

The very first algae encountered by most aquarists is brown film or brown slime. It first appears as brownish or rust-color specks on the glass, rocks, and so forth. As it progresses, it develops into a thin film that tints the glass and decor. Brown slime is caused by colonies of diatoms (*DIE-uh-toms*), which are microscopic organisms with silica cell walls.

Brown slime is typical, and normal, in new setups. It is the very first algae to appear. It will soon disappear, as other types of algae establish themselves and replace it. It is completely natural and temporary. If brown slime obstructs your view, wipe it away. Better yet, toss a few astraea snails into your tank and they will keep it cleared away.

You know you have an algae problem when . . .

. . . your turbo snails have grown to 10 pounds each.

. . . you need a weed whacker to mow the hair algae.

. . . the fish start to scrape the glass themselves.

. . . the only way to see the fish is to look through the little spots where the tangs left lip prints.

. . . your newly acquired algae-eating blenny grabs you by the collar and asks, "What do you think I am, a miracle worker?"

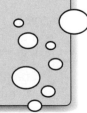

Dinoflagellates (Pyrrhophyta)

The dinoflagellates that interest us most are the ones that live symbiotically within the tissues of living corals. These organisms photosynthesize, producing food for the corals, and are also largely responsible for the color of the corals. They are definitely good guys, and your coral could not live without them.

Light + Nutrients = Algae

As you get experience keeping aquariums, you may notice that some hobbyists always seem to be battling hair algae, others are constantly at war with red slime, and still others have no algae problems at all. In fact, it is a common tale for hobbyists to have one aquarium that always suffers from algae problems when their other tanks do not.

Many factors are involved in this phenomenon. The length of time the tank has been established is one factor. There is a natural succession that takes place in any ecosystem. That is, certain organisms move into a territory first and, once established, help create conditions that make it ideal for other organisms to follow. Succession happens in nature and in the aquarium, too. Brown slime tends to be found in new tanks, green slime comes next, and brush algae is more likely to be found in older, well-established aquariums.

There are two general factors that contribute to excessive growth of unwanted algae: too much light (or too much of the wrong wavelength) and too many nutrients. Controlling one or both factors can create conditions that limit the growth of algae. Of course, it needs to be done in such a way that you don't starve the other plants and animals in your system of light and nutrients, too.

Something's Fishy

Hobbyists sometimes use erythromycin to kill off cyanobacteria in aquariums. I recommend against this. The medication reduces water quality and also kills beneficial bacteria, including those that perform the biofiltration in your aquarium.

Fish and Tips

When brown film algae appears in established aquaria, it should usually be regarded as a sign that light levels are too low. Perhaps the light bulbs are old, have lost their intensity, and should be replaced. Increasing the light will cause the brown film to disappear.

Light

Algae need light to photosynthesize. Without light, they die. Controlling the amount and type of light may control your algae problem. Review your lighting situation. Based on the charts in Chapter 7, do you have too much light? Are you using light of the wrong wavelength? Would running your light for fewer hours per day be beneficial? (You don't leave the light on all night, do you?) Are you using the proper full-spectrum bulbs? Or did you pick a bulb of the wrong spectrum to save money?

Is your tank near a window? Direct sunlight can contribute to unwanted growth of algae in the fish-only aquarium. Although in a reef aquarium, the extra light is probably beneficial!

Nutrients

Like all living things, algae need food. If your system has nutrient overload, algae is going to get a foothold. Is the tank overcrowded? Fish waste adds nutrients. The more fish you have, and the more food you offer, the higher the nutrient levels in your aquarium.

Shortages of nutrients may cause algae problems, too. If nutrients are insufficient or in the wrong proportions to promote growth of desirable macroalgae, there are undesirable microalgae that find those conditions perfect. They will prosper instead.

Something's Fishy

Some manufacturers wash their activated carbons with phosphoric acid during the manufacturing process. This causes them to release some phosphates when used, which encourages undesirable algae. Be sure to purchase a brand that is phosphate-free.

Are you keeping up with your scheduled maintenance, particularly your partial water changes? Partial water changes remove dissolved waste and replace depleted trace elements. Water changes are especially important to maintain healthy conditions in your tank.

Run some water tests. If your tank suddenly has an algae problem, are any of the water-quality parameters testing at abnormal levels? You may find a clue by checking salinity, pH, alkalinity, nitrate, and phosphate levels.

Reef hobbyists often pay special attention to nitrate and phosphate levels in their quest to control algae. Limiting either of these two nutrients can make a big difference. Your dealer carries adsorptive compounds you can add to your filter box to remove nitrates and phosphates. A good protein skimmer removes phosphates, and an ample supply of live-rock will remove nitrates naturally.

Herbivores You'll Adore

Yes, if you control light and nutrients, you can control algae growth, but that is only part of the equation. That discussion left out the fun part! The easiest way to control algae is to get some live-in janitors. Nope, you don't have to call the local employment agency. All you have to do is buy a few algae-eating critters. Not only will they help control algae problems, but you'll also have fun watching them do it.

Algae-Eating Fish

Freshwater aquarists are familiar with the suckermouth catfish (the plecostomus) and its great ability to clean algae from the glass. Unfortunately, there appear to be no equivalents in the marine aquarium. There are, however, many fish species that lend a hand.

The various species of tang will regularly leave their lip prints on the glass as they nibble algae. Most angels and butterflies will nibble some, too, as will many other fish. The algae-eating blenny is also an entertaining choice for aiding in algae control. This fish uses its thick lips to rasp algae from the rocks, decorations, and occasionally even the glass.

Fish and Tips

Even if you are doing nothing different from usual, a sudden bloom of algae may be linked to changes in your local tapwater. Seasonal variances, including heavy rains, can affect the makeup of your local water. Some hobbyists use reverse-osmosis or deionization units to ensure the quality of their tapwater.

Snails

Escargot such as astraea and turbo snails do an especially good job of algae control. A sufficient population will keep even the glass sparkling clean. These little rascals can even mow down a field of hair algae in record time. It will look like a sheep being sheared as they clear a path through the thick mats. Reef hobbyists often keep one snail per 2 gallons of water.

Hermit Crabs

Crabs such as the tiny blue-legged hermits and red hermits are excellent choices for algae control. These tiny guys can get into the smallest places to do the job right. Be sure to get the right species, as most hermit crab species become too large and aggressive.

Some hobbyists keep one per gallon. Hermit crabs are hardly little devils, but emphasizing the word *little* here, it takes many to do the job. Additionally, it doesn't take a very large fish to be able to suck them right out of their seashell homes. So expect to replace a few here and there!

Sea Urchins

These are wonderful algae eaters, but they have a couple of downsides. One downside is that they have the ability to wedge between rocks, where they often exert enough force to dislodge them and collapse the structure. Another downside is that urchins often scrape the desirable purple coralline algae off the rocks, too.

Die, Algae! Die!

Unfortunately, the natural method of algae control doesn't always do the whole job. Even if you've done everything you can to limit light and nutrients, and if you've added enough grazers, you are still going to have to pitch in and scrub some algae yourself.

Something's Fishy

Never use household sponges or scrubbing pads to clean inside your tank. They usually contain toxic soap or chemicals. This even applies to brand new ones. For example, put a brand new cellulose sponge in a sink of water and squeeze it a few times. Look at all those suds!

I highly recommend the algae scrubber pads sold in pet stores. Buy the ones without a handle, as they are much easier to use on the hard-to-reach spots. The scrubber pad can be used on the glass and on some rocks and decorations. For really tough algae on the glass, a razor-blade type of scraper works easily.

A handy household turkey baster works great for blasting sediment off the rocks—sediment which provides nutrients for algae growth.

There are several sizes and styles of bottle brushes designed for cleaning filter tubes. There are rigid versions for straight tubes and flexible versions for getting into the bends of siphon and intake tubes. If necessary, you also can remove ornaments from your tank and take them to the sink to scrub with any soap-free household brush.

Finally, your dealer may carry algicides for saltwater tanks. They are dangerous and should be avoided. Instead, find the cause of the problem and fix it. Use herbivores to control algae. Remember, too, that a large quantity of dead algae will pollute your tank. Yet another reason to avoid algicides.

The Least You Need to Know

➤ Algae is natural and is not necessarily a pest.

➤ An overabundance of algae signals that light and nutrients are out of balance.

➤ Macroalgae are attractive and desirable. Microalgae are undesirable and can be invasive.

➤ Herbivores are the best control for most algae problems.

➤ Keep an algae scrubber pad on hand for touch-ups.

Stress and Disease

I am not a doctor. I don't even play one on TV. Nevertheless, I get to play fish doctor at work. Diagnosing and treating fish diseases is part of my professional life. I wish a chapter on stress and disease in the marine aquarium were not necessary. But it is. Sooner or later, you are likely to encounter problems. No matter how careful you are or how much you stick to the rules, it would be silly to set up an aquarium and not learn how to watch for warning signs or how to deal with health problems.

Our knowledge of diseases of saltwater fish is limited. And fish diseases aren't always treatable. Still, any hobbyist worth their salt will make an effort to help their sick fish. So let's talk about it.

First off, what is it that causes a fish to get sick and die? Your first answer may be that germs are the cause. Sometimes that's true, but usually when disease organisms get a foothold in your tank, it is not so much that they are a cause—more likely, they are an effect.

Don't Stress Me Out!

Notice the title of this chapter. Notice that I listed stress before I listed disease. That's because stress is the major cause of disease and death in fish. How do I define stress? Basically, stress is anything that makes your fish unhappy.

When your fish are under stress, they will be more susceptible to disease. Pathogens are everywhere. There is no avoiding them. However, happy healthy fish are normally able to fend them off quite easily. The fish's immune system does its job well, and the fish stays healthy.

It shouldn't be surprising that the things that stress out your fish are the very same things that stress out you and me. Overcrowding, hunger, overheating, chills, lack of rest, sudden loud noises, bullies, and living in filth are a few examples. These things can be enough to make you, or your fish, sick.

Here is a detailed list of common stressors:

➤ **Hunger.** A fish that is not receiving enough nutrition is a fish with lowered immunity. A starving fish is also more likely to take a cannibalistic nip out of some other fish. Additionally, a starving fish is more likely to be singled out as a weak fish and attacked by the others in the aquarium.

➤ **Improper diet.** Even if you stuff a fish until it is no longer hungry, a diet lacking in essential nutrients will do it little good.

➤ **Overcrowding.** The more crowded your tank, the more territories will overlap, resulting in more fights.

➤ **Bullies.** Constant nips do physical damage, yes, but they also keep a fish from getting adequate nutrition and rest. Bite wounds make easy entry points for infections, too. Bullied fish often jump out of the aquarium, only to die on the floor. While there are many reasons for jumping—and suicide is probably not one of them—breaking the water surface to escape a bully is a primary cause. Mixing compatible species will prevent this problem.

➤ **Poor water quality.** Overcrowding causes your tank to have higher waste levels. I probably don't have to tell you why high waste levels would be stressful. Can you imagine living in a small, closed room with 20 of your best buddies? Imagine that there is no toilet, and the housecleaning staff only comes around every couple of weeks or so to do a partial cleaning. Well, that is sort of what it must be like to live in an aquarium. High waste levels can poison a fish directly, be breeding grounds for pathogens, and affect appetite and immunity.

➤ **Inadequate maintenance.** This can affect an aquarium in many ways besides the accumulation of waste. Failure to top off evaporation can lead to dangerous increases in salinity.

➤ **Rapid temperature changes.** Have you ever noticed that human beings tend to get sick in the spring and fall, when the weather is changing? Fish are more likely to get sick when subjected to extremes in temperature, too. A proper aquarium heater helps prevent dramatic temperature changes. When making water changes, you also need to match the temperature of the new water to that of the old water.

➤ **Lack of rest.** Fish don't sleep quite the way we do, but they do need rest. It is important they get that chance. Be sure to turn out the lights on your tank at night. Can you imagine what it would be like if the lights were on 24 hours a day and you couldn't even close your eyes because you had no eyelids?

➤ **Loud noises.** Sound travels through water much more easily than it travels through air. Sudden, loud noises can be very frightening to a fish, which is why you should not tap on the glass of your aquarium. If you are one of those people who likes to play music at full blast, at least have the courtesy to locate your aquarium away from your woofers and tweeters!

➤ **Not enough light.** This is a stressor for many photosynthetic invertebrates, such as corals and anemones. Without enough light, they starve.

Something's Fishy

Water carries sound better than air, so don't tap on the aquarium glass. It's like screaming in a fish's ear.

What's Wrong with That Fishy in the Window?

In Chapter 11 on picking your first fish, I talked about ways to spot a healthy fish. In this chapter, I'll talk about the ways to spot a sick or stressed fish. Fish are fairly good at giving warning signs of impending problems or doom. You just need to know what to watch for. Following are some danger signals. The same cues apply to invertebrates, too.

➤ **Listlessness.** When a normally active species suddenly starts lying around or hiding, it's a sign that something is amiss. Causes of listlessness include deteriorated water quality, parasites, overeating, injury, and incorrect water temperature. Be aware that territorial species may be quite active in your tank when first introduced, but once they settle in, they will pick a spot and stay there. That is normal behavior, not listlessness. Many species of fish lie on their sides when resting. This also should not be mistaken for listlessness.

➤ **Loss of appetite.** Most fish are hungry practically all the time. Any ravenous eater that suddenly becomes disinterested in food should be viewed with suspicion. Poor water quality, bullies, disease, and spoiled food are possible causes of loss of appetite. Note, however, that cardinalfish and other species are mouthbrooders. If a cardinalfish has stopped eating but has a distended chin,

Fish and Tips

Your fish may refuse food for a day or two when first introduced to an aquarium. Picky species, which should not be kept in the first place, may go weeks before eating.

it probably is incubating eggs in its mouth. It is normal for it to refuse food at this time.

➤ **Color changes.** Many things can cause a fish to change color. For example, some species, such as flounders, change color and pattern to blend into the substrate. Color or pattern can vary according to mood, too. Fish that are angry, excited, or trying to attract mates may take on unexpected colors or patterns. Different patterns for daytime and nighttime are common, too. The foxface changes from yellow to mottled brown. All of these changes are normal.

Watch, though, for color changes that seem abnormal or have no apparent cause. If a fish's color suddenly fades, it is probably under some type of stress. Colors fading over time probably reflect a diet deficiency. Discolored patches may indicate infection.

Fish Tales

Many fish change color at night. For example, yellow tangs fade from bright yellow to an almost tan color and develop a bright white horizontal stripe at night.

➤ **Clamped fins.** The fins of most species will be spread and erect when healthy. If these fish suddenly start keeping their fins folded against the body, it's a danger signal. Other fish, such as the various popular clownfish, may keep their fins folded much of the time, erecting them only when swimming or excited. If you spend time observing your fish, you will know what is normal and what might be a sign of trouble.

➤ **Distended gills.** A fish that is holding its gills open is having major troubles. Many things can cause this, including gill parasites, toxins in the water, and gill damage. High ammonia levels and low pH levels could also be causes.

➤ **Rapid breathing or gasping at the surface.** Both symptoms are signs of a fish that is not getting enough oxygen. Possible causes are low levels of dissolved oxygen in the water, high waste levels that prevent proper exchange of oxygen, gill damage from parasites, or the presence of toxins in the water. Exhaustion from being chased by bullies could cause temporary rapid breathing.

➤ **Split or frayed fins.** Split fins are usually a result of a fight. In most cases, nothing needs to be done. The fins will heal nicely without help. However, if the edges of the fins become ragged or show signs of decay, it could be a sign of disease or even poor water quality. A damaged fish may be singled out for further attacks, too, so always keep tabs on it.

➤ **Sores and wounds.** These can be the result of bites from tankmates or may be signs of severe parasitic infections. One unique problem that is commonly seen with saltwater fish is a small sore on one side of the fish, above and behind the abdominal cavity, where the swim bladder is located. When fish are caught in deep water, they need to be decompressed before being taken to the surface. A common method for quick decompression is to use a hypodermic needle to draw gas from the fish's swim bladder. The site of the needle puncture is vulnerable to infection.

➤ **Cloudy eyes.** Eyes can cloud due to infections, diet deficiencies, scar tissue from wounds, or poor water quality. Occasionally, the problem may be cataracts.

➤ **Swollen stomach.** A swollen stomach may indicate gluttony, a female fish full of roe, internal parasites, or it could mean that your fish has fluid buildup.

➤ **Emaciated stomach.** A skinny fish can be a warning sign. Be sure the animal is getting its share of the right kinds of foods. Disease, old age, and parasites may also be to blame. Poor water quality can kill a fish's appetite.

➤ **Bent spine.** A fish with a bent spine was probably born that way and will likely live a full life. However, a fish that develops a bent spine later in life may be suffering from a diet deficiency or injury. Stray electrical voltage has also been shown to sometimes break the backs of fish by causing strong muscle contractions.

Fish School

The eggs of fish are called **roe,** while the sperm is called **milt.**

➤ **Slimy patches.** Fish excrete extra slime as a defense against infection. The cause of this slime is a little hard to diagnose without a microscope, because protozoans, bacteria, flukes, and just plain lousy water quality can all cause a fish to slime up.

➤ **Obvious infections.** I'll talk in more detail about this in a moment, but you will need to learn to recognize the common types of disease that may infect your fish.

➤ **Erratic or unusual behavior.** Get to know what is normal for the species you keep, and you will catch problems much earlier. A bottom feeder that suddenly spends all of its time hanging at the surface is an example of unusual behavior. When the king of the tank suddenly begins hiding in a corner, something is amiss.

➤ **Hitchhikers.** Some parasites are large enough to spot with the naked eye. Fish lice, which are a type of crustacean, can easily be seen grabbing onto a fish.

Make It a Habit to Check the Habitat

If you spot any of the warning signs I've just described, what do you do first? That's right—clear the room of kids and old folks and then curse aloud! Next, examine the environment. Open your eyes and look for obvious problems. For example:

➤ Has an air line become disconnected?

➤ Is a filter clogged or stopped?

➤ Is the water temperature incorrect?

➤ Is the water level too low?

➤ Is the tank dirty?

➤ Is the tank too crowded?

➤ Are any fish showing obvious signs of disease?

➤ Are there any signs of aggression or incompatibility? Look for ongoing fights, split fins, and ragged fish cowering in corners.

You're not done checking the environment yet! Take time to look for the invisible causes. In other words, check your water quality. Run the tests. You can't judge water quality by eye, no matter how clean and clear the water appears.

➤ Use your hydrometer to check salinity.

➤ Run pH, ammonia, and nitrite tests.

➤ If the fish are gasping, you may want to run a dissolved oxygen test.

➤ Reef hobbyists should run calcium and alkalinity tests.

➤ When did you last change the water?

Fish and Tips

Regular partial water changes prevent problems! Make it a habit.

Obviously, if your water tests show that the water quality is out of whack, you will need to take corrective action. See Chapters 15 and 16 on water quality and cycling a new tank for help with that. Sometimes a partial water change is all you need to correct a problem.

Naturally, if there are visible signs of infection, you will need to medicate. So let's move on to a discussion of diseases and treatments.

Plague and Pestilence

Diseases of aquarium fish can show up as dots, spots, lumps, bumps, patches, and sores somewhere on the outside of the fish. External diseases are the easiest to identify, but even so, a good microscope may be necessary for a proper diagnosis. Diagnosis of internal infections usually requires you to sacrifice and examine the internal organs of the host. Obviously, this won't save the host, but it may be useful in treating its tankmates.

Most marine fish diseases can be classified in the following categories:

➤ Protozoan

➤ Bacterial

➤ Parasitic

➤ Viral

Ick! Saltwater Ich

There are many nasty protozoans that attack fish. Some are true parasites, requiring a host organism to complete their life cycle. Others are merely opportunistic organisms taking advantage of already sick or dying fish.

Saltwater ich, which gets its name from its common freshwater counterpart, is probably the best-known protozoan parasite of marine fish. Ich is so well known that many new hobbyists seem to want to diagnose every disease as ich.

Imagine, if you will, that you are holding your fish in one hand and a salt shaker in the other. Now imagine that you sprinkle some salt on the fish. You have just visualized what a fish looks like with ich—except, of course, that you won't be holding a fish in your hand. Ick!

Fish School

Ich is pronounced "ick" and is short for the name of the common freshwater protozoan, **Ichthyophthirius multifilius.** Saltwater ich, however, is caused by **Cryptocaryon irritans.** Other common names for the disease include **white spot, Cryptocaryon,** and **crypto.**

Yes, ich appears as a spattering of tiny white, salt-crystal-size dots. It may first present itself as a dot or two on the fins or body and later will spread. If left untreated, the fish will eventually look more slimy than dotted—due to massive tissue damage and the production of extra body slime. A fish in this advanced state is probably beyond help.

Before I discuss possible treatments, you need to learn about the life cycle of the parasite that causes ich. When ich first infects your fish, you won't notice it. It is too small. Only after it has had a couple of days to grow will you see the white dots. When attached to the fish in this encysted feeding stage, the parasite is called a *trophont*. This stage lasts three to seven days.

Once full grown, the parasite will drop off the fish, fall to the bottom, and attach itself to objects there. The ich parasite is now in the *tomont* stage. This is the reproductive stage. Depending on temperature, the tomont will divide for 3 to 28 days (8 days is more typical) before rupturing to release up to 200 *tomites* (baby ich parasites) into your tank.

These swarmers seek a new fish host. Without treatment, the whole cycle starts over. Only this time, there will be many more parasites, and your fish will get a much more severe (probably lethal) infection.

A diagram of the life cycle of the ich parasite, Cryptocaryon irritans. (1) infected fish, (2) trophont drops off, (3) tomont attaches to bottom, (4) tomont divides into tomites, (5) tomites seek new host.

Other Protozoans

➤ **Marine velvet disease** *(Amyloodinium ocellatum),* also called rust disease, oodinium, and amyloodinium, has a life cycle very similar to saltwater ich. The parasites are smaller, though, and can survive longer without a host. Infected fish appear to be lightly dusted.

➤ **Brooklynella** *(B. hostilis).* Sometimes called clownfish disease—because clownfish are common casualties of this affliction—this ciliated protozoan infects other fishes, too. Unlike the protozoan infections I've already listed, Brooklynella produces slimy patches rather than spots. These patches can develop into bloody sores.

➤ **Uronema** *(U. marinum)* is another protozoan that produces symptoms similar to Brooklynella. Treatment with an antibiotic to prevent secondary infections is highly recommended when medicating fish with either Brooklynella or Uronema.

Treating Protozoa

Various medications are available for treating protozoal infections. Copper sulfate, formalin, and malachite green are most commonly used. Always treat the entire aquarium when your fish have ich or velvet disease. Remember, though, that *medications for treating these diseases are not safe for reef tanks!*

Copper sulfate is the preferred treatment for saltwater ich and velvet disease. Copper is lethal to invertebrates—use this medication only in a fish-only aquarium! You must treat the entire aquarium, as the medication does not kill all stages of the parasite's life cycle. In fact, it has least effect on the trophont stage, which is the stage where the parasite is embedded in the fish. You must treat for several days *after* the symptoms on the fish disappear to be sure that you kill the other stages.

Fish and Tips

Brooklynella and Uronema infections are usually best treated in a separate quarantine tank. Remove the infected fish from the others to reduce chances of the disease spreading. Besides, a sick fish becomes a target and may be killed by tankmates.

Standard procedure is to dose the aquarium with enough copper sulfate to bring the concentration to 0.15 ppm copper. Yes, you need a proper copper test kit to use this medication! Copper falls out of solution rapidly and is adsorbed by the substrate. Copper levels in the aquarium should be tested every day during treatment, and enough copper sulfate added to bring the level back up to a therapeutic 0.15 ppm. Too little copper won't eradicate the disease. Too much will kill your fish. So monitor copper levels carefully.

Always remove activated carbon from your filter systems during treatment, as it adsorbs many medications and renders them useless. Do not turn off the filters— just run them without carbon. After treatment is complete, do a partial water change and replace the activated carbon in your filters. Special copper-removing resins should also be added to your filter box to remove the remaining medication. Activated carbon does a poor job of removing copper.

Formalin/malachite green solutions treat protozoal infections and are a preferred treatment for infections of Brooklynella and Uronema. Formalin (a dilute solution of formaldehyde) and malachite green (a dye) can be used alone or in combination. They are synergistic, which means they are safer and more effective when used together. Typical treatments require a daily dose in drops per gallon. Various commercial preparations are available. Follow the manufacturer's recommendations for proper dosage.

Something's Fishy

Sharks and rays are said to be sensitive to copper medications. Remove them from tanks requiring this treatment.

Fish and Tips

Avoid chelated (*key–LAY–ted*) copper solutions. You should buy ionic solutions of copper sulfate. Chelated copper contains an additive to keep the copper from falling out of solution so quickly. However, the same action that keeps it in solution greatly reduces its effectiveness against disease.

Dipping freshwater fish into saltwater can cause parasites to die or drop off. The same thing happens when you dip saltwater fish into freshwater. A freshwater dip is a useful treatment that can provide some relief to an infected fish. However, remembering that all stages of the ich parasite's life cycle do not occur on the fish itself, it should be obvious that freshwater dips will not cure an aquarium of ich. I'll discuss freshwater dips in detail later in this chapter.

Bacterial Infections

Bacteria are much smaller than protozoans. You won't be able to detect individuals without a good microscope. However, bacteria tend to grow in colonies, manifesting themselves as slimy or bloody patches developing on the skin or fins of the fish. Bacteria can cause disease in stressed fish, all by themselves. However, most bacterial infections are probably secondary. That is, the bacteria tend to attack where tissues have already been damaged by protozoans, parasites, or wounds.

Antibiotics will be necessary to treat bacterial infections. It is important that you treat quickly, too, as these infections can spread very quickly. Some will kill your fish within hours of the first appearance of symptoms!

Picking an Antibiotic

Your pet supply store should carry a variety of antibiotics. Some are effective. Some are not. In a moment, I will steer you toward the better ones, but you must remember that the best you can do is make an educated guess about which is the right choice. Why? Because no antibiotic treats every bacterial infection. Each will be effective against some bacteria, but not against others.

Something's Fishy

Formalin and malachite green are both known carcinogens. Handle them carefully.

Antibiotics don't work by killing bacteria. Instead, they mess up the reproductive ability of the bacteria so that the bacteria quit multiplying. This lets the immune system of the host catch up and do the job of eliminating the infection.

As you read the packaging of the various antibiotics on your dealer's shelves, you may notice the terms *gram-positive* and *gram-negative*. What does this mean? Well, you need a microscope to see bacteria, and even then, they are colorless and hard to observe. So in 1884, a Danish scientist named Hans Gram invented a procedure for staining bacteria so that you could see them under the microscope.

Just as all medications don't kill all species of bacteria, stains don't affect all bacteria equally either. Gram came up with a procedure that stains most bacteria. Consequently, the stains became known as Gram's stains. The bacteria most affected by the stain turn purple and are called gram-positive. The others, being relatively unaffected, turn pink and are considered gram-negative.

Why is this important? Because most bacterial fish diseases happen to be gram-negative. So antibiotics that are gram-positive will probably not be good choices to treat your fish—which is not to say they will necessarily be useless. Still, you want to steer toward gram-negative antibiotics.

Fish School

In the hobby, the term **antibiotics** is commonly used to include both true antibiotics and antibacterials. Technically, an antibiotic is a substance derived from a living organism and will kill microorganisms. For example, penicillin comes from a mold. Antibacterials are compounds created in the laboratory.

Some antibiotics will have some effect on both gram-negative and gram-positive bacteria. This brings us to another reason you may want to avoid gram-positive antibiotics. It just so happens that the helpful nitrifying bacteria in your filter bed are gram-positive. So the wrong medication may not only do little to cure your fish, but may also have a destructive effect on your biological filtration!

Now I'm going to point you toward some effective antibiotics to try, if the need arises. Since there are many brands out there and I have no way of knowing which ones your local shops carry, I'll just give you the names of the active ingredients. I recommend you avoid choosing medications that don't list the active ingredients. For one thing, you won't know what you are getting. For another, if that medication doesn't work, how do you know that the next thing you decide to try isn't the same medication with a different brand name?

A Cure for What Ails You

Here are some of my favorite antibiotics for aquarium use:

➤ **Furan drugs.** This is a whole group of drugs, including furazolidone, nitrofurantoin, nifurpurinol, and nitrofurazone. These drugs are effective. They will discolor the water a bit, turning it various shades of green or brown. Furan drugs can be carcinogenic, so handle them carefully. Furans treat both gram-negative and gram-positive bacteria.

Fish and Tips

Some antibiotics come as tablets, some as gel-caps. Tablets can be dropped directly into the aquarium without crushing. Gel-caps should be opened and the powder inside should be poured into the aquarium. Dispose of the empty capsule.

➤ **Sulfa drugs.** Again, this is a whole group of drugs, including sulfamethazine, sulfamerazine, sulfathiozole, and sulfaisoxazole. The most common way to find these is in combination sold as tri-sulfa or triple sulfa. Sulfas treat both gram-negative and gram-positive bacteria.

➤ **Kanamycin sulphate.** Many antibiotics don't absorb well and treat only the outside of the fish. Gram-negative kanamycin absorbs well, and it doesn't discolor the water. It's even more effective (synergistic) when combined with oxolinic acid.

➤ **Chloramphenicol.** This is a good one, but you probably won't run across it. Due to some side effects it can have on humans, it is much more highly regulated. Chloramphenicol is gram-negative.

Fish and Tips

If you buy the powdered or gel-cap form of tri-sulfa, it is very helpful to premix the powder in a jar of water before adding it to the tank, because the powder tends to float and may not dissolve properly.

➤ **Minocyline.** This well-absorbed medication is gram-negative.

➤ **Neomycin sulphate.** This treats both gram-negative and gram-positive bacteria.

➤ **Oxytetracycline hydrochloride.** Also known as tetracycline and Terramycin, this drug is not particularly effective in saltwater. However, the oral form may have some benefit. You can purchase "medicated flake" fish food that contains this drug. The advantage of oral medication is that it puts the drug inside the fish, where it will do most good. Of course, your fish must still be eating for it to work.

Here are some other, less favorite medications that you may find. These may be more effective if used in combination with another gram-negative antibiotic, such as one in the preceding list.

➤ **Penicillin.** Gram-positive.

➤ **Ampicillin.** Gram-positive.

➤ **Erythromycin.** Gram-positive. This medication has been shown to have some temporary negative effect on biological filtration.

Pesky Parasites

Many parasitic organisms can infect the animals in your aquarium. Parasites are normally relatively harmless, existing in numbers too small to be a problem. A healthy fish and its parasites achieve a tolerable balance with one another, and life goes on without problem. However, a fish under stress can be more susceptible to parasites, allowing them to get the upper hand. Further, confining several fish in a tiny aquarium—as compared to the vast ocean—can concentrate populations of parasites, increasing the severity of infestations.

The Worms Go In, the Worms Go Out

Worms are not just good food for fish. Sometimes, fish are good food for worms! Of course, I'm not talking about the same type of worms that you would feed your fish. There are many worm species that are internal or external parasites of fish.

Something's Fishy

Do not use antibiotics as preventives. This can result in the development of resistant strains of bacteria. If resistant bacteria should infect your fish, you will have a much harder time effecting a cure.

It should come as no surprise that fish, like many other animals, can be infested with intestinal tapeworms and roundworms. Unfortunately, it is difficult to diagnose these problems without sacrificing a fish and examining the contents of its guts under the microscope. If your fish has internal worms, the odds are that they are present in low numbers. Generally, you need take no action. A healthy fish can live just fine with an occasional intestinal parasite.

With severe tapeworm and roundworm infestations, you can try to medicate, but you will have a difficult time finding worm medications for your fish. You just can't find many commercial preparations available for fish without going to a veterinarian. Besides, the treatment is often more dangerous to the fish than the parasite.

Flukes are an interesting group of worms. Some infest fish from the inside and require one or more secondary hosts (such as snails) to complete the life cycle. These flukes are difficult or impossible to treat, and don't spread in the aquarium anyway. Ignoring them is best.

However, some flukes live on the skin and gills. Skin and gill flukes resemble microscopic leeches, with grasping hooks at one end and a mouth at the other. They move about your fish in inchworm fashion and can do considerable damage. It will take a microscope to make a definite diagnosis, but if your fish scratches on rocks, or if the gills have become distended, it may be infested with flukes. Also, bloody patches may result from a heavy infestation.

Fortunately, skin and gill flukes are easy to treat. Treatments with copper or organophosphates, such as trichlorofon (dimethyl trichloro hydroxethyl phosphonate), are usually effective. Often, a good freshwater dip is all that is required.

Black spot disease is caused by a tiny turbellarian worm on the skin of fish, appearing as tiny black pinprick-size dots. The parasite is most commonly seen infesting yellow tangs. In fact, yellow tang disease is another name for it. Black spot disease is easily destroyed with

Something's Fishy

Always be careful when handling medications and chemicals. Be careful not to inhale dust from them and always wash your hands afterwards to play it safe. You never know what might be toxic, carcinogenic, or allergenic.

a simple three-minute freshwater dip. There are medications that will work, too, but why go through the added stress and expense when such a simple treatment gives a 100 percent cure?

Crustaceans As Hitchhikers

Isopods, commonly called fish lice, remind me of terrestrial pill bugs. They grab tightly onto a fish's back, side, or head for feeding. Fish lice are large enough to be seen with the eye. I've seen them nearly an inch long! Treatment is simple. Merely net out the fish, and use tweezers to pull the little devils off.

Another nasty group of hitchhikers is the parasitic copepods (not to be confused with the tiny, harmless scavengers). There are species of parasitic copepods that attach to the outside of a fish, usually anchoring their bodies beneath one of the fish's scales. Sometimes, only a bump may be seen. Other times, the threadlike body may protrude. Freshwater dips and copper are useful treatments.

Viral Infections

The only viral infection you may be able to identify is lymphocystis. This disease is commonly spotted on angels, butterflies, and other species in dealers' tanks. It may develop on your fish at home, too. When you first spot it, you may think your fish has ich.

The virus causes hard cartilaginous tissue to multiply like crazy, forming little nodules. Usually, the nodules form on the rays of the fins, but sometimes they form on the body, too. They initially appear as single, ichlike dots. As the disease progresses, the dots develop into cauliflowerlike growths. Fish are more susceptible when the body slime has been scraped off—as may happen during capture and shipping. This is why the disease shows mostly on newly acquired specimens.

A damselfish with severe lymphocystis.

The bad news is that there is no treatment for lymphocystis. Sometimes you can take a razor blade, scrape off the nodules, dab the wound with mercurochrome, and the problem may not return. But not always.

The good news is that lymphocystis will usually spontaneously remit in a few weeks. So provide good water quality and a proper diet, and your fish should eventually cure itself. Technically, the disease is considered contagious. In my experience, though, that is rarely the case.

Other Assorted Maladies

➤ **Swimbladder problems.** This manifests itself as a buoyancy problem, with the fish swimming loop-de-loops, floating upside down, or having trouble rising from the bottom of the tank.

The swimbladder is a gas-filled balloon inside most species of fish. It lets the fish maintain the proper buoyancy in the water, and it helps keep the fish in an upright position. However, the swimbladder sometimes fails. There are many possible causes, including infection, injury, genetic defect, and rapid temperature changes. The condition is normally not contagious, but is rarely treatable. Occasionally, the problem will correct itself, but destroying the affected fish is probably a better choice in most cases.

➤ **Pop-eye.** Pop-eye is a condition where gas or fluid builds up behind the eye, popping it from its socket. Sometimes an antibiotic will help this condition. Sometimes it goes away on its own. If a large gas bubble protrudes from behind the eye, it can be helpful to take a small syringe to remove some gas to relieve the pressure.

➤ **Hole in the head.** The common name for this disease, more correctly called *head and lateral line erosion* or HLLE, describes a typical symptom. Fish have sensory pores on their face and running down their sides is a row of tiny pores that forms the lateral line. Sometimes, these pores become irritated and develop into pale open pits. There may be a bit of exudate.

Over the years, many things have been blamed for causing HLLE. One study (the only study of which I am aware) links HLLE to lack of vitamin C in the diet. Over the years, hobbyists have blamed protozoans, viruses, induced voltage, and even use of

Fish and Tips

Consider sterilizing your nets after each use and between aquariums. Nets can transfer disease. There are commercial preparations you can buy to make a sterilizing net soak, or merely mix some bleach and water in a bucket and let the net soak a bit. *Rinse thoroughly* after bleaching.

activated carbon as causes of HLLE. There may be some validity to these claims. But the truth is that no one really knows for sure, and several things may cause this problem. I believe proper diet and excellent water quality will prevent it entirely.

Snake Oil

Your aquarium store probably carries a large selection of fish medications. It will be quite confusing to choose, because every brand and medication is going to make great claims about itself. There are even some brands that make absolutely false claims about what they can do. The fish medication industry isn't as highly regulated as the human medication industry. On one hand, this is bad, because there is less rigorous testing, less quality control, and more exaggerated claims. On the good side, many of these medications are the same ones given to humans but are sold at a fraction of the cost that your pharmacist would charge.

Medication Guidelines

I have talked about symptoms, diseases, and possible medications to use. Now I want to give you some guidelines for using those medications:

1. Before medicating, check the environment. Be sure the filters are working properly and the temperature is correct, and test your tank's salinity, pH, ammonia, and nitrite levels.

2. If it has been more than a week since your last partial water change, change some now. Water changes are very important. Medications degrade water quality. I recommend that you change some water every day during the treatment, but at the very least, you must do a partial water change before, halfway through, and after treatment is complete.

3. Remove activated carbon from the filters. Activated carbon removes many medications!

4. Follow the manufacturer's directions to achieve a therapeutic dose of the medication. Too little of a drug will be ineffective. Too much can be toxic to your fish.

5. Evaluate the treatment. Watch your fish for changes. I recommend that you treat three days before you evaluate.

If the fish is cured, treatment may be discontinued—although it is better to continue for a full five to seven days to play it safe. Saltwater ich and velvet should be treated a full two weeks. If the fish has improved but is not cured, continue the treatment a bit longer. If the fish is the same or worse, the treatment is not working. Change some water and try a different drug.

Freshwater Dip

Just as saltwater is deadly to many freshwater parasites, freshwater is lethal to many saltwater parasites. A simple freshwater dip can be useful in treating or eliminating many problems in obviously sick fish. A freshwater dip is also valuable in treating new arrivals before placing them into a quarantine tank.

To prepare a freshwater dip, use a bucket or other container. Partially fill it with tapwater. Dechlorinate the tapwater, and use some sodium bicarbonate (baking soda) to adjust the pH to around 8 or so. The pH should be near that of seawater. Be sure the water is well aerated. You may even want to hook up an airstone and drop it in the dip bucket.

Freshwater dips work in two ways. The simplest effect is that some parasites are irritated by freshwater and simply drop off their host. You return the fish to the tank and leave the parasites behind. A one- to three-minute dip may be all that is necessary.

Some parasites are more stubborn, though. Longer exposure is required to kill them. Here's how it works. The level of salt inside a fish (and its parasites) is much higher than the level of salt in freshwater. When you place a saltwater fish in a freshwater dip, Mother Nature wants to reach a chemical equilibrium. That is, processes occur that try to make the salt level inside the fish equal to the salt level outside the fish. This is called *osmosis*. The cellular wall is a semi-permeable membrane that doesn't easily let salt out but easily lets water in. So through osmosis, a saltwater fish placed into freshwater will begin to soak the freshwater into its cells. Parasites do the same.

Now here's the cool part. Both fish and parasites are soaking in freshwater. The fish is a much bigger critter, though. It would have to soak up a lot of freshwater to damage itself. Microscopic parasites, on the other hand, quickly soak up enough water to expand their bodies to the point where cell walls burst. Death by explosion! A 3- to 20-minute dip will accomplish this.

Something's Fishy

Most saltwater fish can tolerate a 20-minute freshwater dip without problem. You should always be on hand to observe the dipping process, though, and remove any fish that appears to be abnormally stressed by it.

Something's Fishy

Osmosis is the diffusion of a fluid through a semipermeable membrane until there is an equal concentration of fluids on both sides of the membrane.

Quarantine and Hospitalization

Psst! Want some valuable advice? Before you introduce new fish to your tank (except the very first batch), I recommend that you quarantine them for two weeks in a separate tank. This greatly lessens the chance of introducing a disease into your aquarium. If you ignore this advice, you may regret it. Don't say I didn't warn you!

Fish and Tips

Reef hobbyists should consider a quarantine tank to be a requirement! Medications used to treat common fish diseases are lethal to the invertebrates in a reef tank and cannot be used there.

Quarantine or isolation tanks can be quite simple. A 5- or 10-gallon bare aquarium with an el-cheapo filter in it (I prefer sponge filters for this application) and a rock or plastic plant to provide cover for the fish are all you need. When you're not using the tank for quarantine, you can use it as a hospital tank to treat a sick fish or to let an injured fish recover. You can put together a quarantine tank for around $20. A quarantine tank will pay for itself if it saves the life of a single saltwater fish!

I recommend that you maintain a therapeutic level of copper in the quarantine tank. At the end of the two-week isolation, if the fish appear healthy it should be safe to add them to your main aquarium.

Putting a Fish Out of Its Misery

Sometimes it is necessary to euthanize a fish. If a fish is too badly injured or too far gone to save, putting it out of its misery is more humane than letting it die a lingering death. There may also be times when it is better to destroy a single sick fish than to risk letting it infect an entire tank—particularly if you didn't follow my advice about buying a separate hospital tank.

Killing fish is not fun, but it is sometimes necessary. Here are some common methods to euthanize a fish. Choose the one you find the least distasteful or cruel.

➤ **Freezing.** Put the fish in a plastic bag with some water and freeze it. As it gets colder, its movement will slow until it freezes to death. They say this is the most painless method, but nobody really knows for sure, do they?

➤ **Decapitation.** Lay the fish on a paper towel and crush or whack off its head. Sometimes, both are necessary.

➤ **Suffocation.** Put the fish in a glass of Alka-Seltzer. The carbon dioxide will suffocate it.

➤ **Blunt trauma.** Throw the fish hard at a sidewalk or brick wall. If you do it right, it will only take one throw.

The Scoop on Scopes

I have been working with fish for over 30 years, with as many as 600 aquariums running at a time. So I have developed the ability to spot sick fish by eye and to usually choose the right medication the first time. Still, I can't tell you how valuable a microscope has been to me. Often, it is the only way to determine what course of treatment to take. A good microscope eliminates much guesswork.

You don't need a great microscope to diagnose most fish diseases. If you would like to give microscopy a try, even one of those cheap starter microscope kits for kids can be helpful. You won't be able to see organisms as small as bacteria with the inexpensive models—the quality is just too low— but you can at least spot the larger parasites.

At a magnification around 40X, you can easily see flukes, most protozoans, and intestinal worms. In other words, most everything but bacteria and viruses. So if you can see flukes, worms, or protozoans, you can choose the appropriate treatment. If you can't see those things, your problem is probably bacterial and requires an antibiotic. If it's viral, there will be no treatment, although an antibiotic may be beneficial against secondary bacterial infections.

In many cases, and especially if only one fish is looking sick, you won't need to sacrifice the fish to check it under the microscope. You can net an ill fish and give it a *very gentle* skin scrape with the edge of a razor blade. Smear the resulting slime on a glass slide, add a drop of water and a cover slip, and look through the microscope to see if you can see any protozoans or flukes moving around.

If many fish appear sick, the best thing is to net the sickest fish and do a complete workup on it. In this case, you are asking one fish to give up its life so that its tankmates may live. It's never an easy decision, but sometimes it's the best thing you can do for your fish. Here's how you do it:

1. Lay the fish on a paper towel and sacrifice it by slicing through the brain with a razor blade. Then cut off the head. Do not use a fish that was already dead when you found it, as the parasites you are looking for may have dropped off or died. Also, the dead fish might be covered by protozoans and bacteria that are harmless opportunistic scavengers taking advantage of an edible carcass, possibly leading you to mistake them for disease organisms.

2. Take a skin scrape by gently scraping off some slime with a razor blade. Smear the slime on a glass slide, and add a drop of water and a cover slip.

3. Use tweezers to remove a small section of gill. Mount it on a glass slide as I've already described.

4. Cut open the body cavity and remove a section of intestine to mount on a slide.

Something's Fishy

Dispose of dead fish by putting them in a plastic bag in the trash. Do not flush dead or dying fish down the toilet, as they may carry exotic diseases that could be transferred to native fish via the water supply.

5. Look at the samples under the microscope while they are still fresh. Particularly look for movement. Most of the parasites you seek will be moving, unless your sample is too old and they have died.

6. Mainly, you need to determine if the problem is due to protozoans, flukes, worms, or bacteria and then treat accordingly. If the topic really interests you, consider buying a book about fish diseases so that you can identify what you see.

The Least You Need to Know

➤ Overcrowding and other stresses are the primary causes of disease.

➤ Be familiar with the warning signs of health problems.

➤ When problems appear, check the environment first.

➤ A simple freshwater dip prevents or cures many problems.

➤ A quarantine tank can prevent the introduction of disease to your display tank.

Chapter 23

Fighting Fish

In This Chapter

➤ Things that tick a fish off

➤ Signs of aggression

➤ How to break up fights

➤ Fishy first aid

The world is not a peaceful place. The natural order of things is such that the strong dominate the weak, the jerks torment the gentle, and many animals look upon one another as food. The same applies to your aquarium. No matter how carefully you plan the mix of your aquarium community, there is going to be occasional friction. Sometimes, friction will escalate to the point where it results in serious injury or death.

In this chapter, you will learn why fish behave the way they do. You will learn about the things that turn your angelfish into devils and your triggerfish into assassins. I'll talk about what to do when the bullies in your tank start taking everyone else's lunch money.

My Fish Is Mean!

I can't tell you how many times I've heard customers say this. Personally, I don't really like to say that fish are mean, because meanness implies malice for the fun of it. When fish fight, they have important reasons for doing so. Aggression is normal, useful behavior for fish in the wild. However, when aggression is brought indoors into the confines of an aquarium, it can have more serious consequences. What would have been harmless bickering in the wild may become something deadly.

OK, so if some aggression is normal, how can you minimize it, and how can you recognize when things are getting out of hand?

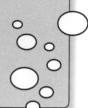

You know your fish is too aggressive when . . .

. . . it spits out a piece of Mike Tyson's ear.

. . . your cat is missing several toes on its front paw.

. . . your pit bull terrier won't come in the house.

. . . you see a story about it on *America's Most Wanted*.

. . . you wake up in the hospital, and the last thing you can remember is reaching into the aquarium.

This Is My Yard and You Can't Play in It

A primary reason animals fight is for control of territory. Many like to pick a spot and call it home, sweet home. The size of the spot they pick depends on the species and the size of the animal. As a fish or invertebrate grows, the territory it claims probably will expand, too. When others wander into its territory, it will drive them out. Usually, this involves a very short, threatening chase—the fishy equivalent of shouting, "Hey! Get off my lawn!"

If the encroacher doesn't move fast enough or wants to challenge, things get nastier. Scales are going fly and fins are going to get nipped. Think about it: If strangers started wandering into your house uninvited, you would probably threaten them to get out. And that might be that. But if they don't heed the warning, you'd get nastier—just like a fish protecting its territory. Some serious butt kicking would likely commence!

That would not make you a mean person. You would merely be protecting your home turf, and that is justifiable behavior—that is, until you start reaching for the assault rifle!

There are many degrees of territoriality. It is not a simple matter of just staking out a spot and laying claim to it against all others. While it's true that some territorial animals will drive away anything that comes near, most are fairly selective about this, driving away only individuals that fit a particular profile—a profile that varies by species and individual.

How does a fish (or invertebrate) determine that an approaching individual is deserving of a chase or a nip? Well, let's pretend for a moment that you are a fish. (This should be especially easy for some of you—I won't say who.) And let's say you are about to encroach upon the home turf of a territorial fish. To decide if you are a threat, that territorial fish might run a mental checklist something like this:

➤ Are you trying to steal my territory?

➤ Are you trying to steal my food?

➤ Are you a rival for mates?

➤ Do you look like me?

➤ Have I seen you around before?

➤ Are you a prospective mate?

➤ Are you an adult?

Claiming a territory is a way for an animal to guarantee that it will have a place to rest, to eat, and to breed. All of these questions relate to those three factors. So what happens when a newcomer enters the claimed space of territorial fish? Several things may happen:

➤ The newcomer may be seen as a threat and will be driven away.

➤ A serious fight may ensue.

➤ If the interloper is of the opposite sex, mating displays may result.

➤ Nothing may happen. Hey, not everyone is a threat.

Sex and the Single Saltwater Fish

The desire to reproduce greatly determines the behavior of all animals. I've already noted how important it may be to claim a territory for breeding, but even more important is claiming a mate. Much of the aggression between fish is based on the desire to obtain a mate.

Many fish, males particularly, see other males as rivals. No male wants the other guy to win the lady, so fights can ensue to drive rivals away from the courting grounds. Prospective mates, on the other hand, may be wooed in wondrous ways.

Sexual maturity is another factor. Species that normally do not get along with each other may tolerate juveniles—knowing that they are not yet rivals for prospective mates. There are a number of ways that fish determine the maturity of another fish of the same species. Size is probably a factor. Smaller fish are generally younger.

Color pattern plays a similar role. Often, different but similar-looking species are aggressive to one another. The visual similarity elicits the aggressive response used to deal with rivals—whether they really are rivals or not. In some cases, vertical or horizontal bands on another fish may elicit an aggressive response. Or it could be something as simple as both fish being yellow, no matter how different they look otherwise.

Fish Tales

Many juvenile fish have color patterns completely unlike those of adult fish. Compare the markings of a juvenile emperor angel with those of an adult. They look like different species. Many species use this mechanism to be sure their juveniles aren't seen as competitive threats to adults—and thus are allowed to grow up.

Finally, familiarity can affect aggression. Two fish that would normally bang heads can become habituated. That is, they get used to seeing each other around and they learn that banging heads gets them nowhere in the confines of an aquarium. So they learn to tolerate one another. In some cases, predators even become habituated to prey and refuse to eat them!

Who Are You Calling a Chicken?

This brings us to pecking order. Fish have them, too. A pecking order can be interspecies or intraspecies. Once everyone settles into your aquarium, they will all know their place. Some fish will be submissive. Some will be dominant. Some will be ignored entirely. It all depends on a complex interaction of species, size, territoriality, and sex.

Fish School

What is **pecking order**? In the barnyard, chickens will peck at other chickens that they consider to have lesser status. Likewise, they themselves will be pecked by the more dominant chickens. A hierarchy results, with the most dominant chickens at the top of the pecking order and the most submissive at the bottom. Some fish do the same.

Sometimes, pecking at another fish is mere opportunism. A fish is hungry, it sees a nice fresh fillet swimming by, and so it takes a nibble. Injured fish are particularly popular targets, although I doubt anyone really knows why. Some say it's because the other fish sense weakness and exploit it. Perhaps it is simply easier to take a bite out of the soft flesh around a wound, or maybe the scent of blood is a draw. Who knows? Maybe it is just a healthy fish's way of telling the damaged fish to get its sickly butt out of here and to take its disease with it.

Officer, I Didn't See a Thing

When damage is done, there aren't always witnesses. Hobbyists commonly describe symptoms of abused fish but swear that they never see any fights. Just because there are no witnesses doesn't mean it didn't happen. For starters, remember that you don't watch your aquarium 24 hours a day. So there is lots of time for the catfish to play while you are away.

Also, when you are in the room where do you think the fish have their attention? That's right—on you! You are the great Lord and Master of the Fish Food Can, the One Who Sprinkles Manna Down From Heaven. So when you are around, and particularly when you are close enough to the tank to see what is going on, the fish aren't going to have their minds on misbehaving. They are going to be thinking about pigging out.

Fish and Tips

Got a mean fish that you no longer want? Maybe a friend has a tank for it, or consider trading with your local pet store or donating it to a school.

Signs of Abuse

You don't have to witness a fight in progress to tell when a fish has been abused. Fish have plenty of ways of telling you after the fact.

➤ **Split and ragged fins.** When fish bite at each other, torn fins are a common result. If the fins have grayish decaying edges, infection has set in.

➤ **Scratches and scrapes.** Sharp fins and teeth cause battle damage. Sometimes, though, scratches result from a fish running into objects as it tries to escape or hide.

➤ **Torn lips.** Many fish lock jaws during their tussles. However, this is sometimes related to courtship behavior.

Fish and Tips

Fish that fan their fins and gills and spread their fins while wagging their bodies at each other may be fighting. Courtship behavior is sometimes similar, though, so they may also be flirting.

➤ **Obvious wounds.** Sometimes an opponent manages to take a pretty good bite! Please note that some infections progress to a point where there are open sores. So be sure that you haven't been overlooking a disease problem.

➤ **Missing scales.** As fighting fish thrash and bite at each other, scales get jarred loose. I've seen fights that made it look like silver rain was falling in the tank.

➤ **Color changes.** These may indicate aggression. Many species display submissive color patterns when bullied.

➤ **Unusual shyness.** A fish that begins hiding may be under attack. Hiding is normal behavior for many species, especially nocturnal ones, but when you find an outgoing fish suddenly sequestering itself, it's a sign that something is stressing it.

Break It Up!

If you do witness a fight, you may need to take action. It will depend upon how much damage occurs. Occasional spats are not reason for alarm, especially if they inflict little or no damage. Sometimes fish just need to vent their frustrations a little, or they just need to reinforce their territorial boundaries. Besides, life will be easier for you if the fish can work things out among themselves. Give them a chance to do so whenever possible.

However, when things get too vicious and major injuries result, you should step in to break things up. On rare occasions, a couple of taps on the glass will distract the fish. More likely, the mere sight of you, oh Lord and Master of the Fish Food Can, will distract the fish. Other times, you can poke a net handle at the combatants to separate them. Of course, that doesn't mean they won't take up later where they left off.

Even when a fight is serious—when one fish is showing damage—things may still work out. Sometimes, a fish just needs to be shown its place in the pecking order. Once it figures that out, peace may return. Be sure to check on the fish, though. Injured fish are targets for more attacks by other fish.

Fish and Tips

When one fish beats up another, it may be better to move the bully instead of the victim. Often, the bully will merely focus on a new victim. In a way, when you remove its victim, you are rewarding the bully by getting rid of its rival.

Off to the Pokey

If you've decided a fish has had enough, you will need to separate it. Perhaps you can move it to a different tank where the tankmates are more peaceful. You may even want to move the fish to a quarantine tank where you can preventively medicate the wounds so infection doesn't set in.

Usually, though, wounds will heal readily without medication. Fish are hardy characters. Still, it is a good idea to separate the injured fish so that it can recuperate without further stress and injury. The easiest way to do this is to hang a net breeder in the corner of the tank. Toss the injured fish into the basket and it will be protected from rivals until it heals.

Joe Aquarist, Fish Paramedic

Here are some things you may want to do for a fish that is badly beaten:

➤ Put it in a quarantine tank with an antibiotic to help prevent bacterial infections.

➤ Use one of the "liquid bandage" water conditioners to help replace its slime coat.

➤ Dab some iodine or mercurochrome on the wounds.

➤ Dim the lights to help the fish relax.

➤ After the victim has rested up and becomes active again, offer some of its favorite live and frozen foods to give it extra nutrition to heal fastest.

➤ Make sure you have kept up with your water changes. Clean, healthy water is probably the best cure.

When New Neighbors Drop In

Just as the new kid at school soon finds out who the bullies are, the newly added fish is most likely to get into a fight. And no, it won't be the one that started it.

The current residents have their territories staked and their pecking order established. They all know their places in the current fishy society. The new fish is at a disadvantage, though. It doesn't have a territory of its own. It doesn't have any friends. It gets dumped in with all these strangers and it has to steal some of their living space to survive. The current residents probably won't be too happy about that. They don't want to give up their territories or their places in the social hierarchy. Sometimes when you add a new fish to the tank, you can almost hear all the others shouting, "Let's get ready to rumble!"

Even worse for the new fish, it is the great Lord and Master of the Fish Food Can dumping the fish into the tank—like manna from heaven! So when the new arrival hits the water, every other fish may think it is feeding time and take a sample nip.

Here are some things you can do to make the transition easier for the new fish:

➤ Feed the existing fish before adding the new one. If their stomachs are full, they will feel less like nipping or fighting.

➤ Consider rearranging decorations in the tank before making the addition, especially if you keep territorial species. Since the new fish may have to fight its way into a territory, you can help it out by arranging things so that everybody has to find themselves a new territory. It puts all the fish on more even footing.

➤ It may help to introduce a new fish late in the day, when the lights are going out. For daytime introductions, turn off the aquarium light to help calm everyone.

Fish and Tips

If fighting causes you to separate a fish that you intend to return to the same tank, using a net breeder to isolate the fish has an added advantage. Since the fish remains a part of the community, it won't look or smell unfamiliar when reintroduced. That way, there will be less chance of new fights.

Fish and Tips

Turn off aquarium lights when adding new specimens to your tank. Darkness has a calming effect that will lessen the chances of aggression toward the new arrival.

Fish and Tips

A well-decorated aquarium helps control aggression by providing lots of hiding places and visual barriers. When it comes to prey and predator, out of sight is out of mind.

➤ Hang around a bit, just to keep an eye on things. Stay until you're satisfied that no one is going to kill the new fish.

➤ If the new arrival takes too much punishment, placing it in a net breeder for a day may help. Tankmates will become habituated to its sight and scent, and will be less likely to attack when you release the new fish into the aquarium.

Petproofing Your Tank

Aggression doesn't always come from within your tank. Make sure that your aquarium is on a sturdy stand that cannot be knocked over by large dogs. Be sure to have a close-fitting cover on your tank to keep kids and pets out. Cats like to walk across the top and paw at the fish.

Not only can pets be a danger to aquariums, but aquariums can also be a danger to pets. I once had a parakeet drown while trying to bathe in the outflow of a filter box. The current washed it into the tank, where there was no escape! This is a really sad story, and one I could have prevented.

The Least You Need to Know

➤ Fish fight for good reasons.

➤ Do your best to pick compatible species.

➤ Know the signs of abuse.

➤ Separate bullies from the general population.

➤ Having lots of hiding places will help keep down the aggression levels in your aquarium.

➤ Petproof your tank.

A Fishy Glossary

absorption   When substances soak into the empty spaces in another substance and are trapped.

actinic bulbs   Bulbs that produce blue, near-UV light.

activated carbon   A special, highly porous carbon product, used as a chemical filter medium.

adsorption   When substances are trapped by chemically bonding with the surface molecules of another substance.

aerobic bacteria   Bacteria that use and require oxygen.

airstone   An air diffuser, usually made of cemented sand grains (although sometimes made of wood) that is porous enough to allow air to pass through it, thus splitting the airstream into tiny bubbles.

algae   Simple-celled microorganisms that photosynthesize. Some scientists classify them as plants, some as protists. *Microulgae* (*micro* means small) tend to be pests, while *macroulgae* (*macro* means large) may be quite desirable.

alkalinity   Synonym for carbonate hardness (not the same as alkaline pH).

ammonia   A poisonous waste product excreted by fish and other organisms.

anaerobic bacteria   Bacteria that do not use or require oxygen.

antibiotic   A natural substance, produced by an organism, that kills microorganisms. The term is often applied to antibacterials, as well, which are artificial agents.

aquarist   An aquarium hobbyist.

bi-metallic strip   A strip made of two different kinds of metal, sandwiched together, that functions as a switch in a thermostat.

bioload   The size and number of waste-producing animals introduced into your aquarium will determine its bioload.

biological filtration   The use of helpful bacteria to break down waste, particularly ammonia that the fish excrete.

biotope   A sample of a particular type of environment.

bivalves   Mollusks that have two shells that come together to protect the animal, such as clams, oysters, mussels, and scallops.

brackish   Somewhat salty. Brackish water is found where rivers meet the sea.

break-in period   The time when a tank is cycling.

brine   Water saturated with salt.

buffer   A combination of an acid or base with a salt that, when in solution, tends to stabilize the pH of the solution.

carcinogen   An agent known to have the ability to cause cancer.

cavitation   The formation of gas bubbles in a liquid, caused when an impeller forms a partial vacuum. Gas falls out of solution in the low-pressure zone, forming bubbles.

check-valve   A device that allows air to flow in only one direction, thus preventing water from back-siphoning through the air lines, should there be a power outage.

chemical filtration   The use of chemical compounds to remove dissolved wastes.

chloramine   A harmful additive found in some municipal water supplies.

chlorine   A harmful additive found in most municipal water supplies.

cnidarians   A group of soft-bodied, stinging saltwater invertebrates, including corals and anemones.

common name or **trade name**   The name you are more likely to know a fish by and the name most people will use.

community tank   An aquarium with a mix of compatible, peaceful species.

crustaceans   A class of aquatic animals with a segmented body, a continuous exoskeleton and paired, jointed limbs. Lobsters, shrimp, and crabs are members of this class.

cycling   Breaking in a new aquarium by starting with fewer fish until enough helpful bacteria develop to handle the ammonia and nitrite loads. The term derives from the nitrogen cycle, which is what is happening chemically during this process.

diatoms   Microscopic organisms with silica skeletons. They appear as brown slime and are often mistaken for algae.

diurnal   Active during the day.

echinoderms   A class of aquatic animals with radial symmetry, internal skeletons, and tube feet, which resemble tiny tentacles with suction cups on the end. Starfish and sea urchins are the best-known members of this group.

emersed   Above the water.

feeding rings   Floating plastic rings that keep fish food from drifting all over the tank.

50-50 bulb   A bulb in which the phosphors inside have been tweaked to produce output that is half daylight and half actinic.

filter feeders   Animals that filter microscopic life and nutrients from the water.

float glass   A type of plate glass that is manufactured by pouring liquid glass onto a bed of liquid mercury. The glass floats on top.

fluorescent bulb   A long glass tube with pins at each end. Internal phosphor coatings glow when electricity is applied to the bulb.

footprint   How much space an aquarium takes up on the stand—in other words, the dimensions of the bottom.

full-spectrum light   Light bulbs that produce both the full spectrum of visible light and small amounts of UV light.

gang-valve   Several valves connected and mounted on a plastic or metal hanger.

gastropods   Mollusks that have a single shell, such as snails and cowries.

gorgonians   Animals with colorful living tissue that surrounds a horny skeleton. They share traits of both soft and stony corals.

ground-fault interrupter   A power outlet that shuts itself off if it detects current leakage—usually caused by splashed water.

hardness   *General hardness* is a measurement of dissolved minerals, particularly magnesium and calcium. *Carbonate hardness* measures buffering capacity.

herbivores   Animals that eat plants such as algae.

heterotrophic bacteria   Bacteria that cannot synthesize their own food and must eat organic matter.

hydrometer   A device that measures the density or specific gravity of your water, and thus indicates whether or not you mixed the right amount of sea salt with your tapwater.

ich   The best-known fish disease.

ichthyology   The study of fish.

incandescent bulb   Old-fashioned bulb with a screw-in base that fits standard household sockets.

inverse square law   The intensity of light decreases by the square of the distance. Put simply, if light travels twice as far, it will have one-fourth the intensity.

invertebrates   Animals that lack a backbone or spinal column. They could be soft like a jellyfish, or hard like a crab.

kalkwasser   Chalkwater or limewater that adds concentrated solutions of calcium hydroxide or calcium oxide to replace aquarium water that has evaporated.

live-rock   Porous rocks that have been harvested from the ocean, along with a healthy growth of attached marine flora and fauna. Live-rock may be *cured* or *uncured*. Cured rock has been in your dealer's tank long enough to have stabilized. Uncured rock is the most recently acquired stuff.

live-sand   Very small particles of live-rock.

marine   Synonym for saltwater or seawater. *Saltwater tank, seawater aquarium,* and *marine aquaria* are all synonyms.

mechanical filtration   Physically sifting out particles of solid waste by passing the water through some type of filter media.

metal halide bulbs   Larger bulbs with a large screw-in base called a mogul base. They have a high light output.

milt   The sperm of fish.

mollusks   A diverse group of soft-bodied animals, most with hard shells.

new tank syndrome   The buildup of ammonia and nitrite during the cycling of a new tank. Also used to refer to some cloudy-water problems in new tanks.

nitrate   A nontoxic (in normal levels) product formed by the oxidation of nitrite.

nitrite   A toxic byproduct of the conversion of ammonia.

nitrogen cycle   When helpful bacteria break down ammonia into nitrite, nitrate, and (eventually) nitrogen gas.

nocturnal   Active at night.

osmoregulate   Adjusting to changes in level of salt in the water.

osmosis   The diffusion of a fluid through a semipermeable membrane, until there is an equal concentration of fluids on both sides of the membrane.

pecking order   A hierarchy, where the most dominant is at the top of the pecking order and the most submissive is at the bottom.

pH   A measurement of the acidity or alkalinity of the water.

photosynthesis   The process by which plants—and corals—use the energy in light to synthesize carbohydrates.

power compact fluorescent bulbs   Fluorescent bulbs that are folded upon themselves into a U shape. They have a higher output.

powerhead   A small water pump.

protandrous hermaphrodites   Fish that mature first into males but can later change to females, such as clownfish.

reef-ready   A glass or acrylic tank available predrilled, with plumbing installed, ready to connect to the proper filter.

roe   The eggs of fish.

rolled glass   A type of plate glass where the liquid glass passes between rollers to make the sheets of glass.

salt creep   The crust that builds up when saltwater evaporates, leaving minerals behind. Also, an affectionate term for a saltwater hobbyist.

scientific name   The standardized Latin name for a species. The scientific name consists of two parts: genus and species. The *genus* usually represents a group of related fish. The *species* is unique for that variety of fish.

sea salts   Minerals that you mix with tapwater to create seawater.

soft corals   Corals that do not build skeletons.

standard length   The length of a fish from tip of nose to base of tail (excluding the tail fin).

stony corals   Also called hard corals, they build a skeleton of calcium carbonate.

submersed   Below water.

symbiosis   A close association between two or more species, especially one that offers mutual benefit.

synergistic   When two ingredients are safer and stronger together than when used alone.

taxonomy   The scientific classification of organisms (Kingdom, phylum, class, order, family, genus, species). In this book, we are most concerned with genus and species, which compose the scientific name.

tempered glass   Glass that is manufactured in a process that makes it stronger than an equal thickness of plate glass.

thermometer   An instrument that measures temperature.

thermostat   A device that automatically controls temperature.

total length   The length of a fish from tip of nose to tip of tail.

two-way valve   A valve that inserts into an existing air line to control its output.

Sample Shopping Lists

My friend Elaine once told me that she wished that there had been an aquarium book with some sample shopping lists when she started her first tank. It would have been easier if she could have walked into a store with a list of exactly what she needed.

Now there is such a book! Here are some sample shopping lists for a few popular sizes of aquariums. I made it even easier by including some brand names where appropriate. I chose quality brands that have wide distribution, so you shouldn't have trouble finding any of the items. Still, these are just guidelines—don't be afraid to let your dealer substitute equivalents.

Each shopping list includes:

➤ A list of equipment

➤ A first batch of hardy fish to cycle the tank

➤ A second batch to fill out the tank after it has cycled

Some Things to Keep in Mind

1. You may want to split the second batch of livestock into a second and third batch, just to play it safe. Adding too many fish too fast can result in dead fish. In no case should the second batch of livestock be added until ammonia and nitrite levels have dropped to zero and remained there.

2. If you add optional live-rock, it must be cured! Otherwise, you must cycle the tank with live-rock before adding the first batch of fish. Ask your dealer how fresh the pieces are. Remember that fresh pieces (new arrivals) may have dying encrusting organisms (caused by shipping damage) that will pollute your tank. Pieces that have been in the dealer's tanks for a couple of weeks can be considered cured and safe.

3. With the exception of the seahorse setup, all the aquariums listed here are for fish-only setups. Reef aquariums are more sophisticated and require further research beyond the information that I have given in this book. I highly recommend that before you buy anything for a reef tank, you get and read the two-volume set *The Reef Aquarium* by Delbeek and Sprung.

10-Gallon Seahorse Tank Shopping List

Equipment	❏ 10-gallon Perfecto or All-Glass aquarium
	❏ 20-inch full-hood with fluorescent light
	❏ AquaClear Mini power filter
	❏ 20-inch undergravel filter (single plate version)
	❏ Mini powerhead
	❏ 50-watt heater
	❏ Thermometer
	❏ 15 pounds crushed coral substrate
	❏ 4-inch fishnet
	❏ Stress Coat water conditioner
	❏ Saltwater test kits: ammonia, nitrite, pH
	❏ Hydrometer
	❏ Sea salt
	❏ Beginner's book (this one!)
	❏ Seahorse book
	❏ Decorations of your choice, including background (Tip: look for decorations that a seahorse can grasp, such as plastic plants)
	❏ Protein skimmer (optional, but highly recommended)
Livestock, Batch 1	❏ 5 to 10 pounds fancy cured live-rock, such as plant rock or reef rock
	❏ 1 pair of seahorses
	❏ Caulerpa algae
	❏ Live food: brine shrimp, ghost shrimp, feeder guppies, etc.
Livestock, Batch 2	❏ 3 astraea snails
	❏ 2 brittle stars
	❏ 1 mandarin dragonet

29-Gallon Fish-Only Setup Shopping List

Equipment	❏ 29-gallon Perfecto or All-Glass aquarium
	❏ 30-inch full-hood with fluorescent light
	❏ Aqua-Clear 200 power filter
	❏ 30-inch undergravel filter (single-plate version)
	❏ AquaClear 301 powerhead
	❏ 150-watt heater
	❏ Thermometer
	❏ 30 pounds crushed coral substrate
	❏ Food: 1 can marine flake food
	❏ 1 can freeze-dried plankton or krill
	❏ 1 or more frozen seafoods
	❏ 5-inch fishnet
	❏ Stress Coat water conditioner
	❏ Saltwater test kits: ammonia, nitrite, pH
	❏ Hydrometer
	❏ Sea salt
	❏ Beginner's book (this one!)
	❏ Decorations of your choice, including background
	❏ Protein skimmer (optional, but highly recommended)
Livestock, Batch 1	❏ 2 damselfish *or* 2 chromis
	❏ A few pieces of cured live-rock (optional)
Livestock, Batch 2	❏ 2 tomato clownfish
	❏ 1 royal gramma, *or* 1 yellow angel, *or* 1 coral beauty angel

55-Gallon Fish–Only Setup Shopping List

Equipment	❑ 55-gallon Perfecto or All-Glass aquarium
	❑ 48-inch full-hood with fluorescent light
	❑ AquaClear 300 power filter
	❑ 48-inch undergravel filter
	❑ 2 AquaClear 301 powerheads
	❑ 200-watt heater
	❑ Thermometer
	❑ 60 pounds crushed coral substrate
	❑ Food: 1 can marine flake food
	❑ 1 can freeze-dried plankton or krill
	❑ 1 or more frozen seafoods
	❑ 6-inch fishnet
	❑ Stress Coat water conditioner
	❑ Saltwater test kits: ammonia, nitrite, pH
	❑ Hydrometer
	❑ Sea salt
	❑ Beginner's book (this one!)
	❑ Decorations of your choice, including background
	❑ Protein skimmer (optional, but highly recommended)
Livestock, Batch 1	❑ 3 damselfish *or* 3 chromis
	❑ A few pieces of cured live-rock (optional)
Livestock, Batch 2	❑ 2 ocellaris clownfish
	❑ 1 auriga butterfly
	❑ 1 royal gramma
	❑ 1 coral beauty angel

75-Gallon Fish-Only Setup Shopping List

Equipment	❏ 75-gallon Perfecto or All-Glass aquarium
	❏ 48 × 18-inch full-hood with fluorescent light (consider buying the extra strip light so that there are two full 48-inch rows of light)
	❏ Aqua-Clear 500 power filter
	❏ 48 × 18-inch undergravel filter
	❏ 2 AquaClear 301 powerheads
	❏ 200-watt heater
	❏ Thermometer
	❏ 60 pounds crushed coral substrate
	❏ Food: 1 can marine flake food
	❏ 1 can freeze-dried plankton or krill
	❏ 1 or more frozen seafoods
	❏ 6-inch fishnet
	❏ Stress Coat water conditioner
	❏ Saltwater test kits: ammonia, nitrite, pH
	❏ Hydrometer
	❏ Sea salt
	❏ Beginner's book (this one!)
	❏ Decorations of your choice, including background
	❏ Protein skimmer (optional, but highly recommended)
Livestock, Batch 1	❏ 3 damselfish *or* 3 chromis
	❏ 2 Clark's or sebae clownfish
	❏ A few pieces of cured live-rock (optional)
Livestock, Batch 2	❏ 1 small yellow tang
	❏ 1 auriga butterfly
	❏ 1 purple dottyback
	❏ 1 flame angel
	❏ 1 juvenile emperor angel
	❏ 1 dwarf lionfish

Where to Learn More

Recommended Saltwater Aquarium Books

I have shelves and shelves of aquarium books at home, but here are some of my favorites. Titles followed by an asterisk (*) are readily available through pet stores (possibly by special order). All titles should be available through your local bookseller, or if you have a computer, check www.amazon.com for fast delivery at a decent discount. Listed retail prices are approximate, in U.S. dollars, and will vary from dealer to dealer.

The Conscientious Marine Aquarist*, by Robert M. Fenner, Microcosm Ltd., 1998, $35.
   Subject: Saltwater aquariums, marine fish, and invertebrates
   Rating: Beginner
   Comments: This is a great book for the new marine hobbyist. It covers all styles of marine aquaria, plus popular fish and invertebrates. Written by someone with experience in all segments of the trade, the book teaches the secrets of an expert aquarist. Over 400 pages; fully illustrated with color photos.

Reef Fishes, Vol. 1*, by Scott W. Michael, Microcosm Ltd., 1998, $69.95
   Subject: Saltwater fishes
   Rating: Beginner
   Comments: This wonderful new book starts with a detailed description of the families of fishes, follows up with information about the habitats found in various zones of the reef, and then begins a compendium of species—complete with information on species and captive care. The author is well-known for his underwater color photos, and this beautiful book is loaded with them! The only bad thing about this book is that it is the first volume in a four-volume set, and the other three aren't available at the time of this writing.

Marine Atlas, Vol. 1*, by Helmet Debelius and Hans A. Baensch, Microcosm Ltd., 1994, $45 per hardcover volume, $30 per paperback volume.

Subject: Aquarium keeping, marine fish, and invertebrates

Rating: Beginner and up

Comments: This book is unbeatable for detailed information on individual species and is loaded with color photos. Both hardcover and softcover versions are available. There are over 1,200 pages in Volume 1, and most of those are dedicated to describing individual species of fish and plants (one per page)! The first 200 pages of the book cover general aquarium keeping. This is followed by 100 pages about algae and over 300 pages of information on species of invertebrates. The remaining pages cover species of fish. Beginners and advanced hobbyists both can benefit. At this writing, only Volume 1 is available in English. Volumes 2 and 3 are due to be translated from German and released in the United States this year. I can't think of a better gift than the three-volume set!

Dr. Burgess's Atlas of Marine Aquarium Fishes*, by Dr. Warren E. Burgess, Dr. Herbert Axelrod, and Raymond E. Hunziker, III, TFH Publications, 1988, $80.

Subject: A photographic survey of marine aquarium fish

Rating: Beginner and up

Comments: This is a very large book, packed with more than 4,000 color photos. Most photos have symbols underneath that signify what the fish eats, how big it gets, and so forth—but that is not the book's strong point. Its strong point is photo identification of marine fish. Stores also carry Dr. Burgess's *Mini-Atlas of Marine Aquarium Fishes* ($36). It's about half the size, with fewer species.

Clownfishes*, by Joyce D. Wilkerson, Microcosm, Ltd., 1998, $30.

Subject: Clownfish and sea anemones

Rating: Beginner

Comments: Clownfish are among the most popular of saltwater aquarium fish, noted for their symbiotic relationship with sea anemones. This book contains detailed information about the various species of clownfish and sea anemones, how to best care for them, and even tells you the secrets of breeding them. Written in language that any beginner can understand, this book is so thorough that professionals and advanced hobbyists use it as a reference. Even if you don't have a big interest in clownfish, you may want to read the book just to get a better understanding of the difficulties and challenges involved in the captive propagation of marine fish.

Marine Plants of the Caribbean, by Diane Scullion Littler, Mark M. Littler, Katina E. Bucher, and James N. Norris, Smithsonian Institution Press, 1992, $25.

Subject: Marine algae and sea grasses

Rating: Beginner

Comments: This book is the field guide to marine algae. Use it to identify species that pop up in your tank or just to drool over fascinating varieties that you will never see. The algae are grouped by color for quick reference.

Recommended Reef Aquarium Books

The Reef Aquarium, Vol. 1 and 2*, by J. Charles Delbeck and Julian Sprung, Ricordea Publishing, 1994–1997, $85 per volume.

> **Subject:** Reef aquariums, marine invertebrates—especially corals, anemones, and giant clams
>
> **Rating:** Intermediate
>
> **Comments:** These two volumes, each over 500 pages, are the undisputed bibles of the reef aquarium hobby. They are the most complete and well-organized reef books available. Volume 1 covers principles of reef-keeping, and contains detailed information about giant clams and stony corals. Volume 2 covers soft corals and anemones. Though not cheap, these books are well worth the money and will pay for themselves by helping you keep your animals alive. I gave them an intermediate rating, but only because I consider reef-keeping to be an advanced topic. Although advanced reef-keeping topics are covered, they are done so well that even beginning aquarists will have no trouble understanding the information. Color photos throughout. Very highly recommended!

The Modern Coral Reef Aquarium, Vol. 1 and 2*, by Svein A. Foss and Alf Jacob Nilsen, Birgit Schmettkamp Verlag, 1996–1998, $85 per volume.

> **Subject:** Reef aquariums, marine invertebrates—especially corals and anemones
>
> **Rating:** Intermediate
>
> **Comments:** These two books were originally published in German, but English versions are now available. Volume 1 (367 pages) covers reefs and reef-keeping in depth. Volume 2 (479 pages) covers corals and anemones. Both volumes are loaded with information and stuffed with color pictures of reefs in the wild. Very highly recommended!

Natural Reef Aquariums*, by John H. Tullock, Microcosm Ltd., 1997, $30.

> **Subject:** Reef aquariums, marine fishes, and invertebrates
>
> **Rating:** Beginner to intermediate
>
> **Comments:** This is a great starter book for someone considering a reef aquarium. Smaller and less expensive than the tomes I've just listed, it still covers the topics very well. The author, a well-known retailer, has much experience teaching hobbyists how to start aquariums, and it shows. He writes in a style that can be understood by anyone. The book is 336 pages long, with color photos throughout.

A Practical Guide to Corals for the Reef Aquarium*, by Ed Puterbaugh and Eric Borneman, Crystal Graphics, 1996, $35.

> **Subject:** Identification of live corals
>
> **Rating:** Beginner

Comments: A great addition to the reef hobbyist's library, this book's primary purpose is to aid in identification of live corals. It is a photographic survey of species commonly sold in shops. Each species is shown with a list of common trade names, level of aggressiveness, and difficulty of care.

Encyclopedia of Marine Invertebrates*, edited by Jerry Walls, TFH Publications, 1982, $80.
Subject: Marine invertebrates
Rating: Intermediate
Comments: This 736-page book is probably the best available for identifying marine invertebrates. Unlike other books for the reef aquarium, which tend to concentrate
on corals and anemones, this one's strong suit is its usefulness in identifying worms, snails, crabs, mollusks, and you name it. When some unknown critter crawls out of your live-rock, you will probably find information on it here.The layout is a bit awkward, though—the photos of any given species are rarely found in the same part of the book as the accompanying text.

Giant Clams*, by Daniel Knop, Two Little Fishes, 1996, $50.
Subject: Tridacnid clams
Rating: Advanced
Comments: This book is geared more for the advanced reef hobbyist. It covers all species of giant clams and their anatomy, reproduction, diseases, and so forth. It even gets into commercial propagation.

Other Reading

Fish and Their Behavior*, by Gunther K. H. Zupanc, Tetra Press, 1985, price varies.
Subject: Fish behavior
Rating: Advanced
Comments: This book is out of print, so you'll have to try used book stores. The online booksellers can also sometimes get used copies. This book helps you get inside your fishes' heads, and helps you understand how they think and why they act the way they do. Both marine and freshwater fish are covered. It makes for interesting reading.

The Manual of Fish Health*, by Dr. Chris Andrews, Adrian Exell, and Dr. Neville Carrington, Tetra Press, 1995, $30.
Subject: Fish disease and treatment
Rating: Beginner
Comments: This book starts off on the right foot by telling you all the things you need to know to keep your fish from getting sick in the first place. It has an excellent section on water quality, a chapter on recognizing warning signs and disease symptoms, and a treatment guide. Plus, it has the best photos I've seen of actual diseased fish, making it invaluable as a diagnosis tool.

Aquarium Magazines

Only a few magazines are available for the aquarium hobby. You may find them in aquarium stores or even at the newsstand, but you'll save money if you subscribe.

Aquarium Fish Magazine
Fancy Publications
P.O. Box 53351
Boulder, CO 80322-3351
http://www.animalnetwork.com/fish/default.asp
>**Published:** Monthly
>
>**Price:** $24.97 a year
>
>**Comments:** This magazine is probably the best choice for the beginning hobbyist. It covers freshwater, saltwater, and garden pond topics. The magazine is full color throughout, beautifully laid out, and filled with articles that you can trust. It does lean more to the beginner's end of the hobby, but it has some technical stuff mixed in and is always written in a way that anyone can follow. Although it is the newest, *Aquarium Fish Magazine* has already achieved the widest circulation of any of the aquarium magazines. They also put out an annual, under the title *Aquarium USA*. (Members of CompuServe's FISHNET Forum can get two years for the price of one.)

Tropical Fish Hobbyist
TFH Publications, Inc.
One TFH Plaza
Neptune City, NJ 07753
http://www.tfh.com
>**Published:** Monthly
>
>**Price:** $40 a year
>
>**Comments:** This magazine has been around for 50 years—longer than any of the others. Freshwater, saltwater, garden pond, and (believe it or not) reptile topics are covered. You will find everything from beginner's articles to technical ichthyological stuff written by one of my customers (yes, I'm bragging), Dr. Stanley H. Weitzman of the Smithsonian Institution. This magazine runs more articles on breeding fish and fish-collecting expeditions than any of the others. The founder, Dr. Herbert R. Axelrod, is probably the hobby's best-known celebrity. TFH Publications is also a major publisher of pet and aquarium books.

Freshwater and Marine Aquarium
R/C Modeler Corp.
P.O. Box 487
Sierra Madre, CA 91025
http://www.mag-web.com/fama/
>**Published:** Monthly
>
>**Price:** $23 a year

Comments: This magazine has more information specifically on saltwater aquariums than the others. On the up side, new ideas and technology tend to appear in this periodical before the others. On the down side, those same avant-garde articles are often full of wild conjecture and outright baloney. Technical editing could be better. They also commit the mortal sin of running April Fool's articles in the April issue without identifying them as such! Be careful that you don't get stung by one. If you want mail-order ads, though, this magazine is full of them.

Practical Fishkeeping
Motorsport
550 Honey Locust Rd.
Jonesburg, MO 63351
  Published: Bimonthly
  Price: $42 a year
  Comments: This is a British import, and I can't help but notice that the layout sometimes resembles a tabloid newspaper. Still, it is full of excellent information and photos. Freshwater, saltwater, and garden pond topics are covered.

Marine Fish Monthly
Publishing Concepts Corp.
3243 Highway 61
East Luttrell, TN 37779-2043
  Published: Monthly
  Price: $22 a year
  Comments: This is the only aquarium magazine dedicated exclusively to saltwater. It's a little on the small side and the articles are often lacking, but you have to start somewhere.

Electronic Resources

The information age is here, and those of you with computers have access to huge amounts of information. There are basically three things you can do online: exchange messages by posting to an electronic bulletin board, download files on desired topics, and chat live with people from all over the world.

Fishnet on CompuServe

Once upon a time, you had to use CompuServe as your Internet provider if you wanted to access any of its communities, but you can now get limited free access to Fishnet, and most other CompuServe forums, via the World Wide Web (http://csi.forums. fishnet). The idea is to give you a taste of what the service offers, so that you will join CompuServe. If you do, you get full access to Fishnet at no extra cost.

CompuServe's Fishnet Forum is, without a doubt, the best place to go for electronic information about fish. Fishnet has been around longer than the other services and has the most information in one place. The founder, longtime hobbyist John Benn, is a visionary in the electronic information business. He has worked hard for many years to see that Fishnet offers good, solid value to its members.

Fishnet has nearly 6,000 aquarium-related files available to download from its libraries, and CompuServe has powerful search engines that let you easily find what you need. Every aspect of the hobby is covered. There are even computer programs for aquariums that you can download.

But if you ask me, the very best thing about Fishnet is the message sections. Message sections are like public bulletin boards. You post a message, and anyone can see and answer it. Likewise, you can see and answer anyone else's messages. (Don't confuse this with e-mail, where people can only access messages sent to their own mailbox.) If you have a question, post it in one of the message sections, and you will almost certainly get an answer—or several! Experts from all over the world can participate, and beginners can, too. It's a great place to go to get relatively quick answers to even the most difficult questions. One section even has fish paramedics.

Fishnet also has chat rooms where you can talk about your hobby, and even weekend parties. Guest lectures are featured regularly, and there are weekly roundtables for beginners and monthly specialty conferences. You don't need to attend a scheduled event to talk to someone else, though. You can page others in the Forum for a chat.

One especially nice thing about Fishnet, and CompuServe in general, is that you will be dealing with real people, using their real names, and behaving the way they would behave if you were face to face. In fact, most areas on CompuServe require the use of real names and will lock out users that refuse to do so.

I should mention that one of the real names you will see on CompuServe, and particularly on Fishnet, is mine. In fact, I was a sysop on Fishnet for over eight years and even did a stint as Message Manager. So feel free to say hello if you are ever in the Forum.

America Online (AOL)

America Online has grown to be the largest online service in the world. In fact, they recently bought CompuServe. Like CompuServe, America Online offers libraries, message sections, and chat rooms. I knew that AOL had a section devoted to aquariums and fish, so I borrowed a friend's account to check it out. I had a hard time finding it, because searches on keywords *fish, tropical fish,* and *aquarium* all turned up blanks. Sheesh! I finally got a hit on *pet,* which pointed me toward the Pet Care Forum. I found the fish section, Fish and Marine Life (F&ML), buried deep within.

Once I found the right place, there was more stuff there than I expected, but much less than on Fishnet. I was surprised to see that F&ML has divided its message sections into many topics. However, I was disappointed when I browsed the messages. So many were either unanswered or had answers that weren't really answers, such as "check out this Web site for an answer." Of course, some messages show no replies, because many posters ask that their replies be sent to their e-mail boxes, instead of being posted in the Forum, where all can benefit. Fish and Marine Life has only four libraries, one of which had only four files in it. I didn't count the actual number of files, but it was certainly only a few hundred.

World Wide Web

If you like pretty pictures and chaos, the World Wide Web is for you! The Web, which is part of the Internet, has brought more people to the online world than anything else. The appeal is that it is a free-for-all. Anyone can have a Web page, and you never know what you will find out there. Interesting Web pages will have links to other Web pages. You click on the link, and off you go to the new site to see what is there.

Believe me, there is lots of information available on the Web, but finding it isn't always easy. You will spend lots of time searching, drawing blanks, searching some more, and maybe finding what you want. It's a lot like a scavenger hunt.

Rather than waste time telling you about some cool sites that may no longer be there when I'm done typing this sentence, let me simply recommend that you visit the many online search engines, such as Yahoo, Excite, Infoseek, and a new one, Google, and search for Web sites, using *aquarium, tropical fish,* and similar keywords. You are bound to turn up something interesting.

Internet Newsgroups

If you are not a member of an online service where you have access to a dedicated fish forum, such as Fishnet, you can use the Internet to access some of the aquarium-related newsgroups. They function like bulletin boards. You post a question and hope for answers. This amalgam of newsgroups is called Usenet.

Usenet is a good idea. It works much the way that my beloved message boards work on Fishnet. However, since it is not a private service and is open to all, it is full of chaos. Typically, you will find that most of the messages in a newsgroup have nothing to do with the topic at hand. Instead, you will find a bunch of ads for silly get-rich-quick schemes and people calling each other jerks. The result is that little serious message traffic occurs there, because people don't like wasting time weeding out all the junk.

However, if you want to check out Usenet, try these newsgroups:

alt.aquaria	rec.aquaria.marine.misc
alt.aquaria.killies	rec.aquaria.marine.reefs
rec.aquaria.freshwater.cichlids	rec.aquaria.marketplace
rec.aquaria.freshwater.goldfish	rec.aquaria.misc
rec.aquaria.freshwater.misc	rec.aquaria.tech
rec.aquaria.freshwater.plants	sci.aquaria

Join the Club

Joining a local aquarium society can be fun. You will make friends who share your interest and who want to exchange information. You will be able to attend lectures given by well-known and knowledgeable speakers, and you will have the opportunity to participate in raffles, auctions, and fish swaps. Other members will be happy to teach you how to breed fish and invertebrates, and may even provide you with some free breeding stock.

Here is a list of aquarium societies that specialize in saltwater environments. It is organized by country and then by state or province, and should give you a good starting point for locating a local society. However, clubs do come and go, and the mailing address is often the home address of a former membership chairperson, so all of this information is subject to change.

Although I have only listed marine aquarium societies in this appendix, there are many aquarium societies that have both freshwater and saltwater members. So even if your local society isn't listed here, you may still want to check it out. Also, my apologies to any marine societies that were omitted from this list.

Nationwide Aquarium Societies

To help further, the first three listings are for master organizations that oversee aquarium societies in the United States and Canada. While you can't join them, your local society can. So they tend to have the most current lists of local aquarium societies. If my itemized list doesn't point you toward a local society, contact one of these groups to see if they have an updated list.

Marine Aquarium Societies of North America
P.O. Box 508
Penns Park, PA 18943

Federation of American Aquarium Societies
4816 E. 64th St.
Indianapolis, IN 46220-4728
102735.2120@compuserve.com

Canadian Association of Aquarium Clubs
c/o Robert Brown
298 Creighton Court
Waterloo, Ontario
Canada N2K 1W6

Aquarium Societies of the United States

Desert Marine Society
P.O. Box 55642
Phoenix, AZ 85078

Southern California Marine Aquarium Society
23010 Lake Forest Dr., Suite 218
Laguna Hills, CA 92653

Marine Aquarium Society of Los Angeles
21915 Wyandotte St.
Canoga Park, CA 91303

Greater Florida Marine Aquarium Society
c/o Museum of Science
3280 S. Miami Ave.
Miami, FL 33129

Marine Aquarium Society of the Palm Beaches
c/o Bob Irvin
2409 S. Haverhill Rd.
West Palm Beach, FL 33415-7327

The Atlanta Marine Aquarium Society
2180 Pleasant Hill Rd., A5/188
Duluth, GA 30136

Honolulu Aquarium Society
P.O. Box 235791
Honolulu, HI 96823-3513

Greater Chicagoland Marine Aquarium Society
c/o Steve Kossack
1520 Hillcrest Ave.
Hanover Park, IL 60103

Kansas City Marine Aquarium Club
512 Fillmore
Topeka, KS 66606

Louisville Marine Aquarium Society
3112 Meadowlark Ave.
Louisville, KY 40213

Gulf Shores Marine Aquarium Society
P.O. Box 6954
Lake Charles, LA 70606-6954

Chesapeake Marine Aquaria Society
1390 Chain Bridge Rd., Suite 99
McLean, VA 22101

Seahorse Hobbyists Society
2821 Hollins Ferry Rd.
Baltimore, MD 21230

Marine Aquarium Society of Michigan
1090 Dye Krest Dr.
Flint, MI 48532

Las Vegas Marine Society
3001 Cabana #283
Las Vegas, NV 89122

Windows to the Sea Marine Aquarium Society
P.O. Box 37
Piscataway, NJ 08855-0374

Cleveland Saltwater Enthusiasts Association
20897 Fairpark Dr.
Fairview Park, OH 44126

Dallas–Fort Worth Marine Aquarium Society
940 Eagle Dr.
DeSoto, TX 75115

Greater Houston Marine Aquarium Society
5510 Foresthaven Dr.
Houston, TX 77066

Marine Aquarium Society of Virginia
2812 Deford Court
Chester, VA 23831

Marine Aquarium Societies of Canada

Vancouver Marine Society
c/o President Barry Higgins
656 Blue Mountain
Coquitlam BC V3J 4R4

Marine Aquarium Society of Toronto
22 Quail Valley Dr.
Thornhill, Ontario
Canada, L3T 4R2

Marine Aquarium Societies of the United Kingdom

Seahorse Study Group
14 Knaves Hill
Linslade, Leighton Buzzard
Bedfordshire, LU7 7UD

The preceding information was extracted from CompuServe's Aquaria/Fish Forum CLUBSUSA.TXT and CLUBSINT.TXT files, compiled by Kevin Done. The online files contain more complete listings, including freshwater aquarium and garden pond societies, and some international listings. Also, thanks to Rob Huntley of the Aquatic Conservation Network, Jim Lilly and Maxine Gorsline of the Federation of American Aquarium Societies, and many others for their input.

Public Aquariums

A public aquarium is like a zoo for animals that live in the water. Many varieties of fish are on display in tanks designed to mimic their natural habitat. You will see some familiar faces, as many fish sold in aquarium stores also can be found in public aquariums—though usually, they will be full-grown adults. The aquariums are much larger than what you will find at home. Most display aquariums are several hundred gallons and larger. Some public aquariums even have large marine mammal tanks with regular shows.

Here is a small sampling of some popular sites. I chose locations from around the country, so one is probably near you. I have visited most of these personally. I promise that you will have fun.

Public Aquariums and Their Features

Public Aquarium	Features
Monterey Bay Aquarium 886 Cannery Row Monterey, CA 93940	Giant Kelp Forest tank; 90-by-15-foot Monterey Bay tank; outdoor intertidal zone
The Florida Aquarium Harbour Island Tampa, FL 33602	Mangrove tidal basin; gigantic artificial reef with artificial surge
Waikiki Aquarium 2777 Kalakaua Ave. Honolulu, HI 96815	Specializes in Hawaiian and South Pacific species; coral propagation research
John G. Shedd Aquarium 1200 S. Lake Shore Dr. Chicago, IL 60605	World's largest indoor aquarium; reef tank with divers; new marine mammal pavilion

continues

Public Aquariums and Their Features (*cont.*)

Public Aquarium	Features
Aquarium of the Americas Woldenberg Riverfront Park New Orleans, LA 70130	400,000-gallon Gulf of Mexico; Amazon Basin exhibit; transparent Caribbean tunnel
New England Aquarium Central Wharf Boston, MA 02110	250,000-gallon giant ocean tank; marine mammal shows; tidepool for kids
National Aquarium in Baltimore Pier 3, 501 E. Pratt St. Baltimore, MD 21202	500,000-gallon ring tank; Shark and ray exhibit with divers; Rain forest on the roof
New York Aquarium for Wildlife Conservation W. Eighth St. and Surf Ave. Brooklyn, NY 11224	First public aquarium in the United States; Innovative Sea Cliffs display; Captive-born Beluga whales

As a former resident of Baltimore, I'm quite familiar with the National Aquarium there and even count some of its staff as friends. I have two favorite spots. One is the lower-level underwater view of the ray tank. The rays swim by so gracefully that it's very relaxing. But my favorite is at one end of the elliptical ring tanks. There are two tanks, one above the other. One has sharks and the other an assortment of reef-dwelling species. To view the tanks, you walk down a huge spiral ramp that goes right down between the tanks.

Fish and Tips

If you want a list of 95 public aquariums, look for this book: *Marine Parks and Aquaria of the United States*, by Anthony L. Pacheco and Susan E. Smith, Lyons and Burford, 1989, $16.95.

The Florida Aquarium is new and quite well done. Exhibits include large mangrove tidal flats, with fish, turtles, and birds all living in harmony. There is a gigantic reef aquarium that is landscaped so that each window makes it appear as if you are looking into a new world. Huge hydraulic pistons on the roof make an actual surge take place in this tank, just like in the ocean. It's very relaxing. And, if you are lucky enough to show up at feeding time, you are in for a real treat. On a recent visit, my friend Denise and I were peering into the reef when the curators tossed some shrimp in from overhead. A view that was at first devoid of fish suddenly became a feeding frenzy as hundreds of fishes rushed over from all around the aquarium. Wow!

The John G. Shedd Aquarium in Chicago is another great stop. They have galleries representing every kind of habitat you can think of. My favorite, though, is one called Tributaries, which features small, well-planted aquariums of a size you could create yourself at home. The new marine mammal pavilion is very well done. The amphitheater where they hold dolphin shows is beautifully designed. The complex is on the edge of Lake Michigan, and large rear windows give the amphitheater an open look. In fact, the design makes it appear as if the water inside merges with the lake outside.

Index

E

F